Hannah Kirshner is a writer, artist, and food stylist whose work has appeared in *The New York Times*, *T Magazine*, *Vogue*, *Saveur*, *Taste*, *Food52*, *Atlas Obscura*, and *Food & Wine*, among others. Trained at the Rhode Island School of Design, Kirshner grew up on a small farm outside Seattle and divides her time between Brooklyn and rural Japan.

* * *

Praise for *Water, Wood, and Wild Things*

"An enthralling personal journey . . . [Kirshner's] lyrical style is soothing and retains the magic of her experiences without being overly effusive. The book is dotted with beautiful illustrations, and exquisite recipes finish each chapter. It's a respectful, insightful, and illuminating work to be savored."
— *The Tokyo Weekender* (an April Book Club pick)

"*Water, Wood, and Wild Things* . . . evokes the best of the nature writing of Rachel Carson and Wendell Berry, as well as the food writing of M. F. K. Fisher and craft writing of Edmund de Waal. . . . [Kirshner's] . . . drawings are charming, and her words, miraculous."
— *The Provincetown Independent*

"[A] sensitive, perceptive, and gratifyingly detailed book . . . A vicarious pleasure for those stuck at home, and a loving tribute to the practitioners of traditional arts."
— *Booklist* (starred review)

"Travel readers who appreciate off-the-beaten-path locales and local cuisine will enjoy this dreamy account."
— *Library Journal*

"Kirshner is both participant and observer, humbly and tactfully weaving a portrait of a history, its mores, and how they've changed. But, above all, she listens—allowing the community to tell their story, and allowing us to view the tapestry she's painted alongside them. *Water, Wood, and Wild Things* is a trove and a boon—we can't help but feel grateful that Kirshner brought us along for the journey."
— Bryan Washington, author of *Memorial*

"With each turn of the page, you can almost hear Kirshner sliding open yet another wooden panel door to reveal a shokunin who refuses to let their craft fade. *Water, Wood, and Wild Things* wonderfully brings a myriad of haptic, visual, and aromatic taste sensations of Japan."

—John Maeda, author of *The Laws of Simplicity*

"*Water, Wood, and Wild Things* chronicles [Kirshner's] time in the mountain town of Yamanaka—and offers a record of what she learned about technique and creation there, from brewing sake to making charcoal."

—Tobias Carroll, *Inside Hook*

"Exquisitely attentive—a lovely and special book."

—Rosie Schaap, author of *Drinking with Men*

"Kirshner's lyric sketchbook provides a glimpse of a mountain town in transition, nurtured by the past while accepting (considered) change."

—Elizabeth Andoh, author of *Washoku* and *Kansha*

"What a luscious book! Lovely illustrations and delicious recipes enhance the multilayered narrative, rooted in deep history and thought."

—Gina Rae LaCerva, author of *Feasting Wild*

"I love this book! Kirshner opens up a window to a Japan that virtually no one from the outside gets to see, and as a hunter, angler, forager, and cook myself, it is fascinating to see that those traditions are not only very much alive there, but also that they are not so different from our own here in the United States."

—Hank Shaw, author of *Hunt, Gather, Cook*

"How does one engage ethically with a culture not their own? Kirshner offers one possible way. . . . Kirshner listened, and allowed me to hear the voices of Yamanaka's people, who are recreating traditions every day."

—Takeshi Watanabe, author of *Flowering Tales: Women Exorcising History in Heian Japan*

"Hannah Kirshner's delicate drawings and uncommon recipes complement this beautiful tribute to rural Japan."　　—Winifred Bird, author of *Eating Wild Japan*

"*Water, Wood, and Wild Things* brings back my memories of growing up in Japan. With her authentic narratives, Kirshner reminded me of countless and valuable teachings from my ancestors and the culture."

—Masahiro Urushido, author of *The Japanese Art of the Cocktail*

Water, Wood,

and Wild Things

Learning Craft and Cultivation in

a Japanese Mountain Town

HANNAH KIRSHNER

PENGUIN BOOKS

PENGUIN BOOKS
An imprint of Penguin Random House LLC
penguinrandomhouse.com

First published in the United States of America by Viking,
an imprint of Penguin Random House LLC, 2021
Published in Penguin Books 2022

All drawings by the author.

"A Saké Evangelist" first appeared in slightly different form as "The Sake Ambassador"
on *Roads & Kingdoms*, February 2016; the Midnight Fried Chicken recipe first appeared
online as "Karaage" in slightly different form in *New York Times Cooking*, July 2018.

ISBN 9781984877543 (paperback)

THE LIBRARY OF CONGRESS HAS CATALOGED THE
HARDCOVER EDITION AS FOLLOWS:
Names: Kirshner, Hannah, author.
Title: Water, wood, and wild things : learning craft and cultivation in a
Japanese mountain town / Hannah Kirshner.
Description: [New York, New York] : Viking, [2021]
Identifiers: LCCN 2020030524 (print) | LCCN 2020030525 (ebook) |
ISBN 9781984877529 (hardcover) | ISBN 9781984877536 (ebook)
Subjects: LCSH: Kirshner, Hannah—Travel—Japan—Yamanaka. | Food
habits—Japan—Yamanaka. | Drinking customs—Japan. | Cooking,
Japanese. | Workmanship—Japan. | Yamanaka (Japan)—Social life
and customs. | Yamanaka (Japan)—Description and travel.
Classification: LCC GT2853.J3 K495 2021 (print) | LCC GT2853.J3 (ebook) |
DDC 394.1'2—dc23
LC record available at https://lccn.loc.gov/2020030524
LC ebook record available at https://lccn.loc.gov/2020030525

Printed in the United States of America

DESIGNED BY MEIGHAN CAVANAUGH

In memory of Yoshiharu Nishiyama;

may we continue his work for the

children's children

Contents

Wild Things

Cultivation

Recipes

*Ingredient measurements are given in metric
units, with U.S. cups in parentheses. Where only cups
are given, either a metric or a U.S. cup is fine.*

A Note on Names
and Pronunciation

In Japanese, one's family name appears first, followed by given name (my name becomes Kirshner Hannah). But most of my friends and acquaintances in Japan use the Western convention when they introduce themselves in English and on English versions of their business cards. I'm following their lead—even for historical figures—to make things easier for English-speaking readers. In this book I call people by the name (sometimes family, sometimes given) that you might use if you, the reader, were to meet them. I've honored the spelling people and organizations use for their own names, even if it doesn't follow contemporary conventions for romanization; I do the same for words already familiar in English.

There is no consistent style of romanization across trade publications, and academic standards may be cumbersome for readers new to Japanese. I've tried to find a middle ground that's consistent and easy to read. Macrons (the short lines above some letters; for example, $\bar{o}$, $\bar{u}$) indicate long-sounding vowels. I use an accent on saké for the sake of clarity, but elsewhere confusion is unlikely. The *e* at the end of a Japanese word is never silent. The pronunciation of vowels is similar to that in Spanish, but syllables are weighted equally. G is always hard. *L* and *r* are pronounced identically—more softly than an English *r* but farther back on the roof of the mouth than our light *l*. I choose not to italicize Japanese words as I introduce them (as is often done for foreign words) because they are not foreign within the context of this book.

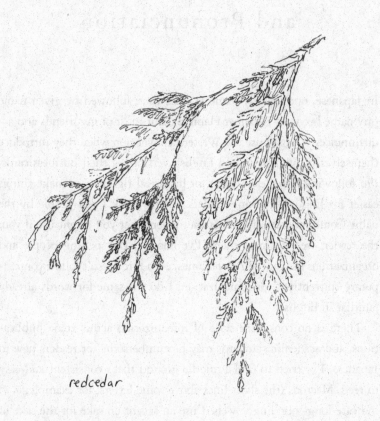

redcedar

Prologue

Yamanaka's forest, draped in moss and feathered with ferns, made me feel at home as soon as I arrived. Like the town where I grew up, North Bend, Washington, there are mountains every way you look, and yet you don't have to drive far to reach the sea.

To get to Yamanaka I traveled three hours on two trains west from Tōkyō. It wasn't my first time in Japan—nearly a decade earlier I'd spent a month with bike messengers in Kyōto and Tōkyō—but I was headed into the deep countryside, far from anyone or anything I knew well. I remember gazing out the window of the new bullet train at mountainsides covered in triangular blue-green conifers. They looked exactly like the motif on the furoshiki (wrapping cloth) my husband carries when he travels. I'd assumed the illustration was stylized; I didn't know trees could be so uniform and symmetrical.

Yamanaka means "in the mountain." Misty ridges encircle tile-roofed wooden houses and weathered shrines. The smell of cypress and saké permeates the air. Artisans and farmers carry on centuries-old traditions, making tableware by hand and cultivating rice and vegetables. I went there hoping that my two-month apprenticeship at a saké bar would be a gateway into deeper understanding of Japanese food and drinks.

At the southern edge of Ishikawa, a prefecture that spoons the Sea of Japan, Yamanaka belongs to a region that's been dismissively referred to as ura-Nihon, the backside of Japan. Because of its isolation, Ishikawa's agricultural, fishing, and craft communities have been slow to give up old-fashioned ways. Now the precise thing that drew disdain makes Ishikawa a destination for avant-garde chefs and discerning travel editors searching for the version of Japan held up in the country's own mythology and romanticized in the West.

Yamanaka claims a thirteen-hundred-year history of tourism because of its hot springs, but most of its visitors still come from within Japan and other Asian countries. Looking at its tourism data over the past hundred years is like watching the ups and downs of the Japanese economy: the number of visitors gradually increased after World War II, then peaked in the 1970s and again in the 1990s. Most years in the past half century about 500,000 people visited Yamanaka.

Fewer than eight thousand people live in the town and its surrounding villages, and that number is shrinking. And yet young artists, designers, and entrepreneurs move there to make a life in the countryside. Students come from all over Japan to study at the wood-turning school and apprentice with master craftsmen. There are few salarymen in Yamanaka: most people are hospitality workers, business owners, or artisans.

THE EVERGREENS I saw from the train are sugi, Japanese cedar, I was told. But they're different from what I know as cedar. The bark of sugi does resemble the strips I peeled off the trunks of western redcedar as a child—bending it back and forth until it became pliable, marveling that indigenous people made clothes from these scratchy fibers. I would crush flat, scaled redcedar leaves between my palms to release their fragrance and find them later crumbled in my pockets. I didn't recognize the spiky fingers of sugi leaves.

It turns out that neither sugi (*Cryptomeria japonica*) nor western redcedar (*Thuja plicata*) is a true cedar: they're both in the cypress family. In Yamanaka, I had many revelations that what I'd been told about Japan was not exactly right. That there weren't always analogues in American culture. That translations were often hasty and imprecise.

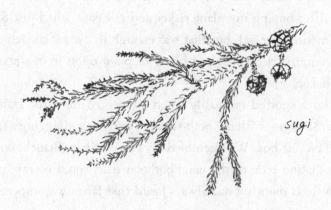

sugi

Another kind of cypress tree, hinoki (*Chamaecyparis obtusa*), looks more like the evergreens I know. Its fragrant wood is used to build shrines, temples, and fancy baths. In Yamanaka, there is a bridge—Kōrogi Bashi—built entirely of perfumy pink hinoki wood, where tourists take photos of fiery-colored maple leaves over the aquamarine Daishōji River. If you look past the picturesque scene, there are clear-cuts on the mountainsides, like the ones I remember from North Bend. Almost 70 percent of Japan's land is covered in trees, but much of this wilderness is in a sense constructed—planted for lumber or stewarded for fuel and raw materials after widespread deforestation.

I WENT TO JAPAN for the first time when I was twenty-two. Since graduating from art school, I'd been working in a bicycle shop and competing in road and cyclocross races. Seeking advice for my trip to Japan, I wrote to an email address I found on a flyer for a bike messenger race in Kyōto. A man named Takuya answered, saying I could stay with his messenger friends in their share house.

I took a second job in the kitchen of a taqueria to save for my trip. After buying my plane ticket and rail pass, I had just $500 for a month of travel, but that was enough to live off convenience store onigiri (rice balls) and bowls of plain udon from stand-up noodle bars.

Takuya spotted me easily when I emerged from the train at Kyōto Station—with my pink-streaked curly hair, dragging a cardboard bicycle box. We assembled my celeste-green Bianchi on the sidewalk and rode to the neighborhood that would be my home for the next month. I had always heard that Japan was impenetrable and lonely for outsiders, but I was immediately welcomed into that cycling subculture.

Takuya introduced me to the cyclocross national champion and arranged for a bike ride with her in Ōsaka. His old art school friend worked with my favorite painter, Yoshitomo Nara, and I got to meet Nara-san in Kanazawa. I partied under the cherry blossoms—with messengers, with young moms, with teenagers who beckoned me to join. They were surprised to hear that I had grown up with cherry blossom picnics too, on the grounds of the University of Washington, petals falling like snow from gnarled old Japanese trees.

After I returned to America, I thought about going to Japan to teach English—I was even offered a job—but instead I started bartending in a gastropub and learned to make cocktails. A good bartender, I thought, can work anywhere in the world.

Over the next decade Takuya and I kept in touch over email and met once in America and once in Japan. I gave up bike racing—even the top pro women are lucky to get a salary of $5,000 a year—and moved to New York, the best place, I thought, to pursue a career in art or food.

I STILL LONGED to live in Japan, but I wanted to go on my own terms, to do something there that I cared about—I am not an English teacher. And I was making a life in Brooklyn with the man I would marry, Hiroshi Kumagai. I'd fallen in love with a Japanese man who had lived in America for decades—since he was eighteen—because he wanted to escape Japan. At the time, he had no interest in returning to the country where I dreamed of going.

We were living together, not yet married, when I got an email from Takuya, asking if I could host Yūsuke Shimoki, the young owner of a saké bar in Yamanaka, a place I'd heard Takuya describe as a magical mountain town. Considering the hospitality Takuya and his friends had shown me in Japan—*of course!*

Shimoki arrived at our doorstep in Brooklyn with a suitcase full of Ishikawa saké. It was his first time outside Japan. I was under the impression that Shimoki had the idea to come to New York to see how saké is served here, but I later learned that he thought I had invited him. I don't know whether the confusion came from Shimoki's hubris or Takuya's scheming to set us up as friends.

Shimoki's weeklong stay coincided with an early-summer dinner party I'd planned. The evening of the party, Shimoki changed into his bar uniform and brought out his framed certificate of expertise—proof of a sommelier-like qualification that fewer than two hundred people in the world held. He chilled half a dozen bottles of saké on ice from a bodega in one of my blue enamelware pots, keeping others at room temperature.

I set the table with colorful mismatched napkins, bamboo chopsticks, an assortment of small ceramic bowls, and a cobbled-together set of white plates that almost looked uniform when dimly lit by a string of white Christmas lights wrapped in jute rope (a misguided Pinterest project that was much harder than it looked). Shimoki brought out five different sets of glassware that he'd carried all the way from his bar and wooden cups made in Yamanaka.

I'd planned to start the evening with miso-grilled oysters in the backyard, but it was drizzling and humid, so the six of us crowded around a worktable in my small apartment, perched awkwardly at different heights on a mix of chairs and stools. I ran back and forth to the grill (down two flights and through the basement).

It seemed presumptuous to cook Japanese food, but I wanted the meal to go well with saké, so I used Japanese flavors in my own hybridized American vernacular. With each dish I brought to the table—kōji-marinated fish wrapped in banana leaves, miso soup with littleneck clams, mizuna salad dressed in Meyer lemon, watermelon with shiso and feta—Shimoki poured saké, explaining it with such exuberance that we barely needed translation.

He wore a waist apron of unhemmed midnight-blue canvas with strands of orange and white woven into the tie—his bar's insignia, depicting rice and a jug of saké, printed in white. I asked him where I could get one like it.

You'll have to work in my bar, he told me, with Hiroshi translating. *Okay*, I said. *You have to come for two months*, he shot back. *Okay*, I said.

He might have been joking, but it quickly became a real plan. Not half a year later, I began my apprenticeship at Shimoki's bar (and I did earn my own apron). I went there certain the experience would open doors, but not sure which ones. While working in the bar, I befriended a master woodturner, a paper artist, and a man making charcoal with a hand-built kiln.

Over the next four years I kept going back to Yamanaka, my visits getting longer and longer until I was living there more than in Brooklyn. I learned about wood turning and carving and got to know hunters and farmers. I'm easily identifiable as an outsider in Japan, but—in part because of my perceived temporary status as a white American woman—I'm privileged with access to people and places that might not be open to a nonwhite foreigner or a native Japanese person.

I knew only a few people in Yamanaka who spoke any English. I was immersed in Japanese—a language that had never really clicked for me in spite of taking classes in college and on and off over a decade. Japanese is written in two syllabaries combined with kanji derived from Chinese characters. Conjugations and vocabulary vary depending on your gender and the status of the person you're addressing. My speaking gradually progressed from halting to conversational, and friends stepped in when I needed help. Hiroshi, now my husband, was my personal hotline for language and etiquette—answering text messages about Japanese vocabulary for art and design or how to politely ask a friend for a ride.

During my long affair with Yamanaka, Hiroshi mostly stayed behind in Brooklyn to run his graphics company and take care of our two backyard chickens. He doesn't appear much in these pages, but he was always in the background, encouraging me to follow my dreams *whole-ass*. And he was the person I couldn't wait to tell about each day's adventure.

This book starts with my first trip to Yamanaka at the onset of winter and ends four years later with the festival at the beginning of autumn. In between, the chapters are organized around the themes of water, wood, wild things, and cultivation. Some stories developed slowly over years, and others are from a few intense months of immersion. There are recipes in each chapter—some to help you bring a little of Yamanaka home, and others to archive foods rarely seen outside Kaga, the part of Ishikawa where Yamanaka is located.

I limited the geographic scope to present-day Yamanaka—to places I could reach by bicycle from my apartment in town—even if this sometimes meant cycling up a mountain. The one exception is "Samurai at the Duck Pond." That chapter takes place in Daishōji, a town downriver, toward the sea. But I followed a Yamanaka man there, and at the time that his archaic sport was invented, the duck pond and Yamanaka were part of the same domain.

I've had a chance to observe things that haven't been written about extensively—or at all—in English, and are little known or taken for granted in Japan. Even in our hyperconnected world, there are still places you can't find on the internet.

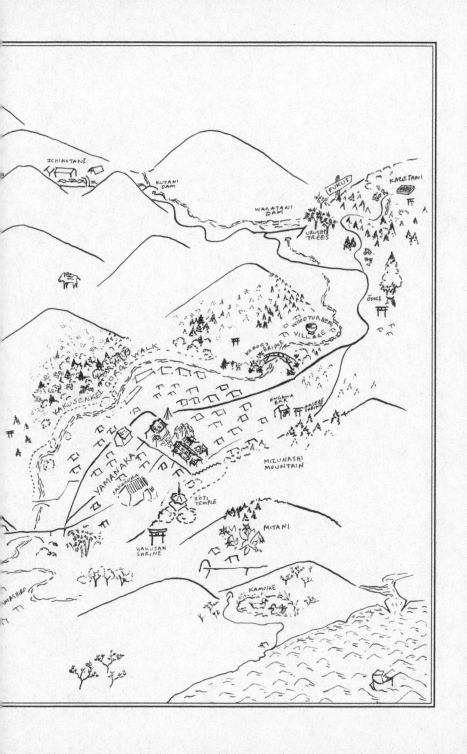

Water

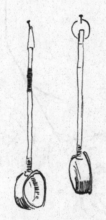

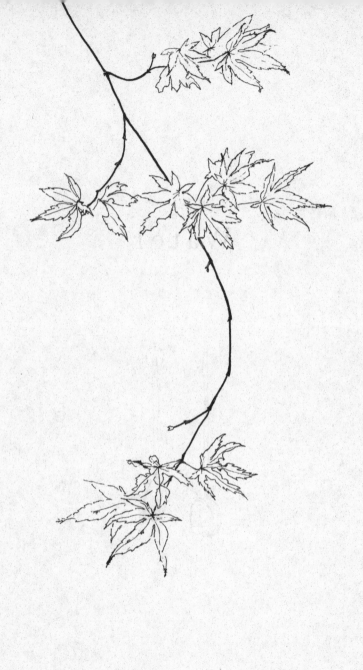

One

A Saké Evangelist

S himoki, in his early thirties, has the aspect of a very serious teddy bear—with a potbelly from spending more than sixteen hours a day tasting, contemplating, and serving saké, and eyes that sparkle when he talks about it. From behind the counter of his tiny bar in the mountains of Ishikawa, he is trying to save the Japanese saké industry, which has been in decline since consumption peaked in the 1970s. His thin, neatly groomed eyebrows dance and furrow as he evangelizes for Japan's national drink. He's hoping to convert me.

He picked me up when I arrived at the nearest train station. It had been a long journey alone from New York to Tōkyō, Tōkyō to Kanazawa, and Kanazawa to Kaga. I was so relieved to see a familiar face that I hugged him, even though I knew that was very American of me—he looked utterly stunned.

Driving the ten kilometers from Kaga Station, we quickly left behind pachinko parlors and chain stores, passing through farmland flanked by a curtain of mountains, the most spectacular of which is snowcapped Hakusan (Mount Haku). It reminded me of catching glimpses of Rainier from Seattle on rare clear days.

The temperature dropped noticeably, and rice paddies gave way to lumber plantations as the road climbed toward Yamanaka. Its downtown is situated in a narrow valley along the Daishōji River, and you can walk it from end to end in less than twenty minutes. Natural hot springs (onsen), a two-thousand-year-old tree at the edge of town, and a meandering stone path along the Kakusenkei gorge are its main attractions.

Dilapidated low-rise hotels overlooking the river are evidence of a 1960s construction boom and the lasting depression that followed. Even the nicest buildings in Yamanaka are in a perpetual state of decay from the moist climate. But it's easy to become entranced by the icy blue river and bright red maple leaves falling softly on mossy rocks and all but ignore the shabby facades on the opposite bank as you walk the gorge.

Shimoki's bar, Engawa, is at the top of a small side street toward the end of town, before the main road heads deeper into the mountains. Where the side street ends, at the entrance to Hasebe Shrine, there's the bar, with its warm light emanating into the damp darkness of late October. I settled into an apartment across the street.

THOUGH I'VE TENDED BAR in some high-end places, my first night of work at Engawa was the first time in my life I had to fasten the very top button of my shirt. I wore a vest, as Shimoki had told me to, and he lent me a tie and a long apron. We matched.

I offered to wash dishes and rolled up my sleeves to get started. *No*, he said, *rolled-up sleeves are for laborers*. I tried to explain that it was a new shirt and the sleeves were too long. *Don't worry*, he said, and—still worried—I unrolled my sleeves. I noticed as I was washing and putting away a water glass that a chip on its rim had been smoothed over and repaired with a bit of gold leaf.

Next, he showed me how to take a coat and hang it neatly facing the wall and how to offer each guest a steaming washcloth called an oshibori in such a way that they can take it with one hand. Then he told me where to stand and watch him, which is how he expects me to learn almost everything.

I'd seen the same thing in fancy Tōkyō cocktail bars, where smartly dressed understudies pour water and wipe the bar for months or years before mixing a single drink. And it was how Shimoki learned too. He spent a year in Kanazawa working temp jobs and going to a whisky bar called Machrihanish every day, ordering two drinks and reading the Japanese translation of the canonical *Malt Whisky Companion*, a guide to more than eight hundred whiskies. Then he moved to Tōkyō and worked eighteen months at a cocktail bar called Mondo. You can see flourishes of cocktail service in the way he presents saké.

With the help of an architect friend, Shimoki renovated a tiny old wooden house into his own bar. Its ornamental carved wooden transom panels called ranma, modern iron and wood chairs with red velvet cushions, and a framed indigo print on handmade paper were crafted by other friends. Under the glass countertop is a miniature garden of raked sand and carefully placed rocks. On a high shelf to the far left, a small television plays old samurai movies on a continuous loop. In the back right corner, there's a tiny shrine just below the ceiling, with a vase of flowers and a cup of saké that Shimoki refreshes daily. Incongruously, a laminated sign for wi-fi is stuck to the backbar.

Besides the five bar stools that Shimoki presides over, there's a small private room painted Kanazawa blue, a shade of periwinkle that used to be reserved for high-ranking lords. A sliding paper door screens the four guests it cozily accommodates: men in suits with the air of good ol' boys who call me in to entertain them by answering questions about what a lady from New York is doing in Japan, or a middle-aged doctor and one of his young nurses (whose drinking together doesn't seem to trouble anyone but me), or sometimes in the late afternoon a family whose toddler daughter uses the same delicate water glass and expensive lacquered chopsticks as all the other guests.

In the narrow space that divides the bar from the private room and bathroom, round stone pavers set into swirls of black and white river rocks echo the path along Kakusenkei gorge. Drunk young ladies in stilettos teeter over the stones precariously, and I imagine the liability this would be in the United States.

It's usually around their second drink when a guest notices that the music playing in Engawa is Scottish. It blends with the old wood and stone, and it matches Shimoki's plaid wool vest. He explains that there's music for beer and there's music for wine, but there's no music for saké. The music he hears in other saké bars is too dour. And while Shimoki himself is comically serious, he's managed to create a space that feels relaxed and casual.

Engawa is a name for a kind of Japanese porch: a place to unwind, drink tea, and catch up with your neighbors. According to Shimoki, the character "en" implies fate or luck, and "gawa" means side—the bar between him and the customers. Engawa is a place for chance encounters.

On any given night the bar draws a mix of onsen-going tourists, saké connoisseurs who've pilgrimaged to Yamanaka, and locals at the end of their workday. There's likely to be a master craftsman or a few students from the wood-turning school (the town is famous for its unique style of cups and bowls), perhaps a government official, or an important guest from one of the fancy hotels. A couple of Shimoki's childhood friends will probably come in later after their soccer game. Once a week, my eighty-one-year-old neighbor Mrs. Kobayashi—a petite woman with a glowing smile—sits at the bar and drinks a saké, a whisky, and a beer. If there's a guest all the way from Tōkyō or Ōsaka, Shimoki dotes on them. Whoever is there, it doesn't take long before they are all talking and tasting one another's drinks.

SIX DAYS A WEEK Shimoki comes in at 11:00 A.M. to tidy and take care of paperwork, and opens around noon to accommodate the occasional afternoon guest. Some time before 5:00 P.M. he'll take a break to restock. He will keep the bar open until the last guest leaves—sometimes midnight, sometimes 5:00 A.M. He doesn't seem bothered that he has time for nothing else: his work isn't separate from his life—it is his life. A neighbor remarks that she has never seen him without his uniform—even at the supermarket or running errands around town.

In a place where your options are typically to take over the family business or leave for the big city (as evidenced by the aging population and growing number of abandoned homes), Shimoki's entrepreneurship is unconventional. When he opened the bar on his thirtieth birthday—a year before I arrived—he already had a reputation for his laser focus on Japanese drinks.

He used to work in my landlady's saké shop, and she recounts with affectionate laughter the time she asked Shimoki to help out with different jobs for the holidays. He refused, saying it wouldn't help him learn about saké. Neighbors speak of him with a combination of awe and bemusement, often calling him Shimoki-kun, like a little brother. But when it comes to matters of saké, they defer to him.

There are no employees at Engawa: my apprenticeship here is out of novelty, not necessity. Shimoki is used to doing everything himself, and I'm certain I get in the way more than I help. He seems glad to have me there, but I wonder what's in it for him. He says he views me as his colleague, not his student. Still, I'm not sure he understands that I've come to Yamanaka to learn about more than saké (maybe because of the language barrier, or maybe because saké is what he cares most about).

IN EARLY DECEMBER, when we've been working together for a month, Shimoki invites me to join him for a daily ritual before opening the bar. I follow him outside up the steep mossy steps to Hasebe Shrine. As we climb, he instructs me to observe the plants, the temperature, and the feeling of the season so we can determine what kind of saké the day calls for. He prays and then tenderly brushes away some fallen leaves and places several coins on the shrine, asking the spirits to bring him good business.

We can feel the cold pressing in as we return to the little bar.

Tonight people will want to drink atsukan, poured hot from a small iron kettle, at precisely 55 degrees Celsius. In the United States, heat is deployed to disguise the flavor of cheap swill. But here, heating saké is an art. Next to the counter Shimoki displays a chart showing how intervals of a few degrees highlight different flavors. Part of my education has been drinking from five or six cups with the same saké heated incrementally warmer in each. At 55 degrees a robust saké burns pleasantly going down, warming you to the core.

Each day, Shimoki has something new for me to taste. In broken English and Japanese—with the help of Google Translate, a saké textbook, and the experience of tasting together—we're developing a shared vocabulary. We've figured out words for bitterness versus astringency, characteristics like tingly or smooth, the names of fruits and flowers, ideal serving temperature and alcohol content. We don't have the language to talk about anything personal, but we can talk about saké.

Before I came here, I could tell that one saké was sweeter, another more delicate, I could see that it was clear or cloudy, but pretty much saké just tasted like saké to me (some better than others). But only a week into my stay I could distinguish all sorts of subtleties and aromas of persimmon . . . kelp . . . pear . . . pine. I quickly fell in love with the fresh and unpasteurized ones often considered too fragile to export, then grew to appreciate rare old saké too, so oxidized it smells like sherry and holds up to dark chocolate.

On days when he's too busy to teach me, people come to ogle at the novelty foreigner and my job is simply to entertain them with my presence. Sometimes they don't even want to talk to me; looking is enough to tell their friends about. It gets worse when the regional paper comes to interview me. *Foreign woman works in saké bar*, they report, with a picture of me dressed like Shimoki and smiling uncomfortably, pouring the local saké called Shishi no sato.

I help translate for the occasional Western guest, but you don't need to speak Japanese to understand when Shimoki describes a drink. *Piri-piri*, he says to describe effervescence, wiggling his fingers near his mouth to express tingly little bubbles. He waves his arm in a grand downward motion, leveling off toward the end and saying, *Loooooooong finish*. He bounces like a cartoon character, and his enthusiasm is contagious. If a guest asks for a recommenda-

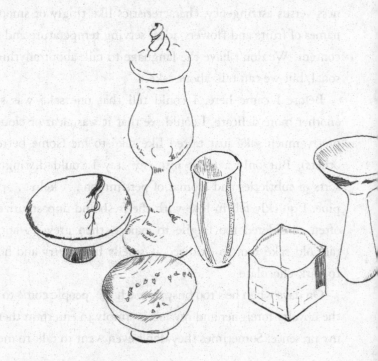

tion, he sizes them up and directs the arc of their drinking like a DJ picking the perfect progression of songs.

One of his favorite tricks is to serve you the same saké in two distinctly shaped cups. It tastes dramatically different, even to the untrained palate. While a scientist might tell you it's a simple matter of how much aroma reaches your nose, in that moment it's magic. Each time he opens a new bottle, he thinks hard about how best to enhance its character, tasting it in various cups. Its expression becomes more umami, earthy, herbaceous, or floral, depending on the shape and material.

A couple from out of town is asking about a glossy blond cup they're drinking from. It's made by Takehito Nakajima, a Yamanaka woodturner, who designed it for Shishi no sato saké, brewed down the street by his friend Fumiaki Matsuura. Shimoki pulls open drawers of the antique wooden cabinet behind the bar and a familiar scene begins: he brings out another style by a different craftsman . . . then another and another until the small counter

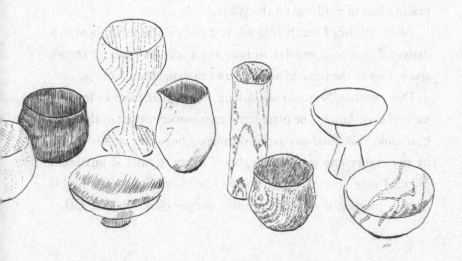

is cluttered with a dozen cups, each with its own story, each capable of bringing out a distinct expression of a single saké.

Every day, he prepares an assortment of otsumami (drinking snacks) using a tiny toaster oven, a torch, an induction burner, and a cutting board. There's roast pork from the butcher up the street, which he heats and mounds on a plate with a blanket of brown sauce and a handful of sliced scallion. There's miso-cured tofu, pungent and creamy as cheese, that he cuts into tiny cubes and stacks neatly in a small ceramic dish. There's tuna that he's marinated in saké and soy sauce, which he sears with a torch before fanning it out on a plate. And there are soy-sauce-cured egg yolks (the eggs from his friend's farm near the seaside), which lately he serves spooned over slices of soft, fresh tofu. Or you can simply have a handful of deep-fried soba noodles to snack on like potato chips, which he transfers from a big plastic jar to a beautifully turned wooden bowl. For guests with a sweet tooth he arranges chilled dark chocolate and yōkan (adzuki bean gelée) on a mirrorlike lacquered stand, dusting the chocolate with a snowfall of powdered sugar that he wipes into a crescent shape and delicately placing bits of gold leaf on the yōkan.

After my shift I neatly fold my vest and tie and leave them in a drawer. I put on a sweater to hide the stuffy uniform. If there's space, I sit at the bar and ask Shimoki to make me a pairing.

One evening, Shimoki sets a long rectangular plate in front of me and says, *Japan*. The plate has three compartments: in the first, kyarabuki (saké-and-soy-sauce-simmered butterbur stems) made by my eighty-one-year-old neighbor; in the second is umeboshi (pickled ume "plums," botanically close to apricots) made by his friend's mother; and in the third a simple okaka (bonito flakes mixed with soy sauce). He pours an old-style saké—more austere and rough than the new fruity fresh brews targeted at wine lovers—into a sugi-wood cup.

The pickles alone would be too salty without saké. The scent of the sugi would be too strong without the pucker of umeboshi and pungent soy sauce. The rough saké is softened by the wood. Together it's poetry.

THURSDAY IS SHIMOKI's only day off. His hair, shaved close on the sides and long on top, is usually slicked back with a handful of gel; today it flops to the side boyishly. We're eating pizza with friends, and I ask him if there's a saké that would pair well with pizza. *Saké never pairs with cheese*, he insists (he will change his mind later). Wine pairing is different, he explains. With wine, you look for contrast, but with saké the ideal match creates a *spiral taste* (he expresses this with an exuberant gesture) where the saké and food enhance each other. You can achieve that with wine too, I counter. His friend agrees, but Shimoki is surprised. *I should study wine more*, he says, looking thoughtful. (But when he goes to France a year later for a saké event, he claims he has no time for wine and cheese, he must keep his focus on his life's work.)

The differences among saké are subtle, in part because of the nature of Japanese food. A Western dinner often comprises a main dish and sides to match—or it's served in courses—so wine can have a strong character as long as it suits the meal. But on a typical Japanese table, there are many small dishes at once, and the saké needs to be pliant enough to complement them all. And while Western food leans on fat for flavor, dashi (broth usually made from kelp and cured bonito) is the backbone of Japanese seasoning. With fatty, bold-flavored Western dishes, saké can become overpowered.

Another evening, before there are customers, we're discussing what would pair best with fresh young saké that tastes like pear and has a faint acidity. Melon and prosciutto maybe? It occurs to me that I am thinking about what food the saké would enhance, but Shimoki is thinking about what food would enhance the saké. I share this with him, and we both laugh at ourselves.

One person at a time, Shimoki makes converts. A thirty-six-year-old cooking teacher from Kyōto, a friend of mine whom I bring to Engawa, confesses that it's the first time in her life she's tasted saké. With her friends, she drinks beer or wine: it's easier, more casual. She wouldn't know how to pick a saké. But Shimoki gently and joyfully guides her, first pouring something from her hometown in Shikoku, reminiscent of the region's famous oranges.

The very same young people who statistics would have you believe don't consume saké fill up half the bar at Engawa most

tsubaki / camellia

nights. Fresh-faced salarymen and hotel concierges, two twenty-year-old aestheticians, couples on a romantic getaway—they drink cup after cup of whatever Shimoki recommends. Still, when I see some of the same girls at a Christmas party, they are drinking beer and wine. Without their master, the flock strays.

But Shimoki's devotion is unshaken. I am his disciple, and I know he hopes I will bring his teachings back to New York with me. While many Japanese people are adopting more Western customs and drinking less saké, the Western world is embracing Japanese cuisine and drinking more saké. Many people, including Shimoki, believe foreign acceptance may be the promising future of this declining industry.

I haven't caught Shimoki's single-minded zeal, but I've fallen for Yamanaka. It can be hard to break through the facade of etiquette and the constraints of hierarchy in Japan, but drinking (or even just being in drinking spaces) suspends rules and cements bonds. I want to loosen the buttons on my collar, roll up my sleeves, and get out into the fields and workshops of the people I've met.

One of the last times Shimoki and I taste together before my apprenticeship ends, he pours two new bottles of saké into small cups for me. The first blooms into the fragrance of a walk in the snow, with soft pine needles and the warmth of white rice cooking somewhere in the distance, a hint of umami from the sea, and a tingly finish that lingers. The second has a similar flavor, but it burns going down, and the finish stops short. The difference, he says, is that the latter wasn't made with feeling.

Shimoki has taught me appreciation for the nuances of saké, but more than that he's shown me how to care for details—all of them. He works with intention in every aspect of his business, from tidying the bathroom to selecting the best saké. Whether it's how to hang a coat or wash a glass or what temperature and cup to use for a particular saké, it has to be done with purpose.

Suko

TIME: *1 hour*
Makes about 1 liter (1 quart)

The pink-red pickles called suko look like rhubarb, but they're made from the stalks of a starchy corm called sato-imo (*Colocasia esculenta*, also known as taro) that's been a staple in Japan since before rice cultivation. Aka-zuiki, red sato-imo stalks as thick as celery, are a local specialty in Kaga, but green ones (*dasheen* in much of the Caribbean and *bac ha* in Vietnamese) can be found at some Asian and Caribbean markets in the United States.

At Engawa, Shimoki serves suko sprinkled with black sesame seeds as a complement to bright dry saké, such as Shishi no sato's Chōkara Junmai. At home, I add a drizzle of good sesame oil. The local grandmas serve them plain, on small dishes, as a tart and colorful contrast to brown winter meals.

There's a market in front of the onsen early on Sunday mornings; it's as much an occasion for old people to drink coffee together as for farmers to sell their produce. When the big bunches of rosy zuiki (sato-imo stalks) appeared in September, I asked Grandma Ishikura, the market boss, to teach me how to make suko. In her Shōwa-era kitchen—with pans and utensils hanging from a wire rack across the filmed-glass window, seasoning and tools crammed into every available space, walls stained tobacco color, and burners blackened from daily use—she taught me this recipe.

1 bunch zuiki (fresh taro stalks), preferably red (450 grams)

3 tablespoons fine sea salt

150 mL (⅔ cup) rice vinegar

6 tablespoons granulated sugar

1. It's easiest to peel the stalks while they are fresh and crisp, as soon as you buy them. Snap them in half, then peel off the translucent ribbons of skin (wear gloves if you don't want to stain your fingers). Discard the skin. If the bottom section of the stalk is much fatter than the top, slice it lengthwise into halves or thirds. Break or cut the peeled stalks into 5 cm (2-inch) lengths, and peel off any remaining threads of skin that this loosens.

2. In a large bowl, rinse the zuiki pieces in a few changes of cold water, then drain. Add enough fresh cold water to cover them, roughly 1 liter (4 cups). Mix in the salt, and put a plate on top to keep the pieces submerged. Soak for about 20 minutes.

3. Drain the zuiki pieces, and pat dry with a clean dish towel. Heat a large nonreactive pot over medium-high heat and add the zuiki to the dry pot (no oil). Stir until the surface of the pieces and the pot are dry, 3–5 minutes; the zuiki should be steaming but not scorching.

4. Add the vinegar and sugar, and stir just until the sugar is dissolved. Red zuiki will turn a shade of rosy pink. Immediately transfer to a glass bowl or container. Cool to room temperature, then cover and refrigerate. Suko will keep, refrigerated, for a few months. Serve as a drinking snack or side dish as is, or drizzle with a little sesame oil and sprinkle with black sesame seeds.

camellia sinensis

Two

The Tea Path

The essence of tea ceremony, it's said, is *ichigo ichie*, an idiom meaning that each encounter is a once-in-a-lifetime meeting. Tea ceremony is Japanese hospitality codified into a choreographed sequence of movements around serving and accepting matcha. In Kakuzo Okakura's 1906 *The Book of Tea*, he calls teaism "a religion of the art of life." Like Christianity in America, even if you don't participate in the way of tea, you're touched by it every day in Japan.

My tea lessons started while I was apprenticing in the saké bar. Mrs. Kitamura invited me to join her. She runs a fancy eel restaurant, called Meigetsurō, where geigi (a more polite word for geisha) sometimes perform for important guests, and she always looks elegant in her sheath dresses and feminine tweed jackets.

I was worried it would be boring: I hated the tedium of violin lessons and math classes when I was a child, and I still don't have much patience for repetition. But tea lessons seemed like a good chance to learn how to move and behave more like a proper Japanese lady—or at least less like a clumsy Westerner.

Japanese people seem to take up less space with their presence, neatly folding themselves into small spaces, speaking in soft voices, and moving through the world with an awareness of how they might affect others. I accidentally slam doors and bump into things.

Much is forgiven because I'm a foreigner. My proficiency with chopsticks draws a baffling amount of praise (given that I have used them since childhood, whenever the cuisine and context called for it). People seem to take pride in etiquette so complex that no outsider could ever fully understand it. But I want to do better than their low expectations of me. I approached tea lessons as "finishing school for foreigners."

Mrs. Kitamura told me to wear white socks and meet her at 2:00 P.M. on Thursday. Since then, I've spent my Thursday afternoons at our tea teacher Ōshita Sensei's house as often as possible, getting an education in much more than manners.

To step through Ōshita Sensei's gate—which frames a miniature landscape of carefully groomed trees and moss—is to step into another world. My attention turns first to keeping my footing over the slippery moss-covered steps carved into the great stone at the gate, and then I'm inside. Unlike the colorful abundance of an English cottage garden or the structured rows of French formalism, a Japanese garden is nearly monochromatic and flows in shapes that seem almost accidental (and yet embody centuries of consideration by tea masters and philosophers). Stepping-stones meander past dwarfed evergreens pruned to look untouched. I had only ever looked over the fence at private gardens like that before I found myself on the dewy path.

There are usually two or three other students. We leave our shoes in the entryway and pad down a long hallway in our white socks, past closed doors hiding any sign of daily life. They showed me, in my first lessons, how to kneel in front of the paper-paneled tearoom door, bow, slide myself over the threshold, and bow again before standing and walking over to appreciate the art and flowers displayed in a small alcove.

We pause to admire the scroll and flowers that Ōshita Sensei has arranged for the day. The scroll, usually an antique, may be an illustration, a poem, or an expressively drawn word that captures the feeling of the season. In a vase, two or three stems of carefully selected flowers or foliage bring the outdoors in. These aren't exuberant bouquets but quiet compositions. The more fleeting a flower, the more highly prized. Sensei keeps a calendar of Japan's seventy-two seasons, and the flora and fauna that appear, to help with his choice of flowers and teaware.

Seventy-two seasons may seem excessive, but if you are a farmer or a hunter, or if you walk an hour a day as Ōshita Sensei does, you'll notice that the starfish-shaped clusters of waxy leaves in the stone wall send up green shoots one week that bloom into purple flowers the next. Tiny green uguisu flit from branch to branch calling *hō-ho-KE-kyo*. The forest lights up with wild shaga iris, branches of golden yamabuki, and miniature mountain hydrangea.

As the days become humid, four-pointed white flowers bloom on the pungent dokudami that grows low along the edges of buildings. Frogs serenade each other through the rainy season, until the big blue cultivated hydrangeas give way to orange lilies, and the insects hum louder each day.

The sound of cicadas fades after the first chill days of fall. Spidery

higanbana bloom atop bare stems. Wet vermilion leaves stick to the cobblestones and
wash down to the river. One day the gray silk
moths of summer are gone, replaced by fuzzy
yellow ones mimicking the shape and color
of the last golden ginkgo leaves fluttering to
the ground. The calls of summer swallows
and bulbuls cease. Hawks circle against the
gray sky.

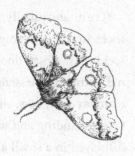

Improbably pink camellia blossoms come into full bloom the
week of the first snow. Fluorescent green fuki-no-tō force their
way through the frosty soil when spring still seems a far-off dream.
Before the cherry trees burst into thunderclouds of pink and white
petals, timid white wild ume and their bolder pink cultivars are
the first signs of spring. Ōshita Sensei brings a little of this into
the tearoom each time we meet.

Once I've taken in the essence of the season from the alcove, I'll
stand again and shuffle flat-footed to my seat on the floor, forming
an L shape with the other students. I haven't yet mastered this
grace, but at least I'm becoming more aware of my feet, less pon-
derous. I've heard it takes the landscapers who tend gardens like
Ōshita Sensei's years to perfect the way to walk softly in their flexible tabi shoes so as not to hurt the moss.

Toshio Ōshita Sensei is spry and intellectually curious. He looks
professorial in his pleated khaki trousers and wool vest, with his
gray hair neatly combed and parted. He tells me that he and his
wife enjoyed practicing tea together after their two sons left home.
He'd married into the Ōshita family—taking his wife's name because her family had a history of more than a thousand years in the

area, and her grandfather was a famous maki-e artist. (Maki-e, ornate lacquer painting dusted with precious minerals, is often used
to decorate teaware.) His mother-in-law and wife ran a tea school
to train young women in manners. When his wife died at sixty, he
decided to carry on her work, welcoming young men to learn too.

He brings the tea utensils into the room and kneels in front of
an iron kettle, sunk into the floor. Besides the scroll and flowers,
the iron kettle and tea utensils, the room is nearly bare. The walls
are colorless, not white but a warm shadowy absence. The floors
are padded with tatami mats and a narrow runner of faded carpet
to sit on.

Tea making begins with the crisp snap of the purple silk cloth
that Sensei takes from his waistband, pulling the two corners taut,
then folding it to wipe utensils that are already gleaming clean.
There's the low hum of the kettle, not quite simmering. His bamboo ladle sinking into the water, and then the trickle of water into
the bowl. There's the swish of the bamboo whisk, the chasen. He
turns it over to inspect it for broken tines and then rests it on
the edge of the tea bowl with a clink, repeat, and then he rests the
chasen softly and silently. Another swish and then the pouring
sound of the water being discarded into the kensui, a low wide
ceramic vessel.

Sensei opens the lacquered wooden container of powdered green tea, almost sound-
lessly, revealing the most vibrant color in the
whole room. It evokes the moss in the garden
outside and leaf buds in early spring. With a
chashaku, a narrow bamboo spoon, he scoops
the tea powder twice into the bowl and then

raps the chashaku twice against its rim. Again there is the sound of the ladle dipping into the kettle, the trickle of water, and the swoosh, swoosh, swoosh of fragile bamboo tines brushing briskly against the bottom of the bowl, frothing tea dust into hot water. He sets down the whisk softly. He serves the tea to the first guest, and I study their movements to see what I must do.

When the guest is done drinking the tea, Sensei works in reverse: rinsing the bowl, discarding the water, pouring in more water, swishing the whisk. To finish, he ladles cold water from another vessel into the kettle, silencing the roar of tiny bubbles against iron.

In the beginning, I always played the role of guest. I learned to bow with my fingers on the mat in a chevron, my palms softly curved as if cupping an egg; to accept the tea with two hands, bowing again to the guests at my right and left; to lower my head in gratitude, and then with one palm supporting the bowl rotate it clockwise so my lips won't touch the front (the most beautiful part); to lift the bowl two or three times to drink the frothy matcha, and then wipe the rim with my finger, before rotating the bowl back and setting it down in front of me.

The matcha is barely bitter, not grainy or harsh. It's grassy and bracing—tempered by the simple sweets we enjoy with it (the timing and technique for eating these still confound me).

This reverential proceeding befits a tea as labor and resource intensive as matcha. To make the best matcha, *Camellia sinensis* shrubs are shaded—traditionally with straw shelters—so that they receive only the faintest dappled light in the weeks before harvest. This concentrates umami-imparting theanine in the leaves that would otherwise be converted into astringent-tasting catechins.

The most tender leaves are plucked by hand, steamed, and dried. The dried leaves are stone ground into a fine powder. (At least, this is how it's supposed to be done: cheap matcha is not good, and good matcha is not cheap.)

After turning the empty bowl's front to face me again, I set it down gently. I cock my head from side to side admiring the design. Then I lift the bowl and gently rotate it to appreciate its features. Once, at a formal tea gathering in a Yamanaka garden, I drank from a bowl made in the sixteenth century. I'm used to seeing art and antiques behind glass in a museum; an artifact takes on a new resonance when you hold it in your hands.

If our lessons are a rehearsal, then a formal tea gathering—like the one where I held that five-hundred-year-old bowl—is the performance. At the real thing, the host serves everyone, but in our lessons we take turns playing host and guest.

Miki-chan, Ōshita's niece, goes next. She's in her thirties but dresses and talks like a sweet teenager. In floral leggings and pigtails, she's bubbly and cute, with big eyes, pretty long hair, and a playful skip in her step that she can't seem to contain in spite of more than a decade in the tearoom.

After some months, I'm asked to try to make tea too. Miki or Mrs. Kitamura sits beside me translating for Ōshita Sensei (with gesture and onomatopoeia as much as actual English). I learn how to hold the ladle in the most graceful manner and where to put my hands as I prepare the tools. The others correct me, and it's a relief: the tearoom is the one place where someone will actually tell me if I'm doing something wrong. I can let go of the constant anxiety I feel as a foreigner, that I might unknowingly offend someone.

The feeling that everyone in Yamanaka is watching me is not just in my head. I often hear from people I'm meeting for the first time that they saw me going for a run or having lunch with so-and-so. Sometimes, I embrace this, painting on red lipstick and pretending to be a movie star. If they're going to look, give them something to look at! Other times I wish I could be invisible. In America we say, *The squeaky wheel gets the oil*, but in Japan the saying goes, *The peg that sticks out gets knocked down*.

NEARLY FOUR YEARS into taking tea lessons on and off, I'm still a total novice; Tozaki-san, my serious elderly classmate who has been practicing for decades, would say the same thing. That's because tea, like martial arts, is a path, not something that you master and finish learning. To call it tea "ceremony" is a bit of a misnomer. In my lessons it's more like tea "practice," closer to a meditation than a celebration.

Chanoyu, as this practice is often called, means hot water for tea. In English, we use only one word for water, but in Japanese there are many. Mizu is the most general. Shimizu (shōzu in local dialect) is the purest, freshest water, and chōzu is for washing hands. Ohiya is chilled water to drink. Suidōsui is tap water. Oyu (the *o* is an honorific) is hot water for bathing or for making tea, ocha.

Chanoyu can also be called chadō or sadō. The *dō* part of the word (as in karatedō or jūdō) means way or path. You are always on it, never at the end. Though, arguably, my teacher and the other students are much further down the path than I am.

As Ōshita Sensei reminds me where to place each tool, I can see that the arrangement is correct in terms of what looks most pleasing. And there's an efficiency too, like a chef's *mise en place*, so you need not ever reach for something awkwardly. The details are exhausting, but I become aware of an aesthetic logic. When you finish making tea, you turn away from your guests to carry something dirty out of the room. If you carry something beautiful and clean, you turn toward your guests to leave.

Chanoyu is like a play in which the tea master has written directions for the set design, the dialogue, and the stage direction. We are the actors practicing our parts. Or it's like Sol LeWitt's wall drawings, for which he sent instructions for the museum staff to execute his work in graphite on the white walls. It's relational aesthetics—a living artwork about the interaction of host and guests—from four centuries before Nicolas Bourriaud wrote the book on it, or Rirkrit Tiravanija served noodles in a gallery. It is a vessel for social exchange.

The script that chajin, tea people, follow today originates with Sen Rikyū, a sixteenth-century tea master employed by the military leader and imperial regent Hideyoshi, though tea ceremony itself is much older. Sen Rikyū's one hundred rules for making tea read like a poetic Miss Manners. Here is a section, as translated in *Cha-No-Yu*, by A. L. Sadler:

If anyone wishes to enter the Way of Tea he must be his own
    teacher. . . .
No pains must be spared in helping anyone anxious to learn.
One who is ashamed to show ignorance will never be any
    good.
To become expert one needs first love, second dexterity and
    then perseverance.

In putting down a utensil after using it, do so regretfully as if
   you loved it.
When you give anyone flowers they must not be fully open,
   for it is impolite to the recipient.

Perhaps Rikyū became too powerful or too critical of his pa-
tron's excesses: he was ordered by Hideyoshi to commit ritual sui-
cide for suspected treason. After his death, his disciples quietly
carried on the way of tea. The most popular styles today are named
according to where Rikyū's great-grandsons became the next generation of influential tea masters. The two who shared the historic
Rikyū residence founded schools named for the position of their
houses. There's Urasenke, literally the back family, and Omote-
senke (which we practice), the front family. A third great-grandson
founded Mushanokōjisenke, named for the street where he taught.
A long family tree of masters descends from them.

Most modern Tokyoites have never entered a tearoom. It's a
classy hobby more associated with Kyōto, where traditional arts
thrive. But in fact, Ishikawa prefecture has the highest percentage
of tea students per capita of anywhere in Japan. Even in the tiny
town of Yamanaka, I have my pick of teachers and styles. High
schools have tearooms for their chanoyu clubs, and until the
1960s it was a typical part of premarriage training for young
women.

In Ishikawa, art appreciation and samurai culture run deep.
Toshiie Maeda, who built the Kaga Domain in the late sixteenth
century (which came to include Yamanaka), learned tea from Sen
Rikyū himself. Rikyū's way of tea aligned with samurai ideals of
discipline and simplicity—with living each day as though it

might be your last, which in a violent era was more fact of life than philosophy.

The Maeda clan—who ruled over the Kaga Domain for three centuries, until Japan was consolidated under central rule and samurai status dissolved in 1868—channeled their wealth into the arts so as not to threaten the shōgun, the military ruler who loosely united Japan's independent domains. The Maedas built Kenrokuen garden in Kanazawa, an expansive and beautiful disguise for training grounds, with moats masquerading as decorative ponds. They kept craftsmen close at hand, ready to fabricate the costumes and weapons of war: elaborately decorated helmets and swords. In peacetime, the craftsmen turned their attention to table- and teaware.

Tea was to the Japanese military class what cocktail parties later were to twentieth-century American socialites: an opportunity to show off your good taste and sharp wit. Teaware and works of art were as valuable to some of these military men as large pieces of territory, and rulers were quite happy to pay them in bowls, scrolls, and caddies rather than land.

After the Meiji Restoration in the late nineteenth century, Western hobbies like ballroom dancing took on prestige. To bolster their ranks, chanoyu masters welcomed more women, who make up the majority of tea practitioners today. Chanoyu has never entirely fallen out of fashion with the erudite and elite. To this day, it merits its own section in bookstores, and some athletes practice it to sharpen their focus.

EVERY WEEK, as two o'clock on Thursday afternoon approaches, I think I'd rather take a nap than go to my lesson. But I shower and put on nice clean clothes and walk a narrow cobblestone road through a grove of maples, crossing the arched hinoki Kōrogi Bridge over the Daishōji River.

The moment I walk through the gate into Sensei's garden, I'm glad I came. Samurai would put down their swords to enter the tearoom, and I put away my phone. At some point early on, Ōshita Sensei gave me a small fan, which I'm meant to place in front of me as I enter the tearoom, and then behind me once I take my seat. This is one of the rare places I'm fully present, disarmed from distraction. The plainness and precision of the practice enforces attention.

I learn, one day, how to open and close the sliding paper door to enter the tearoom. Kneeling in front of it, pulling it two-thirds open with my left hand, then pushing it the rest of the way with my right. And then, to close it, reversing the motions. Next I practice gliding across the tatami mat in six small steps, starting with my left foot.

Chanoyu is everything I'm bad at. I remember when as a teenage artist, full of energy, I was advised by a more mature painter that I had great ideas but I needed to practice teinei, handling my materials with respect and patience (it was a concept she had learned from Buddhist monks). Unless I am in nature, I have a hard time focusing on one thing for any length of time. In spite of better intentions, I'm a bit careless with the way I handle my belongings. Chanoyu trains us in grace and intention.

If it's starting to sound like mindfulness meditation, that's no coincidence. Both are secular practices intertwined with Zen Buddhism and Taoism. There are wild tea plants in Japan, but tea cultivation, along with these religious philosophies, came to

Japan from China (and via the Korean Peninsula). The eighth-century Chinese poet-priest Lu Yu wrote the first scripture of tea, *Chajing*, in which he emphasized mirroring the universal in the particular, speaking about tea with a reverence for the harmony in all things. It was during the Song dynasty that powdered tea whipped into water came into vogue, in parallel with the spiritual conviction that a process has greater meaning than its product.

But chajin are not ascetic monks, and they are free to surround themselves with beautiful worldly things. In autumn the natsume (tea container) we use is Yamanaka shikki, lacquered woodenware, decorated with gold chrysanthemums. In winter Sensei might switch to one with a silver moon. He rotates through various bowls with the rustic texture favored for tea, and earth-toned drippy glazes or spare illustrations of natural things—for the new year, a pale red sun rising over Mount Fuji. By chajin's standards, his tools are not luxurious—mostly acquired by his late mother-in-law for her students—but they are beautiful. At the end of teatime, the host places the tea utensils in front of the guests. The first guest, representing the others, admires each item and asks the host questions about it.

The spirit of this interaction, I believe, is for the host to show the guests the fine things that were prepared for their pleasure, and for the guests to show the host their appreciation. But vanity can easily intrude. Some practitioners buy new clothes and wares for each important gathering. This ostentatious, wasteful showing off seems to me to be at odds with the essence of chanoyu.

Japanese people (past and present) are not inherently averse to vulgar and garish decoration, but the rules of chanoyu helped spread minimalist and restrained taste in architecture, gardens, and ceramics. Ironically, the demand for naive rustic tea bowls by anonymous craftsmen, such as the plain Korean rice bowls favored by Sen Rikyū and his followers, drove up their price and prestige. It encouraged the development of whole schools of Japanese pottery: Raku, Shino, and Oribe.

In the words of Sen Rikyū:

> If you have one pot
> And can make your tea in it
> That will do quite well.
> How much does he lack himself
> Who must have a lot of things.

Frivolity disguised as frugality is nothing new (I wonder if even Rikyū succumbed to vanity at times). Some lords went to great lengths to construct modest tearooms and dress in peasant-like garb. Tea can easily slip from stylized meeting into ridiculous charade.

There's an allegory about a collector who bought a weathered vessel encrusted in oyster shells that appeared to be a rare antique and used it to hold flowers in his tearoom, hoping to impress his guests. Instead of the envy he hoped for, they showed surprise: it was a Chinese chamber pot.

I'm not sure if it was vanity or modesty that guided me when, committed to my lessons, I bought a wallet for my tea things (the fan Sensei gave me and kaishi, paper for sweets). I chose a rough gray silk. It looked plain, but it was not cheap.

Occasionally, I get glimpses of my teacher's life through a door accidentally left ajar (an exercise bike or a newspaper). He's shown me pictures of vacations to India and Spain with his children and grandchildren. Once he invited me to look at some dolls, set up for Hina Matsuri (Girls' Festival), that had been passed down in his wife's family since the Edo period. But I know little of Ōshita Sensei's life outside the tearoom: that too is concealed or made irrelevant by the formality of our interaction.

Tea feels removed from the world, but the things I've picked up by practicing are actually practical. On important occasions I can now politely sit seiza, kneeling with my knees together and feet crossed under my bottom, long enough for welcoming remarks to be made before a meal or a performer to be introduced. I can stand straight up from kneeling without flailing or lurching forward. (If you are not accustomed to sitting on the floor, try this, and you'll understand how far I've come!)

I can enter a restaurant, sliding a fragile door open and closed with care, without it rattling off its track or slamming into the door frame. And holding cups and bowls politely with two hands feels intuitive rather than awkward. The other day, a woman said my way of using chopsticks is more elegant than the manners of most young people in Japan, and I felt that it was a real compliment this time, not just that I'm doing well for a foolish foreigner. All that picking up and setting down of tea tools has put some grace in my hands.

I still can't remember all the steps for making tea—neither can Miki, who has been practicing since high school. But I get it now when I see a barman prepare a drink with elaborate and careful choreography. Each step has a purpose, but the purpose may be more aesthetic than practical. I see the way of tea in the fourteenth-generation saké brewer, still striving to improve his craft, or in the multiple-award-winning woodturner, still challenging himself to make something more beautiful. I notice how construction workers watch with intention as a colleague works, supporting them psychically. Tea mentality influences the culture in all kinds of ways. Or maybe it's the other way around: tea distills the values of Japanese culture.

In chanoyu there's even a protocol for the preparation before guests arrive and the cleanup afterward, which they will never see. When I finish making tea, I return all the tools to the mizuya, the room for washing and storing tea utensils. I rest the bamboo ladle on a hook on the wall and return the natsume and chashaku to the shelf. I kneel and scoop cool water from a clay basin into the kensui and tea bowl, washing them gently with my hands.

In summer, Sensei mists the garden with water before we come, to make it feel cool. We switch to a different tearoom. This one is screened in with reed doors that let through filtered sunlight and the sound of the river. We use shallower bowls in cool colors and patterns that evoke breeze and water. The kettle and basin are a different style, in a different position, and the choreography for making tea is different. I have to learn all over again.

With the different schools, the seasonal changes to tools, the varying methods for men and women, you could get lost in the apocrypha. But the structure is there to smooth the way for hospitality from the heart. Without sincerity, chanoyu is an empty vessel.

One bit of tea lore that sticks with me is a story about Sen Rikyū traveling to Uji to attend a tea gathering, with the nobles who were his students in tow. The host was thrilled to make tea for the great master and noblemen, but so nervous that he knocked the spoon off the natsume and then dropped the whisk, letting it roll across the floor. The nobles exchanged bemused glances, but Rikyū was pleased. He praised the host for being so focused on serving the tea at the ideal temperature to guests who'd traveled a great distance that he didn't even notice those small mistakes. In the end, the best etiquette is true thoughtfulness, and for that no training is better than simply paying attention.

When I leave the tearoom, the world feels fresh and bright. The mountain line seems more crisp, each tree in focus. I walk home across Kōrogi Bridge on light feet, wondering if this high is from caffeine, theanine, or the practice of chanoyu.

Kuri Yōkan

TIME: 30 *minutes, plus 2–3 hours to set*
Makes 36 small pieces

This sweet bean gelée, called yōkan, is studded with candied chestnuts colored yellow by gardenia petals. The father-daughter team at Sankaidō, a century-old wagashi shop in Yamanaka, taught me this recipe. Their subtle sweets change with the seasons. Kuri yōkan appears in mid-autumn, when urchin-like chestnuts fall from the trees.

During tea ceremony, sweets counter the bitterness of matcha. Instead of the flour and butter, chocolate and vanilla, that Western confections are made of, wagashi are concocted from rice pounded into mochi or milled into flour, sweet bean pastes, starch from fern roots, or gelatin-like seaweed. Their subtle flavors complement Japanese tea the way doughnuts do coffee.

  2 teaspoons kanten (agar-agar) powder

  75 grams (generous ¼ cup) brown zarame, turbinado, or raw sugar

  500 grams (2 cups) koshi-an (smooth adzuki jam), store-bought or homemade (page 325)

  Pinch of salt (optional)

  8 kuri kanroni (candied chestnuts in syrup), cut into 5 mm (¼-inch) slices

1. You'll need an 8-inch square pan, ungreased and unlined, preferably with a removable bottom. In a medium saucepan, whisk together 250 mL (1 cup) water and the kanten powder. Bring to a boil over high heat. Add the sugar and simmer, stirring, until dissolved. Lower

the heat to medium. Whisk in the koshi-an a little at a time (4–5 additions) until smooth. Mix in the salt if using.

2. Adjust the heat to keep the mixture bubbling but not sputtering. Stir frequently with a heatproof silicone spatula so the mixture doesn't scorch. The mixture will thicken and become glossy after about 10 minutes. Lift the spatula: when the mixture spills off in ribbons that slowly melt back in, turn off the heat.

3. Ladle a little of the mixture into the square pan—tilt the pan to spread it out into an even layer that just covers the bottom. Arrange the sliced chestnuts, spaced evenly, on top of the layer of yōkan. Slowly pour the rest of the mixture over the chestnuts. Spread it out with your spatula, then jiggle the pan so the yōkan settles.

4. Let the yōkan cool for about 20 minutes before transferring the pan to the refrigerator. Refrigerate until completely set, at least 2 hours. Once the yōkan is chilled, cover the pan with plastic wrap; it will keep in the refrigerator for 3–5 days.

5. If your pan is constructed with a removable bottom, lift it out before cutting the yōkan (if not, you may end up with some imperfect pieces, but it will be fine). Cut vertically into 6 sections, then horizontally, so you have 36 squares. Serve with freshly whisked matcha or other Japanese tea.

kuri / chestnut

geta

Three

Chrysanthemum Water

If you're not used to it, it's a bit awkward running into your landlady when you are completely naked getting ready to bathe. But in an onsen (hot spring) town, it's part of daily life. At the public hot spring bath I'm likely to exchange greetings with the shopkeeper I buy vegetables from, the serious older lady I know from tea lessons, my hunter friend's daughter or wife, or the clerk who sells me coffee at the convenience store. The onsen is the town's social, economic, and cultural center.

Until recently, any home within walking distance of the onsen didn't have a bath or shower, and some still don't. My apartment, in a modern cement building, has both, but like most of my neighbors I prefer the onsen. Why strip in a freezing-cold musty bathroom when I could instead step on warm clean stones and be cloaked in steam as I soak in mineral-rich hot spring water? It's only a five-minute walk from my place. I flash my pass to enter, stow my clothes in a locker, and carry my pink perforated bag of toiletries inside.

A high wooden ceiling arcs over a wide pool, ten paces by twelve paces across warm granite floors, with a small fountain bubbling in the middle. A glass wall along one side faces a narrow enclosed courtyard with a small pond where a few spindly stalks of bamboo bounce in the breeze. At the far end of the cavernous room, a bank of showers form an L-shaped corridor. The place hums with the sound of running water, punctuated by the echo of plastic stools and basins set down in front of the small round mirror at each shower station. There's the kind of ambient noise and chatter that breaks loneliness, even if you speak to no one.

At the busiest times of day, when all forty showers are running at once, the steam is so thick you can't see across the room. In the early morning hours, old ladies rule the onsen, marking their favorite shower spot with their pastel plastic caddies; they scrub each other's backs and swap gossip. Midday, there's a steady trickle of tourists, retirees, and hospitality workers. In the early evening, families and housewives bustle in and out, children meeting their friends and mothers relaxing for a moment before shuffling the kids off to dinner and bed.

Everyone has their routine. I avoid changing the time of day I go because if I do, some meddling grandma who mistakes me for a tourist will try to make sure I use enough soap or tell me how to wash my hair. This nosiness isn't all bad. If someone doesn't show up for a few days, people notice, worry, and ask after them. It is a safety net for elderly neighbors who might otherwise be isolated.

Often I meet my friend Mika, a papermaker and photographer, during the lull while most people are at dinner, a time when it's easy to find an open shower. We chat intermittently as we wash our hair, then soak in the onsen, sitting on the interior stone bench with hot water up to our shoulders. When we start to overheat, we perch on the polished granite ledge, worn down in places like the well-trodden marble stairs of a New York walk-up, our legs dangling in the water. Children play with bath toys, and old ladies do calisthenics.

If the water were any hotter, it would be scalding. The winters here are damp and chill you to the bone in a way that I remember from living in the Pacific Northwest. It's different from the harsh cold of icy Northeast winters—less shocking, but insidious. I leave the onsen feeling warmed to the core. The glow lasts long enough to walk home without a coat, drink a nightcap, and tuck into bed before the chill can catch up with me.

I once met a doctor who claimed the onsen could prevent cancer and heart disease. He might have been a quack, but I like the idea of a curative soak. If the minerals are healing me, that's nice, though maybe it's really the steam and warmth that makes me feel renewed each time, my face a little younger. Soaking in the onsen is a kind of daily meditation—away from work, the chores of home life, and communication with anyone who's not actually present. Some locals bathe there twice a day; their skin looks baby soft, and their countenance is calm.

An American friend asks me over the phone, *How do you have time?* It takes no longer to walk to the onsen than to run a bath. And the public bath is always sparkling clean without my having to lift a finger. Entry costs ¥460, an unlimited annual pass ¥22,000 (about $4 and $200, respectively). It's a much cheaper way to unwind than getting a massage or some kind of spa treatment. And

I'd rather use my leisure time going to the onsen than watching TV or scrolling through Instagram.

One night, as I left the onsen with Mika, I saw a flyer for "Culture Class" posted on the bulletin board outside, pinned among posters advertising golf for seniors and a multiday walk to Tōkyō to commemorate the annual Edo-period journey of samurai lords. Culture Class offered two options—singing or dancing—for studying the local folksong called "Yamankaka Bushi" and its musical offshoots.

I knew "Yamanaka Bushi" only from the recorded music piped through loudspeakers along the main street from morning to evening every weekend. To my untrained ear it sounded like the mournful wailing of a sea siren, layered over sparse percussive strumming and melodic plucking on the strings of a shamisen. The lugubrious otherworldly sound floats over the tile-roofed houses like the low clouds snaking through the mountains.

I'm terrible at singing (and "Yamanaka Bushi" is said to be the most difficult Japanese folk song), so I signed up for dance class.

Mika explained that I would need to wear a kimono or yukata; the flyer said I could borrow one from the teacher. Hardly anyone wears silk kimono as everyday clothing. Still, kimono is the most formal attire for important occasions, and it determines the shapes and movements of folk dance. There are courses in how to properly wear these traditional clothes (though the rigid rules for wearing them are only a few hundred years old) and rental shops that will dress you for wedding photos or a special day out.

If kimono is varsity level, yukata is JV. During festivals and fireworks displays, young people like to dress up in the colorful cotton garments, patterned with flowers and butterflies. But putting on a real yukata is still much more complicated than the loosely belted yukata robes (equivalent to a bathrobe) that you get from a hotel. I would need help. Mika called the teacher to tell her I wanted to borrow clothes. My landlady, Yoshiko, excited that I was interested in the local culture, offered to take me to the first class.

AFTER THE ONSEN, I sometimes have dinner or a drink at one of the bars or restaurants nearby (and that is how I began to learn the history of "Yamanaka Bushi," the town's folk song). They stay open late, buoyed by tourism. I can eat gyōza at Chōraku, the skins hand rolled to order; grilled whole fish at Gyoshin, impeccably fresh because the port is less than thirty minutes away; or teishoku at Eimi, homey side dishes crowding the tray of salt-cured fish, rice, and miso soup.

If I'm feeling down, I'll choose Saraku, a sushi shop on a dark narrow side street. The sushi is fine, but it's the conversation with the ebullient chef, Kenichi Hibino, that lifts my spirits. He has rectangular scholarly-looking glasses, a ring of short gray hair around the sides of his head, a riotous laugh, and an insatiable curiosity about astronomy, Yamanaka history, the Beatles, and the human beings who come to his shop. He's written a book on Yamanaka's folk music. And his wife, whose darkly painted eyes and magenta frown look like the face of someone who doesn't tolerate nonsense (actually, she's funny and kind), is an expert in singing it. With the slightest encouragement Hibino will launch into lively stories about the history of "Yamanaka Bushi."

Until a century ago, walking through Yamanaka, you might have heard the voices of young women singing outside an open-air bath in the center of town. Between voyages, merchant seamen came inland from the ports of Hashidate and Shioya to spend a week or two relaxing at the onsen. Following the same road that carried salt, fish, and seaweed from the coast into the mountains, they brought with them folk music from the places they traveled. They sang with the bath attendants called yukatabe—girls who carried guests' towels from their lodgings and kept their robes dry while they bathed. Their songs became part of the Yamanaka folk songs, Hibino tells me, and geigi (geisha) became the keepers of that musical tradition.

The outdoor bath, and the girls singing beside it, are long gone. In 1931 all of Yamanaka's downtown burned in a great fire. The co-ed onsen was replaced with separate men's and women's facilities (by then, Western/Christian body shame had seeped into Japanese consciousness) and a wide plaza spreading between them. Each hotel or ryokan now has their own onsen, so there's no need for yukatabe to escort guests to the public bath.

In front of the men's onsen, steam rises from an outdoor fountain with a statue of a white egret. In the plaza, a weeping willow that's grown taller than the high green tile roofs of the bathhouses nearly dips its branches into the ashi-yu, a shallow pool where travelers can sit on a stone bench beneath a shelter, soaking their weary feet in onsen water. Swallows nest in the eaves of the grand building housing the women's bath, welcome center, and performance hall. Well-fed koi swim lackadaisically in a moatlike pond.

The singing yukatabe and merchant seamen have been replaced with the recording of Yamanaka folk music broadcast along the main street on weekends. This soundtrack coincides with an influx of tourists arriving by bus and taxi. In fall and winter they are mostly from Japan, China, and South Korea; they come to eat crab from nearby ports, take pictures of autumn leaves, and watch the snow fall from the warmth of a hot spring bath. In spring, a few of the Americans and Europeans who come to Japan for cherry blossom season make it all the way to Yamanaka (few enough that they are sometimes mistaken for me, or assumed to be my friends). Tour groups and solo travelers follow in the footsteps of the seventeenth-century poet Basho Matsuō, visiting the sites of his beloved haiku (and perhaps having a plate of omuraisu or pancakes at the smoky coffee shop named for him).

They stroll through town in the yukata robes provided by their hotel or ryokan. At night, hearing the clip-clop of their geta (thonged wooden sandals) on the stone sidewalks, you can easily imagine you've slipped back in time.

Inside the ladies' locker room at the onsen there's a reproduction of a mid-nineteenth-century map of Yamanaka. The town doesn't look so different now—constrained on one side by the Daishōji River and on the other by Mizunashi Mountain—with one long main street cutting north to south, the onsen and a plaza at the heart, and the temple, Iōji, on the mountainside above.

An original print of that map is housed in Iōji, along with many of the town's most important artifacts, including a set of painted scrolls from 1812 that tell Yamanaka's origin story. (The set is a reproduction of an earlier one that was lost in a fire long ago.) It is the only physical record of a history that was otherwise preserved by storytelling, person to person, generation to generation.

One morning, I went to see these artifacts at Iōji. Kyoukou Kano, the head monk, asked me to kneel before the grand altar as he chanted a prayer. Then he led me into the temple's interior, the

sheer black robe that shrouded his cotton tunic and pants fluttering ever so slightly as he walked. He knelt, unrolled the set of
yellowed scrolls on the floor, and narrated the story.

According to the mint-green-and-ocher-painted panels and the
inked text, the hot spring was discovered by a monk named Gyōki
around 700 C.E. Yakushi Nyorai, a god of healing, appeared to him
as an old man and told him where to dig. A bathhouse was built
around the spring that Gyōki discovered there, and he established
a temple on the hill, in the place where we are now looking over
the scroll. In the centuries that followed, Gyōki's temple and hot
spring were destroyed by fire and war, and forgotten.

The next scroll tells of the samurai lord Hasebe hiking toward
the forgotten onsen with his twelve attendants on a falconry expedi-
tion in the 1190s. They encountered a beautiful young woman,
Yakushi incarnate. As Hasebe's men crouched in waiting, one of them
holding a gray-brown goshawk, Yakushi told Hasebe to look for a
white egret healing its wounds in the hot-spring water, and dig
there. She urged him to rebuild the bath and the temple on the hill.

In the next panel we see the lively hot spring bath, surrounded
by guesthouses. Kano pointed to a woman covering her head with
a scarf, an indication that she's wealthy, and other ordinary people
with no shoes. *All classes of people, men and women, bathed in the onsen*,
he said. There's a blind monk playing a biwa, a sort of lute. Yamanaka was a destination for pilgrimages, from Kyōto and farther
afield. *The onsen was like a salon*, said Kano, a place for the exchange
of ideas and culture.

By the time the poet Bashō Matsuo visited on his famous journey north in the late seventeenth century, writing haiku along the
2,450-kilometer trek that would become *Narrow Road to the Inte-*

rior, Yamanaka was well established as a retreat for physical and spiritual healing. Neighboring Yamashiro Onsen had developed into a red-light district, selling sex and entertainment. Yamanaka was where you went for a quiet cure (but even the ailing and exhausted crave pleasure, hence the yukatabe and geigi to delight them). Bashō stayed in Yamanaka nine days and wrote an ode to its hot spring, referencing the Chinese legend of longevity-granting dew on a chrysanthemum's petal. Looking up from the image of the public bath, Kano recited the poem:

> At Yamanaka
> no need to pick chrysanthemums
> fragrance of hot springs.

Some years after Yamanaka was immortalized in *Narrow Road to the Interior*, Yamanaka's hot spring was renamed Kikunoyu, Chrysanthemum Water. Phrases from that poem were incorporated into folk songs. *Yu no kaori*, the fragrance of hot springs—I hear it sung longingly, the last syllable stretching toward something.

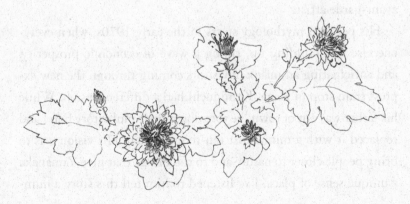

Kano turned to the two-hundred-year-old map, which lists the industries that grew alongside onsen tourism: among them, charcoal making, forestry, and wood turning. Crafts flourished because travelers wanted souvenirs.

It's about thirteen hundred years on and off that Yamanaka has been a tourist destination. Somehow it has thrived on that tourism without becoming phony. (And onsen tourism is the most popular kind of domestic travel in Japan.)

In no small part, this is thanks (in recent decades) to the visionary owner of one particular ryokan, Kayotei. Even at eighty-seven, Masanori Kamiguchi is a strikingly handsome man—with snow-white hair and unblemished skin. Maybe it's the onsen water, or that he long ago gave up alcohol, coffee, and most animal products (for the pleasure of being contrary as much as for his health). His clothes are understated but for the flourish of an ascot or an interesting hat (he's especially fond of the lambskin cap his daughter-in-law bought him in Canada). I don't know if I've ever met anyone as sure and consistent in their aesthetic sensibility—as absolutely correct. He's all social grace and impeccable manners, but bubbling under the surface is the mischievous temperament of an avant-garde artist.

His personal mythology starts in the early 1970s, when everyone else was building up, riding a wave of economic prosperity, and anticipating an influx of visitors coming through the new express train stop in Kaga. Kamiguchi had a different vision. While his father was out of town, he tore down their multistory hotel and replaced it with a minimalist ten-room ryokan. His vision was to bring people closer to nature and to the things that give Yamanaka a unique sense of place. I've listened to him tell this story a number of times, over wild herb tea, sipped out of a china cup in Kayōtei's lounge. (I can't afford to stay at Kayōtei, but sometimes Kamiguchi invites me to stop by for a chat or to use their onsen.) Wrapped in the calm of a comfortable chair with a view of the forest, I feel as if I could hear a leaf drop.

Kayōtei's aesthetic is so complete that to stay there (even just for tea) is to inhabit a work of art. His philosophy is that a ryokan should provide something you can have only there, in that town, on that land, with those things growing. He curates an elite group of local artisans—craftsmen, artists, and food producers—whose work gives shape to this philosophy.

There's the rice farmer who uses no pesticides or herbicides and instead has ducks in his fields. To get by, he must sell his crop for double the price of heavily subsidized conventional rice, and Kayōtei buys most of it. There's the nori maker who handpicks only the best buds of the young seaweed, who is still in business solely because of Kayōtei. There are the top woodturners, whose delicate cups and bowls show the natural grain of the material; Kayōtei uses these wares to serve sweets, miso soup, and saké. My friend Mika's handmade paper, installed in a wood-slat screen, glows with warm lamplight in one of the peacefully dim hallways.

The things these artisans make enrich guests' experience of Kayōtei. And that experience cultivates connoisseurship. Guests can request to visit one of these woodturners, take a papermaking workshop, or see how tofu is manufactured. Through Kayōtei's patronage, the artisans are able to make a living selling their work to collectors and gourmands from all over the world.

Kamiguchi's influence extends beyond the ten rooms of his ryokan and the people who stay there. He's worked in and with local government to shape policies that preserve the history and scenery that make Yamanaka beautiful.

As in so many rural towns the world over, the population of Yamanaka is aging and diminishing. I buy notions from the small sewing store, marveling that the shopkeeper has enough business to stay afloat. I've bought pens, their plastic caps so sun bleached and brittle that they crumbled when I got home, from a small stationery shop open only a few days a week. On the way to the supermarket I pass a sign for a bookstore, but the windows are covered. There used to be a movie theater, a bowling alley, a cable car, and a small ski slope. Even in the past few years I've watched businesses disappear and empty houses get torn down when they became fire hazards. I wonder sometimes if the town will eventually return to wilderness.

IT WAS POURING RAIN the first day of Culture Class, so my landlady, Yoshiko, drove me in her boxy bright pink Hustler and helped me get settled in. Class was held in the same building that houses the women's onsen, in a practice room behind the theater. In the entryway, there were umbrellas and half a dozen pairs of zori, the shiny sandals worn with kimono. They belonged to my classmates, mostly housewives in their fifties and sixties whose children were grown. They seemed excited to have a new young person join them. I wondered where my peers were—did they not care about the folk traditions of their town?

Even sixty years ago, there were still two hundred geigi in Yamanaka. Now there are five. Twenty-something-year-old Konoha is the only new member in at least a decade. These sophisticated entertainers—versed in music, dance, hospitality, and conversation— are the keepers of Yamanaka's folk traditions. They don't like the word "geisha," which conjures stereotypes and misconceptions that what they do is sex work. Geiko sounds old-fashioned and is strongly associated with Kyōto, so they call themselves geigi, skilled entertainers.

Like most old folk songs, "Yamanaka Bushi" has many variations. A geigi named Yonehachi (the first) standardized the lyrics and melody of "Yamanaka Bushi." She recorded it in 1931 to preserve it for posterity. Her successor left for Tōkyō to become a pop star. *I am to blame*, she has said, *for spoiling this fantastic folksong*, for letting this beautiful music fade.

I'd seen refined geigi, most of them old enough to be my grandmother, singing and strumming shamisen in the fall festival. But Culture Class was the first time I'd met one in person.

Botan Sensei, Yamanaka's most senior geigi (whose name means Peony), teaches the class. She is stout, with short gray hair and a bit of pink eyeshadow brushed from the inner corner of her eyelid to her tidy eyebrows. She's pleasingly blunt and has a reputation for scolding customers who show up late or misbehave.

Geigi Botan (born Chizuko Matsuzake) grew up in nearby Fukui prefecture, and her friend's mother was a geigi. She admired the woman's beautiful clothes and elegant manner and saw becoming a geigi as a way to escape home. During her first month in Yamanaka she trained every day in singing, shamisen, taiko, and dance. Then she started trailing more experienced geigi to learn how to pour saké, lead drinking games, and entertain guests. She has continued, over the six decades that followed, to earn certifications in teaching various kinds of dance. *I will never finish training,* she says. *There is no ceiling, no goal. If you stop making an effort to improve, you will lose your skill.*

As the most senior geigi, Botan has no special title but has extra responsibility. I've heard people say Yamanaka's geigi tradition will collapse without her. Her daughter, known as Geigi Kiyono, became a geigi later in life, after getting married. Her husband urged her to help her mother as the number of geigi in Yamanaka dwindled. *What customers want has changed*, says Botan Sensei. *They're more likely to hire a hostess and sing karaoke.*

Geigi Kiyono helped me into a blue and white yukata and belted it with a navy and gold obi. It was barely long enough to reach my ankles (ideally, it would nearly brush the tops of my feet). Thankfully, I'd guessed (correctly) that I should wear the white split-toed socks I wear for my tea lessons. I was grateful too that tea lessons had taught me to kneel and stand with control. The narrow straight lines of the skirt required me to keep my knees together and my feet tucked neatly under me. As we knelt on the tatami floor, Kamiguchi (owner of Kayōtei ryokan) arrived to make remarks for the beginning of this year's class. Thirty years ago, he established a preservation society for "Yamanaka Bushi." *I'm eighty-seven*, he said, *so I have about ten more years to do my best for supporting Yamanaka's culture.*

Everyone else had taken the lessons before, and they expected me to follow along as they began dancing. I had no idea what I was doing! But tea lessons had prepared me for that too. I followed the teacher's movements as best I could. We acted out the stories told by three songs: "Yamanaka Bushi" ("bushi" means "folk song"), "Yamanaka Yakyoku" (nocturne), and "Yamanaka Shigure" (rain shower).

The first one we practiced was "Yamanaka Bushi." The lyrics and choreography lead a guest through town and on a romantic walk across the Kōrogi Bridge, pointing to the temple on the hill, the fish in the river, and the mountains in the distance.

Botan Sensei tried to help me by calling out right and left in English, but it was actually harder for me to switch back and forth between languages. She had the idea that counting off the steps would help me, a Westerner, but it only confused me because what I heard in the music often had nothing to do with fours or eights. The class lasts an hour with a short break in the middle for tea. The slow movements are surprisingly strenuous. After the first lesson, I went home and lay down on the floor, mentally and physically exhausted.

The next week, I felt no less awkward and clumsy, but wearing a yukata and moving to the wistful music, I tried to channel the poise of a geigi. I watched the straight lines that the most graceful dancers made with their torsos, the way they glided across the floor, taking small steps. I've spent most of my life trying to break my natural habit of standing pigeon-toed, but Botan Sensei instructed me to point my feet in, ladylike. She told me to keep my fingers together and thumbs tucked under, and I was glad, for once, to know what to do with my hands.

This dance has none of the playful flailing or sexual gyrations that I associate with dancing, no quick footwork or fancy spins. Instead, it's like the slow elegant movement of an egret across a rice paddy. Any eroticism is contained in a contemplative cocking of the head, the seductive modesty of obscuring one's face with a hand.

Usually, Botan Sensei's daughter, Geigi Kiyono, or another

young (fortyish) geigi would attend, and I watched them carefully. Geigi are masters of facial expression: they maintain a look that's at once movingly emotive and utterly unreadable. When I caught a glimpse of my face in the mirror, it was comically serious and strained. But I could see my body making the mannered shapes that I thought were some royalty-like grace bestowed only upon the most cultured Japanese women, pictured in black-and-white photos of powder-faced ladies holding parasols and fans.

For some dances, we hid our hands inside our sleeves, and our arms became wings, fluttering back and forth and closing over our chests. I struggled to withdraw my hands into the too-short sleeves of my borrowed yukata. If I was going to continue the classes, I thought, I should get a yukata that fits, and I began asking my friends where I could buy one.

Before I had a chance to go shopping, my neighbor Noriko (my landlady's sister-in-law) appeared at my door with a yukata and a satin obi wrapped in a dry cleaning bag. She'd heard I needed a longer yukata, and she too is tall (by Japanese standards; I am five feet six).

She didn't use it often, she said, handing me the warm gray yukata, patterned with lilac dragonflies and pale green rippling pools of water. The obi was deep orchid and gold green, with birds taking off in flight. It was almost the colors I'd choose if I bought my own yukata, and it was plenty long.

It wasn't strictly necessary, but I bought a pair of geta to complete my outfit. At the local sandal shop, I picked out a set of wooden soles and woven lilac thongs that the shopkeeper attached. As soon as I slipped my feet into the geta, my gait transformed from a purposeful stride to a modest shuffle.

Still uncertain of how to put on the yukata, I shuffled to the onsen for a bath before class. I was sure I'd find guidance there. In the locker room, as soon as I began to struggle with the yukata, a group of grandmas swooped in to help me. They straightened me out and belted me in and fussed over the best kind of bow, deciding on a chōchō (butterfly), like the ribbon on a fancy present.

It wasn't until the fourth or fifth lesson that I realized that the silk tenugui (hand towels) we use as props for the dances really are towels. Towels: because these dances came from women who worked beside the onsen.

For the sad love song called "Yamanaka Shigure," we swish our towels like a gymnastics ribbon as the song describes steam rising off the water. We unfurl the blue and white rectangles of fluttering silk and coyly hide behind them. I imagine yukatabe playfully flirting with guests. As the song ends, we wave the towel like a flag of surrender, while the singer wails, *The music of Yamanaka hot spring town, it sounds like weeping.*

I'VE LEARNED BY NOW how to tie a chōchō myself, but I'm still late to class most weeks, because I think that I have figured out how to put on my yukata, but mess up and have to watch YouTube clips to learn it again. A yukata or kimono is constructed of straight rectangular lengths of cloth, and the shape comes from how you wrap and tie it, adjusting it to your own body.

I raise the hem to my ankles and cross the left side of the yukata over the right, pulling it tight at my hips. There are two white cotton under-belts to hold it in place. I tie the first one low around my waist to shape the skirt. Then I adjust the top part of the yukata so it folds neatly over the skirt, like a blouse. I pull down the collar to a fist's distance from the back of my neck and adjust where it crosses in front to make a high V-neck. I tie the second belt around my true waist to keep the upper part of the yukata in place. Sometimes, at that point, I realize the hem is too high above my ankles, or the seam in back is crooked, and I have to start all over.

Once I've got that sorted, I prepare to tie the stiff silk obi around my waist. I crease one end in half lengthwise and drape it over my shoulder. The other end drags on the floor. I pick up the long end and wrap it around my waist two times and pull it tight. I tie it off with the part that was draped over my shoulder, folding the extra length into a carefully constructed bow. I slide this around to the back, by rotating the obi clockwise, and check myself in the mirror.

I don't have the petite, long-waisted, narrow-hipped, flat-chested physique that these clothes are made for. But when it's belted and tied right, my yukata is surprisingly flattering. I stand up a little straighter.

I trot down the alley toward the onsen, taking the back way because I still feel shy about dressing in Japanese clothes, unsure if it's acceptable (even though it's required). I hope that I look more like one of the refined Kyōto ladies who dress in earth-toned kimono regularly than like the tourists posing for photos in too-bright costumes. Or maybe like one of my cool counterculture friends, who blend kimono with everyday yōfuku, Western clothes, wearing it as easily as the hippie-inspired outfits they've appropriated.

My favorite dance tells a story of seduction and separation, set to the song called "Yamanaka Yakyoku," about a young woman's affair with a traveler who must leave. She kneels at her vanity applying lipstick, then opens the doors to greet her lover. At first, she falls back, covering her face shyly. Then, next thing you know, he's gone. She calls after him, *Remember the town of love, Yamanaka.*

This has always been a place where people from far and wide come and go, meeting at the hot spring. It has inspired music and haiku. Yamanaka may be a small town, but its history is one of exchange, not isolation. The onsen is still a place for the transmission of culture.

When the classes end, I try to return the yukata to my neighbor. *Oh no,* she says, *it's a gift! I would be glad if you take it back to America and wear it there.*

Saké Kasu Ice Cream

TIME: *20 minutes, plus chilling and churning*
Makes about 1 liter (1 quart)

One of the great pleasures of life in Yamanaka is eating a saké kasu soft serve after a soak in the public hot spring, Kikunoyu. They sell the cones year-round at Shishi no sato, the local saké brewery, just a block away from the baths. Its refreshing and not-too-sweet flavor has all the floral yeasty aromas of saké without the alcoholic burn. Here's a homemade version: eat it straight from the churn for that airy almost-melting texture of soft serve, or let it firm up in the freezer and serve creamy golden-tinted scoops atop wafer cones.

> *Note*: Saké kasu is sold at Japanese markets in sheets, crumbles, or paste. Sometimes you can get it directly from a saké brewery. It will continue to ferment in your refrigerator but can keep almost indefinitely in the freezer. If you purchase sheets or crumbles (most common in the United States), make a paste so it's easy to work with: smash it with a fork, adding saké or water as needed until it is the consistency of miso paste. Store in a glass jar; leaving it loosely covered at room temperature for a day or two will help the paste soften and integrate. After that, keep it refrigerated with the lid sealed and use within 3 months. (It may never spoil, but the color and flavor will change.)

5 egg yolks

100 grams (½ cup) granulated sugar

70 grams (¼ cup) saké kasu paste (see note)

725 mL (3 cups) half-and-half (pasteurized or ultra-pasteurized)

½ teaspoon fine sea salt

1. In a large bowl, whisk together the egg yolks and sugar until the mixture is pale and no longer feels grainy, about 3 minutes. Place the saké kasu in a medium heavy-bottomed pot or the top of a double boiler and gradually mix in the half-and-half (some lumps are okay). Whisk in the egg mixture and salt.

2. Warm the mixture over medium heat, stirring constantly, until it thickens to a custard, about 10 minutes. (To check if it has cooked enough, dip a spoon in the custard: a finger swiped across the back of the spoon should leave a clear trail.) Strain the custard through a fine-mesh sieve into a large bowl.

3. Before churning, chill completely: either in the refrigerator for at least 6 hours, or over an ice bath, stirring occasionally, for about an hour.

4. Churn the custard in an ice cream maker (according to the manufacturer's instructions) until it reaches the texture of soft serve. Eat immediately, or freeze in a loaf pan, tightly covered. The flavor is best within a few days of making it.

Four

Saké Goddess

The spirit of saké is female. Her name is Matsuo. Some people say the reason for the old prohibition against women entering a sakagura, the building where saké is brewed, is that Matsuo Sama could get jealous. I was told it was the saké brewer's wife who would be suspicious. Whatever the real reason for the long-standing exclusion of women, it was unimaginable that I would actually get to work inside Yamanaka's saké brewery: in fourteen generations the Matsuura family had never employed a lady—or a foreigner.

But now I carry in my wallet a small folded slip of paper inscribed with a prayer to the spirit of saké: a protective talisman called an omamori. It was given to me by the kannushi, the Shintō shrine keeper, who came to bless the sakagura on the first Sunday in November, the start of the saké-making season.

Shishi no sato, the brand name of the saké that has been brewed beside the hot springs of Yamanaka since 1772, means village of the lions. It's named for the yukatabe girls who would wait beside the open-air baths, attending to visitors with dry towels and songs for entertainment. With the guests' yukata draped over their heads to keep the cloth dry and free from wrinkles, it was said the girls looked like shishimai, lion dancers. A lyric in an old Yamanaka folk song talks about looking down from Iōji, on the hill above town, at the lion girls around the hot spring.

I arrived at the sakagura on the first Sunday in November a little before 7:30 A.M., with my own mane of unruly curls tamed into two tight braids, self-conscious about leaving even one strand behind in a place usually closed to women. Fumiaki Matsuura, the fifty-year-old owner and tōji (brewmaster), ushered me into the

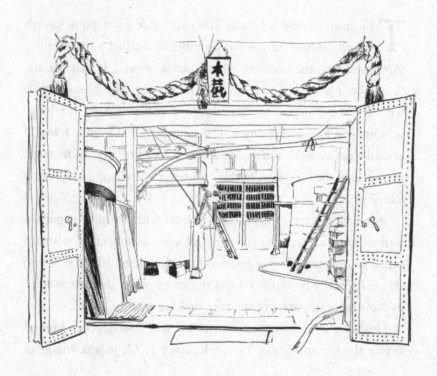

2,640-square-meter warehouse where six men brew and bottle fifty kiloliters of saké each year. That's enough genshu (undiluted saké) to fill about thirty thousand big party-size bottles—enough to serve all the residents and tourists in Yamanaka and a loyal following in Tōkyō too.

I hoped, if I was lucky, to watch their work for a few days, but Matsuura had prepared a navy blue work jacket with "Shishi no sato" embroidered in white script above the breast pocket, a white mesh hat, white rubber boots with my name on them, and a pair of slippers for break time—a wardrobe that made me part of the team, a kurabito (brewery worker). In the small break room, he introduced me to each of the five kurabito, who were gathered around a kerosene heater, sitting cross-legged on a worn raspberry-colored carpet. Even the men who wouldn't start work until later in the winter had come that morning for the blessing.

The kannushi arrived, dressed in wide pants and a robe of crisp silk dyed muted eggplant and embroidered in platinum chrysanthemums, with long kimono sleeves—their inner cuff banded in vermilion—that nearly brushed the floor. A tall glittering black hat conferred a sense of majesty. We followed him past rows of battered aluminum buckets and a network of water valves and steam pipes, through a set of heavy doors with a thick rope of rice straw hanging over them like the entrance to a shrine. Housed inside were dozens of enameled steel tanks painted institutional gray green. We climbed eighteen ominously steep wooden stairs that took us above the tanks to the second floor and sat in a row facing a modest shrine on the wall.

The kannushi chanted and waved a stick feathered with fluttering strips of white paper, an ōnusa. Periodically we bowed at his

indication. With my head lowered, I studied the tangles of black scratches on the floorboards—which looked to me like an exuberant abstract expressionist painting—etched into the wood over a century of labor (the original sakagura burned down with most of Yamanaka in 1931).

After some time, the kannushi finished speaking and pressed play on a small portable speaker. Ancient-sounding music came out of the white plastic cylinder. I watched carefully (thankful for my place second to last) as he handed each person a waxy green branch of sakaki leaves to place in front of the shrine. When my turn came, I stood to accept the branch, bowed, walked to the table in front of the shrine, bowed, placed the branch atop the others, bowed twice, clapped twice, bowed, and returned to my seat.

Finally, he poured us each a small cup of saké. There were remarks about a good year ahead, and then we drank. It was not yet eight in the morning. We proceeded to follow Matsuura and the kannushi around the brewery so each important place could be purified, the swoosh of the paper tassels cutting through the quiet of the cool morning air.

Shintō is a belief system in which everything has a spirit. If there is a god in water, a god in rice, a god in saké, then a sakagura is like a shrine. Our work is worship. The most devotional act of all is cleaning. For the first two days, we wash every tool, tank, hose, and cloth in the sakagura. Thoroughness is prized over speed; as we run our hands over every surface, we encounter cracks and tears and repair them. I get to know each room and each piece of equipment as we take them apart and wash them (though I don't yet understand how they are used).

The warm wet smell of sugi wood fills the air as we scrub the big lids the tanks using stiff-bristled tawashi brushes, their palm fibers making a satisfying *swoosh, swoosh* across the sudsy wood. We work in tandem, dancing around each other to rinse, scrub, rinse, lift. Soapy water pools around our white boots on the concrete floor.

Caring for your space and tools is something everyone here has done since elementary school, when they were taught to clean their own classrooms, so there's no sense that *someone else will clean it up* if you leave a mess. Cleaning isn't a task relegated to low-skilled laborers: everyone pitches in, including the boss, Matsuura.

Matsuura is confident and purposeful inside the sakagura, setting an energetic example for his team, but he seemed painfully shy when I first met him. It was the winter I apprenticed at Shimoki's bar, at the height of the saké-brewing season. On a rare night off, Matsuura had come to drink beer. He wore khaki dad pants and conservative wire-rimmed glasses. Shimoki wanted me to ask all my questions about saké, and he pushed us together like an awkward couple on a blind date. As we talked, Matsuura kept his eyes politely averted, occasionally glancing up through fringed bangs that had grown a little too long since his last haircut.

In a mix of Japanese and halting English, he explained that Shun, my favorite saké, took years to perfect because he wanted it to be unassuming, not showy or complicated. Like a good bottle of Rhône table wine, it's intended to drink easily, transforming to suit whatever food you want to eat. That balanced simplicity, the illusion of effortlessness, is the hardest thing to achieve, he told me.

It was clear, though, that Matsuura wanted to relax and not think about saké that night. We escaped Shimoki's overeager encouragement, leaving with a couple of friends (Nakajima the woodturner and Mika the papermaker) to eat midnight fried chicken and drink beer and highballs. By the time we parted ways, Matsuura had promised I could visit his brewery. But in the sober clarity of morning he changed his mind.

There were a couple more drunken promises—broken by morning—before I did finally get my tour. He walked me past steam billowing through cloth in the dawn light and let me taste saké scooped straight from the tank. A few years passed, with many shared bottles of saké, beer, and wine, before I gained Matsuura's confidence to see more than a glimpse of how saké is made. Now here I am: a kurabito—or at least dressed like one.

WE ALL TAKE BREAKS at the same time: thirty minutes at 10:00 A.M., lunch at noon followed by nap time until 1:15, and another thirty minutes at 3:00. It might seem like a lot of downtime, but the work is both physically demanding and mentally taxing (I am often in bed by 8:00 P.M. after a nine-hour day of lifting bags of rice and recording precise measurements). The kurabito need to stay sharp so they don't get hurt or make a mistake. Over green tea and instant coffee, I get to know my co-workers.

Kajiya-san is the most senior, in years and experience. He has big teeth and baby-smooth skin, perhaps from four decades of being awash in steam and kōji at various sakagura where he worked. On every break he falls asleep and starts snoring, but when he's awake, he loves to write things on the whiteboard and lecture to no one in particular about the technical details of making saké. In the off-season, he grows adzuki beans and a local variety of saké rice, called Ishikawamon.

Kitano-san is a sixty-seven-year-old retired ironworker with a weathered face who spends his summers hobby fishing. He has a knack for using whatever is lying around to make clever repairs and modifications. Worried about his paunch, he claims to be on a diet, which entails eating Cup Noodle and an onigiri for lunch every day. (Sometimes he has cake instead of onigiri.) Occasionally, he speaks a word or two of well-timed, clearly enunciated English.

Gato-san, thirty-nine, is the only year-round worker and the youngest. His love of soccer and baseball translates to an athlete's physical ease. He's tall, with a strong nose and a ready smile— often bemused but cheerful with his co-workers. He doesn't talk to me much, but greets me heartily in the morning, and in the break room he graciously passes napkins or fills my coffee. With good-natured teasing, he reminds the other men to be respectful of the lady in their midst.

In January, fifty-year-old Nakaya-san and Kimura-san will join. The former, a lumberjack, looks nothing like the bearded flannel-clad woodsmen in my hometown. Fresh-faced and svelte, he plays bugle in a military-style band and is always ready with a goofy joke. His wife makes him cute bentō lunches that I envy. Kimura has deep-set eyes and salt-and-pepper hair. He's busier than usual this year with his main job: high-end carpentry. When our paths do cross briefly, the impression he makes is of sophistication and calm.

Break is over when Matsuura announces, *Yarō!* Let's do it! And everyone sweeps into action. From November to April they will transform rice and water into twelve kinds of saké, and I will see each step: kōji, shubo, moromi, pressing, and bottling. When we leave the sakagura a little past five, bats swoop and circle in the darkening sky.

ON THE THIRD DAY, we begin the afternoon routine of washing and soaking the next day's rice. Matsuura and his men will go through six tons of rice by April, carefully measuring it into buckets, tumbling it in a whirlpool of water that runs off cloudy, feeding it into mesh sacks, and bathing each sack in its own orange plastic tub before spinning it dry in a wire basket hanging from a beam on four white ropes. Gato spins the basket and water droplets fly off.

They weigh each bag of soaked and spun rice to calculate the water absorption (though Matsuura can get a pretty good idea by watching the grains turn opaque in their bath). The ideal soaking temperature is 10 degrees Celsius—the same as the water rice plants soak up in a paddy in early spring. But each day they adjust the soaking time to the day's conditions. The mesh bags rest on racks overnight, swaddled in foam insulation.

If saké has something like terroir, it's from the local water, not from the rice. As much as twenty-one thousand liters of water pours through this warehouse in a day. Most of it is piped down from Mizunashi Mountain (a name that means no-water mountain, curiously) through an aqueduct built under Iōji. Only the sakagura and the temple use this water.

Most sakagura order the best rice from wherever it's grown, and that can change year to year. With few exceptions, yeast is cultivated in labs, and kōji spores come from one of four companies. And yet each region— each sakagura—has its own characteristics. Matsuura dreams of one day making saké entirely with material from Yamanaka, but for now only a small portion of rice comes from around here, the Ishikawamon from Kajiya's farm.

Rice is delivered once a month in thirty-kilo brown paper sacks, labeled with the polish rate: the percentage of the grain that remains. Like rice for eating, saké rice is hulled and milled from brown to white. But then they keep going, polishing away the outer layer of proteins and lipids toward the starchy core until less than 65 percent of the grain remains. That inner core that would be food for a germinating sprout is also perfect nutrition for the microbes that transform it into saké.

Like wine and beer, saké relies on yeast to convert sugar into alcohol. Grapes, already sweet, need only be crushed for wild yeasts to get to work. Beer brewers coax starch-converting enzymes out of barley by letting it begin to germinate. For saké, enzymes from a miraculous mold called kōji, *Aspergillus oryzae*, break down rice starch into food for yeast.

Before you let your mind stray to the blue-green growth on old sandwich bread, think of the healing powers of penicillin, the delicious streaks of blue in Stilton, the powdery rind that's evidence of good salami. Kome kōji, rice inoculated with kōji spores, is opaque with white peach fuzz and sweet smelling. Mold can do beautiful things.

Various strains of kōji work in the fermentation of miso, soy sauce, and saké. Matsuura has named one of his most refined bottlings after it: Oryzae, with a big calligraphic *O* brushed on the label. *Kōji makes rice into fruit*, he says.

To enter the kōji-making room, the muro, I will change my shoes three times. Upon arrival at the brewery, I leave my street shoes in the office (which Matsuura has designated as the ladies' locker and nap room) and put on my white rubber boots. I'll wash my hands as I enter the work area where steaming and washing are done. I'll pass through the threshold of the warehouse full of gray-green fermentation tanks and leave my boots at the base of the stairs, where I'll change into black faux-leather slippers. At the top of the stairs, I'll wash my hands again, and mist them with alcohol. I'll sanitize my hands again before entering the muro and leave my slippers at the doorway, stepping into a pair of knockoff athleisure slides.

Of everything that happens in a saké brewery, kōji making is the work most closely guarded. The slightest disturbance of the microbiome in the muro could make it all go wrong. Visitors are rarely allowed inside, and kurabito are prohibited from eating nattō (sticky-slimy fermented soybeans), kimchi, or shiokara (fermented cuttlefish) because of the powerful microbes these foods transmit.

I am not religious or particularly superstitious, but I pay my respects to the saké spirit every day that I'm in the sakagura. In front of the small shrine where the kannushi officiated the opening ceremony, I bow twice, clap twice, and bow again. *Thank you for letting me be here, please don't let me screw anything up*, I pray. I like to think that, rather than a rival, Matsuo Sama is my ally in the sisterhood of saké. Recently, more women are entering the industry, and making some of the finest brews. And women, after all, made the first saké by chewing rice—the enzymes in saliva doing the work that's now done by kōji.

The three-day process of making kōji rice starts in the morning. Steam billows into the white cloth covering a metal vat the size of a small hot tub, which holds enough rice to fill about a thousand bowls. It puffs toward the ceiling in a great white cloud, as if from a smokestack, tickling the thick wooden beams and rusted green exhaust pipe high overhead and then escaping through chicken-wire-covered windows where the high ceiling comes to a peak. Shafts of daylight filter through the windows, reflecting on tubs of water where Kitano or Gato—haloed in a soft haze—wash the mesh bags and cloths that swaddled the rice since soaking it the previous night.

It's all hands on deck to shovel the steamed rice into bundles of cloth netting, which are hoisted in a metal tub to the second floor by a motorized winch. Upstairs, outside the muro, the hot rice is spread out on loosely woven cloth in wooden boxes lined with bamboo slats. Now the upstairs is shrouded in steam too.

The rice for kōji is firm and bouncy—almost gelatinous—not cooked soft and sticky like the rice we'll add to the mother and mash later. We break apart the clumps by hand to let off heat. It takes only a few minutes to cool from hot to warm, and then we gather the cloth and carry the bundles of rice into the muro.

The warm rice is mounded on a canvas-covered steel table (actually eight tables zip-tied together) that nearly fills the room. We fold more canvas over the pile of rice, then tuck it in under layers of breathable insulating cloth, fleece blankets, and a twenty-year-old sheet of Gore-Tex (a formula to let it cool slowly without losing too much moisture) to rest until the afternoon.

After lunch, we return to the muro. In the days prior, there had been a bit of fuss about what I should wear. The men often go shirtless or wear loose happi that ties at the waist and hangs open at the chest. Matsuura decided that I should have a T-shirt instead, and provided one for me. Gato-san had advised me to bring *half pants*, which I assumed meant shorts.

I'm wearing the T-shirt and a pair of three-quarter-length running tights under my jumpsuit, because I'm not really sure where I could change privately (and making a fuss over it would draw more attention to my difference). The men simply strip to their boxers and put on a happi and apron. Having spent a lot of time camping and bicycle racing, I'm not fazed by co-ed immodesty. I peel off my jumpsuit, take an apron from the hook with my name on it, and follow them into the muro.

Inside, it feels as hot as a sauna. Towels twisted into hachimaki and tied around our foreheads catch beads of sweat as we spread the rice out on the table.

Puffs of gray-green spores drop in tendrils from a mesh-bottom pan that Matsuura shakes with one hand—as if dusting an enormous cake with powdered sugar—his arm outstretched and gaze focused. A few minutes later we mix the grains by hand and then dust them again. This time, I sprinkle the spores, called kōji-kin, and Matsuura snaps photos, eagerly documenting the first time a woman—a foreigner—has worked in this room.

We mound the kōji-kin-dusted rice into an island in the middle of the table, forming sheer cliffs down its sides. Again, we wrap it in sheets and blankets, putting it to bed for the night.

In the morning of the second day, the rice is softly matted and sweet smelling. We break up the velvety white grains—opaque now—and ferry them to the second chamber of the muro, where they're spread out on a bed of loosely woven cloth.

Two boards hold the inoculated rice in a ten-centimeter-deep layer, and the cloth is folded over to protect it. We return to the muro again after lunch, and before going home for the night, moving the boards a little farther apart to spread out the kōji. Matsuura will come back again at night when everyone else has gone home.

Each time, we run our hands through the kōji to let off heat and gasses. As *Aspergillus oryzae* works its way into the rice—transforming starch into sugar—it can generate enough heat to kill itself, or mature to gray green (useless for fermentation) before penetrating all the grains. It needs careful tending.

On the third and final day, the kōji smells sharper, almost sour. We leave it alone to let it grow roots, threading the rice into a fuzzy white mat. I follow Matsuura upstairs to check its temperature every few hours (he wants the kōji rice to get to 42 degrees Celsius, but not too quickly). By lunchtime it smells like roasted chestnuts, and by mid-afternoon, when the kōji is ready to take out, its scent resembles shimeji mushrooms. It's grown what looks like thistledown in miniature.

Rice is planet, says Matsuura, noticing me studying a clump of kōji rice on my palm. *Kōji is trees*.

Other kōji, which we make for the moromi (mash), will be harvested earlier when it's still snow-white, but for the mother it's allowed to ripen to soft yellow, as if lit by incandescent lamps. It looks especially luminous on the naturally golden Ishikawamon rice from Kajiya's fields.

We break up the spongy mat, crumbling the soft clumps in our hands until the fragrant grains fall through our fingers. The heat makes me sleepy and light-headed. I want to lie down in this fuzzy warm bed of kōji rice! I want to bathe in its perfume!

We scoop up the kōji rice and shuttle it outside to the drying room, where it will wait in suspended animation until being added to the shubo, or saké mother, tomorrow.

This work gets more intense as the days get colder and the batches get bigger. The muro is nicknamed Hawaii, and it can be a shock to the system going there from the cold of the warehouse (especially if you've been in Hokkaidō, the drafty uninsulated wing where the pressing machine lives). On particularly long hot days spent in Hawaii, Matsuura sometimes treats us to ice cream on our afternoon break.

In Hawaii, I make my first big mistake. I'd wondered if the three-quarter-length tights and T-shirt I'd been wearing in the muro might make the guys self-conscious. It's like if I went to a swimming pool fully clothed: That would be weird, right? Kajiya is often shirtless and in short boxer briefs (he'll put on a happi for some small measure of modesty if I'm around). So I get myself some flyless women's boxers made of thick cotton that seem to me not unlike the tiny shorts taiko drummers and festival performers wear, or the shorts favored by marathon runners, and wear them the next time I work in the muro. The new boxers are certainly more comfortable than the three-quarter-length tights that hold the sweat behind my knees.

A few days later I go out for dinner with Matsuura and our bilingual friend Takuya. Once we've all had a few drinks, Matsuura asks Takuya to explain that what I wore in the muro was too tight or revealing and he was worried the guys would find it sexy. *But don't worry,* he assures me, *this is just between us.* Takuya tries to make light of the situation, suggesting I wear a burka. Red-faced, I change the topic.

I'm mortified. I've been trying so hard not to intrude and I totally screwed up. As much as I might want to be, I am not one of the guys. How had I so misjudged the situation? The last thing I want to do is cause trouble! Did I ruin everything? I save my tears for when I'm home by myself, but it keeps me up at night.

I'm also furious. There's a reason the men wear so little: it's really hot in the muro! My body is what it is—why should I have to hide it?

But I put my outrage in check. How can I expect Matsuura and his men to understand third-wave feminism when the second wave is still working its way through the general population of Japan? And I'm here to learn about what they do, not to change them. Fair or not, the rules are different for men and women.

The next time I come to work, Matsuura has a pair of knee-length baggy basketball shorts for me. He apologizes that he hadn't prepared something before. From now on, I change my clothes around the corner from the muro, in the room with the shrine (Matsuo Sama is a lady too, so it's fine). I still don't know if it was the running tights or the boxers that were too sexy, or both. But I didn't lose my job, and eventually I got my sense of humor back.

WE TAKE TURNS tending the kōji in pairs, and that's where Matsuura and I talk, while kneading spores into steamed rice or running our fingers through clumps of kōji rice to cool it. *It's amazing,* he marvels, *that people could converse with the microbiome before they had modern science to explain it. They did everything by observation.*

Matsuura is curious about my childhood, my parents, the movies and music I like. When he was young, he didn't plan to take over the brewery. He wanted to escape. He loved James Bond movies and dreamed of traveling the world, so he studied hard and went to college to become a diplomat.

But before he could follow in the footsteps of his rakish hero, he felt the pull of the family business. His ancestors had come to Kaga from Imari (where the famous porcelain is made) as oil merchants in the seventeenth century. They opened the sakagura in 1772. Now the legacy of the family business depended on him.

Inspired by (and competitive with) his good friend Takagi, who was also born into a saké family, he decided to become a tōji, a brewmaster. He studied for two years at the brewing institute in Hiroshima, spent a few months working at Takagi's sakagura, Jūyondai, and then a few months at another sakagura outside Tōkyō.

He returned to his family brewery to support their tōji, Yaegashi. (Until recently, the owner of a sakagura did not make his own saké; he hired a tōji.) Yaegashi was from up north in Iwate, a man so tough he gnawed on chicken bones, prone to mood swings, but always gentle with the kōji and yeast. As Matsuura set to work cleaning the old neglected equipment, a strange thing happened: the saké started to smell like mold.

The next ten years were hell. They had to filter all the saké with charcoal to get rid of the strange smell, but the filtering also took away most of the flavor. That had been the style in the 1990s, but in the new century people were interested in rich-tasting unfiltered saké. The health department directed Yaegashi and Matsuura to use more bleach, but the smell only got worse. The brewery lost two-thirds of its business and nearly went bankrupt. Matsuura brought in visiting tōji and scientists from all over Japan to try to solve the problem. They could not find mold, and yet the smell persisted.

Meanwhile, he tried adding yeast to the filtered saké after bottling, so the flavor wouldn't be so flat. It didn't work how he expected, but he accidentally created what might have been the first bottle-fermented sparkling saké. (Later, he'd refine that recipe into the slim blue bottle of bubbly he calls Sen.)

Finally, one of the scientists had a breakthrough: there is a chemical reaction between wood, bleach, and kōji enzymes that makes saké smell like mold. Together, this scientist and Matsuura persuaded the health department to change the rules. They stopped cleaning the muro with bleach, and the problem was solved.

But by then, the business had lost so much they couldn't afford to pay a tōji. Yaegashi graciously resigned to let Matsuura take over. Cautiously, incrementally, Matsuura made operations more efficient. Once he eliminated unnecessary tools and clutter, they needed fewer people. Over time he found he could shift the rhythm of the microbiome so it didn't require all-night tending (as had been the norm in old saké breweries). He dedicated himself to making saké that is as fresh as mountain air and makes you want to eat and drink more and more. When someone tastes Shishi no sato, he says, he wants them to know it's Shishi no sato.

Two decades later, Shishi no sato has been praised by saké writers including the preeminent English-language expert John Gauntner and featured in trendy Japanese magazines; most important to Matsuura, it's beloved by gourmands. He has been asked more than thirty times to export to the United States, he says, but his small sakagura is already at capacity. Quality is more important to him than growth, and he doesn't want to be beholden to banks or investors. Matsuura has transformed the brand, but the influence of Yaegashi, the former tōji, can still be felt inside the sakagura—particularly when it comes time to mix the shubo.

THE CHARACTERS FOR "shubo" literally translate to saké mother. Like levain for sourdough bread, the mixture provides a nursery for yeast to grow and multiply. A week before making the moromi, or mash, in one of the big tanks, Matsuura mixes up the shubo in a smaller vat. He doctors the soft water—piped down from beneath the temple on the hillside above—with minerals to encourage healthy yeast and lactic acid to guard against intruders. He pours in bottles of yeast that he's been culturing and incubating in a tiny bio lab at the south corner of the sakagura. The men ferry down kōji and stir it in. They steam rice, wetter and softer this time, and spread it out to cool; then into the vat it goes.

Gato, because he's tallest and strongest (or at least youngest), is in charge of mixing the shubo by hand. This method is from Iwate, where Yaegashi was from. Gato stands on two wooden crates, his legs spread wide for stability, and folds himself over the edge of the vat, reaching his long arms to the bottom to bring up the kōji that's sunk to the bottom. The mixture is like soggy cereal now, bits of steamed rice and kōji floating in cloudy liquid. His arms are submerged nearly to the shoulder, his face turned sideways to keep his nose from dipping into the slosh.

By afternoon the rice has sucked up the water, and the mixture is thick as porridge. The second stirring is even harder work. But by the third time, in the evening, the kōji has nearly softened the rice, and the shubo is fluid again. By tomorrow, it will be a bubbling liquid fragrant with yeast.

Matsuura is certain that no one else in Ishikawa mixes their shubo this way. Even in Iwate, hardly anyone mixes the shubo by hand anymore: there are laborsaving machines that can do it. But hands are gentler on the rice; hands can tell you more about texture and temperature and whether the kōji is evenly mixed through.

Over the next week and a half the shubo will bubble and expand as yeast colonizes the vat and the enzymes from kōji dissolve the rice. It smells at first of its ingredients, and then like white bread, Asian pear, lemon, alcohol, ripe peach, and sour apple candy—changing every few hours until it settles into maturity and smells like the beginning of saké.

Soon there's a second shubo going (I get to mix it when Gato has the day off to take his son to soccer, reaching my arms deep into the cold porridge until my cheek nearly touches the milky surface), a third batch of kōji, and then another and another. The pace picks up as the tasks layer, cycling over one another.

BY THE END of November the first shubo is teeming with yeast (400 million per milliliter, were you to count). It's ready for making moromi: the mash of rice, kōji, yeast, and spring water that will become saké. So as not to break what remains of the grains, we transfer the shubo to the big tank by the bucketful rather than pumping it through a hose.

The next morning, kōji tumbles into the tank from a trapdoor in the second floor. Steamed rice, vacuumed through a giant hose, falls like hail. Carbon-filtered water floods the tank until the mixture reaches about one-quarter of the way up. This is the moromi— much like the mash for beer or whisky—on its way to becoming saké. Over the course of days, as the yeast multiplies, it will get three more feedings of rice, kōji, and water.

Matsuura strides around the brewery making notes on temperatures, analyzing samples scooped from bubbling vats of shubo and moromi, plotting data points on graphs, assessing what adjustments need to be made, and directing the flow of work.

A shift of one degree in the temperature of the moromi at the wrong time could be catastrophic. There are some thirty enzymes in kōji. To activate the enzymes that bring out the flavors he wants, Matsuura manages the arc of temperature change throughout the fermentation. It's warmer than usual this winter. Matsuura adjusts the thermostat on the cooling coils that wrap each tank. If he needs to heat a moromi, he puts a lightbulb or an electric burner beneath the tank.

By mid-December there are four tanks full of moromi. I trail Matsuura up a wooden ladder to the planks that run alongside the tanks. At first, I was afraid of tumbling to the cement floor three meters below. But then the body memory of childhood days spent scrambling around in barn rafters for the pure joy of being up high came back to me.

From this vantage point, you can see into the tanks and smell their constantly morphing perfume that hints at pear, apple, mo-chi, narcissus flowers, and banana cream pie. A thick froth of big bubbles caps the younger batches of moromi. Yeast rests suspended in this foam, while kōji settled at the bottom converts starch into sugar to feed the yeast. There are newer foamless yeasts that work faster and more cleanly, allowing tōji to fill the tanks higher with-out risk of overflow. But Matsuura prefers the complex flavors achieved by a slow, stratified fermentation.

Peering into the more mature tanks, I see that the froth has sub-sided and the mixture looks milky and smooth, with little air bub-bles popping audibly at the surface as in a simmering pot. The yeast is more active now throughout the moromi, making sugar into al-cohol. Today the one named Muku smells like a forest after rain.

Matsuura teaches me to stir the moromi with a long pole called a kaibō, like a gondolier's paddle. He shows me how to scoop up the moromi with a hishaku, a cup on a stick like the one you use to wash your hands before entering a shrine, ladling it into a cloth-lined funnel so the liquid can drip into a beaker for analysis.

Analysis is my favorite job. Usually, only Matsuura does it, but he has taught me how. And today he leaves me alone in the small room of beakers, flasks, pipettes, and syringes—like a high school chemistry lab. Matsuura apologizes for the rudimentary equip-ment: there are fancy tanks that measure all this for you, display it on a digital screen, and even automatically adjust the temperature. But later, when I ask him about those high-tech tanks, he says they are toys. There are so many variables—the moisture content of the rice, the humidity, the character of the kōji—that the tech-nology cannot account for.

I test the samples for sweetness with a delicate glass Baumé hydrometer calibrated for saké and then drip in red dye to measure the acidity, recording the data in Matsuura's notebook. He returns to help me distill a small amount to measure the proof. We test for amino acid released by the yeast as they die off: when amino acid is high, it's time to stop fermentation. *The timing for pasteurizing and bottling*, says Matsuura, *is like the timing for taking a picture.*

LATER, AS MATSUURA feeds the first moromi of the year its final dessert—a saccharine mix of rice and enzymes—he tells me that the mash is like a party (that lasts for a month). First, there's a speech from the host (the kōji) to greet the guests (yeast). This is when things are just getting going; not much is happening yet. Then there's a dance performance, a burst of activity. The guests begin eating the rice, cooked by kōji's enzymes. It quiets down while the host makes another lengthy toast. Then the party ramps up, building and building, everyone eating and dancing. After everyone gets drunk and passes out, a few guests (yeast) are still dancing. There's sometimes dessert for the last men standing.

It sounds exactly like the kind of rigid Japanese event that I find trying, but it helps me visualize what's going on in the tank. I'd better not do anything to spoil the party if I want to be invited back.

WHEN THE PARTY is over, it's time to press the saké. Matsuura uses a machine called a Yabuta that has been in service here for more than four decades. It looks like a giant accordion of pressurized cushions. These cushions are fastened to metal panels, and a great arm pushes the bellows together. This makes a kind of segmented tube for the moromi to pour into. The cushions expand with air, sandwiching the solids and pressing the liquid out. The moromi pours into the accordion through a tube at the top looking like porridge, and clear saké drains out another tube at the bottom. From there, it's pumped into a clean holding tank to await pasteurization and bottling.

We've just pressed the first saké of the year, a junmai made from Kajiya's Ishikawamon. Matsuura ladles out three cups with a small hishaku. The first taste is for Matsuo Sama, and we hurry upstairs to place it on the altar and bow in gratitude. *Thank god my presence didn't screw it up!*

Next, Matsuura hands a cup to me. Sharp and unsettled, it's effervescent and faintly reminiscent of whisky, hinting at vanilla. As it pours into a holding tank, it shimmers straw yellow, evoking fields of Ishikawamon under the late summer sun. The rest will mellow in the tank for a few days, awaiting dilution, pasteurization, and bottling.

The next day, we pull apart the cloth-covered metal frames of the accordion and peel off the saké kasu—the sediment of rice, kōji, and yeast—that's left behind. It comes away in segmented sheets, thick as a wool blanket and the color of ivory, that we stack in turquoise plastic crates and weigh. It will be packaged and sold for stirring into miso soup, for pickling daikon radish, or for cooking into sweet ginger-scented amazake as the days get colder.

The first saké to be released to the public will be Muku, unpasteurized and unfiltered, meant to be consumed while it's fresh as the snow that's falling now and drunk before the spring thaw.

When we press it, Matsuura reserves five buckets (10 percent) of the moromi and passes it through a loosely woven cloth, straining out just the solid pieces of rice. He adds this milky liquid back to the tank of clear saké, to round out and soften Muku's flavor and give it a faint white glow.

Muku will be released on the solstice, a full moon this year. Its name means purity. Matsuura mentions a prolific television and film actress, and a Kabuki actor famous for his roles as women, who are waiting for Muku. *Pressure!* he says, but I can tell he's proud.

A FEW DAYS before the new year, I come down with a cold. Matsuura sends me home early with two bottles of Muku. It's good with fish, he says, or osechi ryōri—the salty-sweet dishes eaten in the first few days of the year to bring luck and health. That sounds nice, but I expect I'll ring in the new year with instant noodles and herb tea. Then, on New Year's Eve, a friend comes to my door to deliver a shiny stacked bentō of osechi ryōri, wrapped in a red silk cloth.

On January 1, feeling a little better, I untie the red cloth and open a bottle of Muku. In my glass, the particles of sediment refract a moonlike glow. The fragrance is reminiscent of snowdrops. The flavor of the saké blooms as I put gems of tazukuri into my mouth, tiny crisp fish candied in soy sauce and sugar, studded with sesame seeds. I bite into a piece of oily fish wrapped in soft simmered konbu, and now Muku tastes like the sea, cold and bracing, bringing to mind arms of kelp dancing in crystal clear water. Eating lightly pickled strings of daikon radish and carrot woven with threads of yuzu, and thin lacy rounds of peppery vinegared renkon (lotus root), I taste the mellow sweetness of kōji in the next sip of saké. A chestnut wrapped in mashed sweet potato calls forth the smell of forest floor that Muku's moromi had in the tank, evoking crumbling wet leaves beneath my feet, mushrooms growing among fallen pine needles. It drops deeper into the soil as I eat chikuzenni: chicken, burdock, and carrots cut like flowers, simmered in deeply seasoned dashi. With candied black soybeans it tastes briny.

All this, and yet it's as easy to drink as cool mountain water (which, after all, some 80 percent of it is). All this, from a quiet saké in an unassuming bottle.

IN JANUARY AND FEBRUARY, nearly every sakagura in Japan is making daiginjō. Technically, what defines daiginjō—and makes it precious and expensive—is the high polish of the rice. Often 40 percent or less of the grain remains, at most 50 percent. But the starchy pearls get special treatment through every step, from kōji making to squeezing. Matsuura says technique and heart are as important as the polish rate. He named his daiginjō for the rice it's made from: Aiyama.

If Yamada Nishiki is the king of saké rice (it's what almost everyone uses for their daiginjō), then Aiyama is the queen. Robust, elegant, and not easily manipulated, she doesn't get the recognition she deserves. The cultivar was brought into being during World War II and obscured by the events of that era. For decades, Aiyama was raised by one farm, for one sakagura. But in 1996—when Matsuura was becoming a tōji—an earthquake destroyed that sakagura, and they halted production for a year. Matsuura and his peers bought the rice to support the farm, and his romance with Aiyama has continued ever since.

For his daiginjō, Matsuura dusts the steamed Aiyama sparingly with kōji spores bundled in a purse of gauze. He incubates the kōji rice in small wooden boxes instead of all together on the table and ferments the shubo (which smells like strawberry) in a smaller-than-usual vat so he can control the temperature precisely. The moromi (the big mash) has its own room, apart from the other brews. It's the only one that gets daily analysis, and he plots the points on a complex graph, meticulously monitoring the arc of fermentation, coaxing the moromi to follow an ideal curve. He makes only one tank of daiginjō per year; it cannot fail.

In early February, standing on the catwalk above the tank of creamy immature daiginjō, Matsuura asks me what it smells like. I lean over the edge and inhale. It evokes a cold blue stream running over mossy rocks. He ladles out a cupful and gives it to me: it's sweet and astringent, like the skin of Asian pear. Matsuura never tastes the saké before it's done, but he likes me to try it and tell him what I think.

There was a time when his daiginjō won contests seven years in a row, but that's not what he's going for now. *The saké that wins contests*, he says, *tastes like perfume*. And saké that wins in spring is not good by summer. He wants to make something that enhances—and is enhanced by—food. *Saké that's a breath of clean mountain air to refresh city people*. That blooms in spring, but doesn't peak until much later.

I think it tastes lovely, but Matsuura says this daiginjō is off track. He wanted to keep the daiginjō rice whole to make a delicate flavor, but it's melting. It's because the rice dryer was broken.

February is his least favorite month. As tank after tank matures, he can see his mistakes. He looks perpetually tired. The first batch of chōkara, extra dry, is sweet because of a few warm days. And there are hoses that need to be replaced, but he can't do it until summer because new hoses leach off-flavors. Still he says, *I will never give up*. After the ten years of struggle and near bankruptcy at the beginning of his tenure, nothing seems insurmountable. *You have to control your mind before you can control the saké*, he says.

Meanwhile, more tanks bubble away. There's another batch of Muku, a chōkara that really is extra dry, and a junmai called Shun—that understated food-friendly table saké that first made me appreciate Shishi no sato. For fun, Matsuura tries making a saké with two kinds of yeast. *I want to surprise Shimoki*, he says. The moromi is hyperactive and smells like rye; he aims fans at the tank to keep the bubbles from overflowing. Altogether, Matsuura makes twelve different kinds of saké.

One afternoon I help him blend a five-year-old junmai, the color of weathered bronze, into a fresh tank of pale yellow junmai. When we add water, the color changes to green gold. It doesn't dilute the flavor: it opens it, like a few drops of water in a fine scotch. It tastes lemony and bright. This is the bottling of Kizuna he'll release for cherry blossom season. The one that everyone will drink at the town's fall festival is still wild in spring; it needs to mellow over the summer.

Upstairs the shubo for Sen smells like white bread. Sen—the sparkling saké he created by chance during the hardest years—is Matsuura's favorite child. A gift from god, he says. Later, its moromi smells like chiffon cake. It won't be ready to drink for another two years.

TEN DAYS BEFORE squeezing the daiginjō, we begin preparation. Instead of sending it all through the Yabuta press, we'll drip a portion of the daiginjō through heavy cotton bags. We soak the bags in cold filtered water, washing them daily and changing the water. We clean big 18-liter glass jars, drying them on a wooden rack in the daiginjō room. Nearly three weeks into February we rinse the bags and jars one final time and cut lengths of nylon twine. Matsuura shows me the graph: it's back on track. The moromi tastes like chilled pear.

The next day Nakaya and Kajiya stand on the platform stirring and scooping; Kimura balances on the ladder below them, holding up a bucket, and from the bucket fills bags that Matsuura hands up one at a time. Gato and I balance on wooden crates next to a big stainless trough, tying off the bags and hanging them from wooden rails across the top. Saké drips slowly into the trough and then spills into the waiting jars.

Fukuro-shibori, bag squeezing (dripping really), is labor intensive and low yield. We press just a small portion of the daiginjō this way, and the rest gets pumped through the Yabuta so Matsuura can sell it at a reasonable price. The fukuro-shibori tastes at first like dandelion flower and cold fruit salad, almost viscous like seaweed broth, with a tingle that reminds me of grapefruit peel. The one pressed through the Yabuta has less gas; it's mellower but not as nuanced and delicate as the fukuro-shibori. When I drink it a month later, the perfume of ripe kōji fills my glass, and it tastes like maitake mushrooms.

Saké, says Matsuura, is like a flower. You can enjoy it as a bud, in full bloom, and even as it begins to drop its petals. Each phase has its own beauty; each one blooms at a different time.

AFTER THE LAST PRESSING in late March, we all go out to an izakaya for an end-of-season party. Matsuura has a fresh haircut and new glasses. He looks well rested for the first time in months. Outside the sakagura, everyone is relaxed, and they talk to me more than they ever have.

Matsuura, his father, and Kajiya make remarks about a successful year behind us, about brewing good saké in spite of a warm winter. Pouring bottle after bottle of the saké they made, the men consider their work; the social code is that alcohol allows you to speak freely, even to the boss. They discuss what qualities make a good saké, until they are all too drunk to discern the difference.

Matsuura says I'm starting to look like Matsuo, the saké goddess. I just thank her that I didn't create any problems at the sakagura, that I actually made myself useful. I will never be one of the guys, but I am part of the team.

FOR THE FINAL MONTH of the season, work shifts to bottling and cleaning. We fill a thousand bottles with summer junmai one day, seventeen hundred bottles of autumn-release chōkara another day. It takes a week to disassemble and wash the Yabuta press. Each section of the bellows—a thick aluminum plate covered in heavy cloth—is as tall as a picture window and takes two kurabito to lift. Soon, Matsuura must change roles from artisan to businessman, concerning himself with money and marketing instead of the poetry of fragrance and flavor.

I arrive one sunny April morning to help Kitano wash the

cloths from the Yabuta. Kajiya has the day off to prepare for planting rice. Nakaya has returned to work as a lumberjack, and Kimura
is busy with carpentry. Matsuura took the day to drive his daughter back to college in Kyōto. And Gato is filling in for the delivery
guy. I've never seen the sakagura so still. In the warm spring air,
the room doesn't fill with steam. There's only a faint smell of kōji
and yeast.

Kitano fills two tubs, like stainless steel kiddie pools, with
forty-degree water. The two of us pull five sheets at a time from a
trough of bleach water and put them in one tub. For fifteen minutes we push the sheets with kaibō so the water spins like a washing machine. We transfer the sheets from that cloudy water to the
fresh tub and push at them for another fifteen minutes. Finally, we
spin them for five minutes in cold water. It takes a whole day to
wash twenty of the eighty sheets from the Yabuta.

The aluminum plates take another week. We splash them with
hot water, scrub away the remnants of saké kasu with surgical
soap, using three kinds of brushes, and then rinse the plates clean.
Five months ago, I didn't know what they were for, but now each
tool, each piece of equipment, has meaning to me.

When the washing is done, I say goodbye to Matsuo, the saké
goddess, walk out of that shrine to saké, and let my hair down.
The sky is still light, and I can smell flowers (whose names I don't
yet know) on the breeze.

Matsuura says it was a onetime thing, having a foreign woman
work in the sakagura—there won't be others—but I can come
back anytime. He hopes I will. I asked him why he agreed to make
an exception for me: *Because Nakajima vouched for you.*

Miso-Cured Eggs

TIME: *15 minutes, plus 3 days for curing*
Serves 6 as a snack or side dish

One of my jobs in the sakagura was peeling the saké kasu—the lees, or sediment—from the press after the saké was squeezed clear. It came off in big sheets that were then cut and packaged to sell in the store. The broken pieces were put in a barrel, and we stomped on the kasu—with a specially designated pair of clean boots—until it fermented and loosened into a soft paste. My boss, Matsuura, often sent me home with bags of saké kasu to use for cooking.

I stir it into miso soup and use it to flavor sweets like pound cake, but my favorite things to make with saké kasu are these gently cured jammy eggs. The recipe comes from Dankura, a soba restaurant in Yamanaka. Straight miso is a more typical pickling medium for boiled eggs; cutting it with saké kasu makes the result less salty, more nuanced. I like to use a reddish-golden-brown awase miso (that means it's made with soybean kōji and rice kōji) or inaka (country) miso—something with lots of umami and complexity, but not dark and overpowering. If your supermarket has only red and white miso, you can mix them.

7 large eggs
70 grams (¼ cup) saké kasu paste (see note, page 70)
75 grams (¼ cup) miso
Scallions, thinly sliced on a diagonal, for serving

1. Fill a medium saucepan with enough water to cover the eggs (but don't put them in yet), and bring to a boil. Using a spoon, lower the

eggs one at a time into the boiling water. Adjust the heat as needed to keep the eggs at a simmer, not a full boil (you want to consistently see little bubbles, but not big ones), for 8 minutes. Immediately pour off the hot water and fill the pan with cold water two or three times, until it stays cool.

2. Meanwhile, in a small bowl, mix together the saké kasu and miso to make a uniform paste.

3. As soon as the eggs are cool enough to touch, crack each one all over and carefully peel it under cool water. Select the 6 nicest-looking eggs; the remaining one is a cook's snack. (If you managed to peel them all perfectly, congratulations!)

4. Tear off a piece of plastic wrap large enough to wrap one egg. In the center, spread a generous tablespoon of the kasu-miso mixture into a thin layer, so you can cover the whole outside of the egg. Place the egg in the middle of the paste, fold the plastic around the egg lengthwise, squishing around the paste so it completely enrobes the egg. Twist the ends of the plastic closed and set aside. Repeat with the remaining 5 eggs.

5. Cure eggs in the refrigerator for 3 days (wrapped in paste and plastic, the eggs will keep for a long time, but the flavor is best within 3–5 days). Before serving, gently wipe off the paste as best you can (I do this with the plastic wrap or my fingers), saving the paste for another use (such as soup or marinade). Slice the eggs into quarters, and scatter a few slivers of sliced scallion on each piece.

Wood

Five

Wood and Whisky

T he first time I met Nakajima-san I remember noticing his fingers, elegant and strong like a pianist's—on them, a set of "brass knuckles" made of horse chestnut—and his quiet masculinity. He wore a brown leather jacket and periodically swept his salt-and-pepper hair away from his forehead in a gesture that could be interpreted as either cocky or shy. I was apprenticing at Shimoki's bar that winter, and on my days off he would often call me in to meet some important person. He introduced Takehito Nakajima as one of the most skilled woodturners in this town known for its handmade lacquerware. Shimoki proudly explained that he thought Nakajima, in his mid-forties, was already a Living National Treasure and should soon be officially designated as such by the government, the highest honor for a craftsman.

I drank that night from a cup Nakajima had made specifically for the local saké. A whorl of wood grain glimmered like a panther's eye through the translucent black finish, different from the opaque coating of black or red that makes most Japanese lacquerware nearly indistinguishable from plastic. The lip was so thin it seemed I could crush the cup in my hand, and yet it felt strong. Instead of the shape curving toward a typical foot on the bottom, the cup's graceful arc continued unbroken to where the base flattened only long enough for it to rest steadily. Admiring the pleasing tension in its lines, I marveled that a cup could make me feel something more intense and complex than appreciation for its beauty.

Later, I asked him about that subtly unconventional saké cup. Tradition, says Nakajima, is dynamic. It's not something in the past, but something we are always creating. *I want to make forms that will have significance one hundred years from now*. This could sound like bluster, but the quality of his work backs up the reach of his ambition.

I never had any particular interest in learning wood turning (it looked both frightening and tedious), but when a top craftsman offers you lessons, you don't say no. And I was curious about this aloof bad boy who made such beautiful, delicate things.

A VISIT TO his studio always starts with coffee. I worry about taking too much of his time, but it would be rude to get straight to work. We pass through towers of concentrically stacked rough-hewn bowls (the raw material for Nakajima's work) that nearly reach the ceiling. It feels as if one careless brush of the shoulder could topple the whole room, but these stacks have withstood earthquakes. He'll pull up a couple of folding stools and stoke the stove with sawdust while an assistant drips hot water through those single-serve Drip On coffee filters ubiquitous in Japan. We attempt small talk or just stare out the window at falling snow or budding foliage, depending on the season. (One afternoon, as we are drinking coffee by the fire, he casually moves away a smoldering scrap of wood, placed a little too close to the stove.)

For my first lesson, he gives me a tenugui (a multipurpose length of cloth that can be a hand towel, scarf, or gift wrap) to tie around my head. This one has a pattern of saké bottles on it, because I'm apprenticing at the bar, and it's high quality—dyed all the way through, rather than printed on one side.

After coffee, we climb the stairs, stepping between bowls and cups lined up on either side, to a narrow loft. To the right are four lathes: his father's, then his two assistants', and under the window is Nakajima's. To the left, extraordinarily refined pieces are stacked precariously on the crowded shelves among the controlled chaos of hundreds of prototypes and samples for clients. He makes it look effortless to turn out multiples with machinelike precision, each piece identical within a fraction of a millimeter.

The job of a craftsman like Nakajima is to flawlessly produce specific types of tableware and teaware, but his work space is cluttered with experiments: a saké cup with black-light-sensitive painted stripes, a bowl that's been stained and then reshaped on the lathe, and an incense box (for tea ceremony) with silver inlay. There are playful failures, which he regards with amusement: a large bowl whose red lacquer is far too garish for his taste, a wooden beer stein that just doesn't seem quite right.

On his bench, bullet shells are disassembled for making into rings and pens. A cup so thin it's translucent rests over an LED. There's always a pack of cigarettes, a full ashtray, and a coffee cup covered with a wooden lid that looks like an acorn top. Model fighter planes hang from the low rafters. Chunks of mammoth ivory and precious black persimmon wood are tucked onto a ledge within his sight line, waiting for the right use to strike him.

First, a demonstration. Nakajima slides into a cockpit beneath the floor-level lathe to operate it with foot pedals controlling the speed and direction. Blades that he forged himself line the wall. The ones he uses most are half-buried in a heap of sawdust behind the lathe, and he sharpens them periodically on a stone as he works. His uniform is a U.S. Air Force flight suit that broadens his shoulders but hangs loosely from his slight frame. A tenugui tied over his head is the only protection he wears: no safety goggles, no dust mask.

It's mesmerizing to watch him work. Sometimes he wraps his fingers gently around the outside of a spinning bowl while a blade carves out the inside, millimeters away. His hand is so steady he can

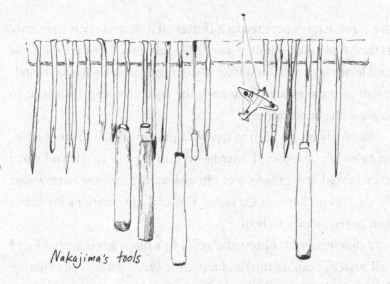

Nakajima's tools

shave wood eggshell thin. He dips his fingertips in ash from the slim cigarettes he smokes and applies it to the tool rest to keep the handle of the gouge from slipping. There's a satisfying whir as metal makes contact with wood; shavings fly off in long thin curls, and the form of a bowl emerges from what was a hunk of tree trunk.

He deftly engraves two thin stripes in the bowl, five centimeters apart. Then he picks up another tool: this one is flexible and bounces rhythmically, drawing vibrational waves on the bowl between the two lines. When it stops spinning, the waves resemble bowing stalks of rice. Nakajima looks relaxed, but his precision is astounding.

He picks out a scraper from a cigar box; what looks like a razor is actually a slice cut from a saw blade, attached with electrical tape to a bamboo handle, and sharpened into a curve. This tool is unique to Yamanaka's style of wood turning. Holding the tool in his right hand, he steadies it with his left. When it scrapes against the bowl, long papery tendrils flutter off. (When I try it later, only flakes of sawdust crumble away.) He takes the bowl off the lathe and hands it to me; the surface is so smooth and flawless that sandpaper is unnecessary. *Tsuru-tsuru*, he says, touching his cheek to explain the onomatopoeia.

Suddenly it's my turn to try. Nakajima hands me a pair of safety goggles (*for foreigners*, I later heard him explain to a friend when they looked at pictures). I climb awkwardly into the narrow seat in the cockpit beneath the lathe. The assistant positions my hands and hovers nearby to help.

Apprehensively, I press the pedal (it's like a sewing machine, I tell myself, I can do this) and move the blade toward the spinning hunk of oak. The tool jumps, chatters, and bites the wood. Nakajima patiently demonstrates how to steady the handle with my elbow and shift my torso as I move the blade left to right, rotating my wrist to follow the curve. We switch back and forth on the lathe: him demonstrating, and me trying to copy his movements.

Soon I get a feel for it: like making a form from clay, or whittling away a stick but at high speed. I start to transfer an approximation of the curved line in my mind to the hunk of wood, and the outline of a saké cup emerges. *Umai!* exclaims Nakajima. *She's really good at it!* I'm not sure whether to be flattered or insulted by the praise that I'm certain would be withheld from a serious student. Nakajima and I are both surprised by my aptitude and a little giddy (though I'm trying to hide it).

Tensai! the assistant exclaims, and Nakajima looks pleased. *Genius*, she translates on her mobile phone. Hardly. They don't realize I studied art and grew up on a farm—making things is what I have always done. This is a new set of tools and materials, but the principles are the same. Clearly the bar is low for an interloper like me: Nakajima expected me to only hack out a straight line. I didn't expect much either, but I'm starting to like this.

Delighted, he sets up a nicer piece of wood for me to make a cup out of (the first one was for practice). He's done this so many times he doesn't need a level to set it perfectly straight on the lathe chuck. We discuss the shape, and he puts me to work, watching closely and coaching. *Don't think; feel*, he instructs when I tense up and lose control of the tool.

Some four hours later, I've satisfactorily accomplished what would take him ten minutes, if that, to do perfectly. I shaped the outside to my own design, but he took over for the more risky work of carving out the interior. My arms are shaking and my mind is exhausted. I gather that he's pleased with my *sense*. He invites me back to make a bowl.

Often, even after he's given up half a day to teaching me, Nakajima will hesitantly ask if I have dinner plans (I always keep them open, just in case) and then take me out. We're wrapped up in the intensity of fresh creative admiration, but without the words to share what's on our minds, we show our enthusiasm by eating and drinking together. We're never without a chaperone—his assistant or one of his friends. It's a small town with intense social norms, and neither of us needs scandalous chatter about the married American lady cavorting with the divorced master craftsman. (Still, it's a point of pride from both our perspectives to be seen together, he with Hannah-from-New-York, and me with this standoffish shokunin.)

There's camaraderie and competition among woodturners. I get the sense that those most closely matched in skill would rather not associate much and that by befriending Nakajima, I have declared my loyalty. After hours, Nakajima keeps the company of the celebrated maki-e artist Mushū Yamazaki, who has a rather coarse manner but makes delicate lacquer paintings of nature, and the gentle and observant monk-by-marriage (whose father-in-law is head of Iōji) Yūichi Kano, who also administrates the local chamber of commerce and is a talented amateur photographer. All of them are enthusiastic drinkers.

The more drunk everyone gets, the more easily we communicate, becoming willing to make mistakes in English or Japanese with lowered inhibitions. (I learn, for example, that Kano is conversant in English.) Stoic Nakajima becomes loquacious, earnestly telling me his thoughts about design and craftsmanship. I listen thoughtfully, even when I don't understand. If nothing else, we bond over our love of whisky. Nakajima and I always drink highballs: a tall glass of iced Suntory Kakubin topped with cold prickly soda.

Never am I allowed to pay a dime. (I've tried to invite him out for drinks that I would pay for to show my appreciation, yet to my chagrin he always insists firmly on picking up the tab.) Certainly there's an old-fashioned gender dynamic at play, and in Japan the oldest (or highest-ranking) person is often expected to pay—but still!

Sometimes these evenings progress from one place to the next, finally ending with ramen or sushi well past midnight. We might make dinner of little grilled and fried things shared while we drink at a greasy izakaya, then sip fancy whisky in a dark sultry jazz bar, then stumble to our favorite ramen shop to share fried chicken and gyōza under too bright lights before parting ways. After one particularly enthusiastic night out, Nakajima gifts me one of his bowls: a wedding present, he says. I'm grateful for his prideful propriety.

I daydream about becoming a woodturner. The focus and flow I feel at the lathe, the satisfaction of making something beautiful and useful with my own hands, is unparalleled. I wonder if this master, now my friend, who has let me into his studio would take me as an apprentice. How many years or decades would it take to become competent, if not truly skilled? It's a beautiful daydream, but the truth is I don't have Nakajima's singular focus.

My nature is to dive deep into something for a time—roller derby, bicycle racing, pastry baking, cocktail bartending—until I feel as though I understand it enough. I could spend a few years studying wood turning full throttle and probably make some nice things under the guidance of my teachers. But they would never be as refined, with each detail tenderly considered, as the work of Yamanaka's best craftsmen. I'd get distracted by a shiny new opportunity and be on to the next thing, while they continue their lifelong journey of getting better at their craft.

Nakajima grew up in his father's workshop but didn't intend to follow in his footsteps. He went to a technical high school and trained to be an auto mechanic. But when he started working in a garage, he was disappointed to find he rarely got to do interesting mechanical work: it was cheaper and faster to replace parts than to repair them. Disenchanted, he gave up on his dream of being a high-level mechanic. He spent a few years working in a gas station, drag racing a Nissan Skyline DR30, and customizing his vintage reproduction Lotus Super 7. It was the beginning of the 1990s economic bubble, and he saw that you could make money selling anything: he may as well learn his father's trade.

In 1991 his father won a national prize, and Nakajima went with him to Tōkyō for the award ceremony. Kijishi, woodturners, make two kinds of work: wares to fulfill orders, and sakuhin, works of art. Their sakuhin still take the form of table- and teaware, but expression and beauty are emphasized. It was the first time he'd been to Tōkyō, and seeing his father's sakuhin on display, Nakajima decided to become an artist. *My first goal was to become as good as my father.*

After six years of learning from his father, he was ready to become a professional. The wood-turning school opened that same year, offering a two-year advanced course, like a master's degree in wood turning. Nakajima enrolled and studied under Ryōzō Kawakita, the first kijishi to be designated a Living National Treasure. *All the students admired and imitated Kawakita*, says Nakajima. Nakajima was capable of making work that pleased his teacher.

He graduated, began entering contests, and won every year. Ten years into his career, for the first time, Nakajima's sakuhin didn't win the national craft competition. *Winning is nice*, he says, *but it's pressure*. It makes it hard to take risks. *If you're addicted to winning prizes, you're not free.*

He'd always shown his new designs to Kawakita for approval. *I thought I would try the opposite of what Kawakita said was good; then it became fun.* He won more contests, but that wasn't what mattered anymore—he was chasing his own ideal.

Over highballs and yakitori, Nakajima complains about Yamanaka: the small-town gossip, the provincialism. I ask him if he'd ever considered living somewhere else. He replies, *Why would I?* The best resources for his craft are here. The school where students come from all over Japan to learn turning and lacquer is here. The best practitioners are here. The wood is here.

Kijishi used to move from town to town, felling what trees they could use. Forest resources and stewardship were shared, and legend has it these woodturners carried a logging permit from the emperor's family. They'd sell their wares to the local people, then come back around several years later, when those people needed new things. By the end of the sixteenth century, land use was becoming more regulated, and the woodturners could no longer roam freely. A group of kijishi moved in and set up shop upriver from what is now Yamanaka, at the source of their material.

The woodturners gradually moved their workshops closer to town, where they could sell souvenirs to travelers. Lacquer and then maki-e artisans followed, settling in Yamanaka and decorating the woodenware with chrysanthemums, stalks of rice, and swallows—dusted in gold powder and jeweled with mother-of-pearl and iridescent beetle wings. Yamanaka became known for wooden lacquerware as well as its onsen.

Over generations, these woodturners developed a unique style. Avoiding the very center of a log, they cut their blanks so the wood grain runs vertically, the same orientation as the bowl. Though the practical reason is to prevent warping in this humid environment, it makes for beautiful asymmetry in the wood grain patterns that emerge. (In other places, a typical turned bowl blank is cut perpendicular to the grain, so the resulting patterns are symmetrical.) The variations are further emphasized with translucent lacquer: a technique born out of frugality that persists as an aesthetic choice. Even the lathe setup is peculiar. When I show photos of Nakajima's workshop to New York woodworker

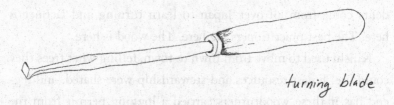

turning blade

friends, they are amazed at how different the tools are from what they use.

There are little pockets like this all over Japan where craftsmen pride themselves on a very specific way to make things, practiced only in their village. But in the internet age, these craft villages are no longer unconnected from each other. Some four thousand people follow Nakajima's (thoroughly hashtagged) work on Instagram, and he exchanges messages with woodworkers around the world. He borrows ideas from guitar makers and furniture builders. Nakajima is willing to risk giving away some ideas for the lively exchange that it invites.

Some craftsmen guard their techniques jealously. Their workshops are private; their methods are secret. They fear, perhaps, that the little things that make their work special could be stolen from them. Nakajima, on the other hand, welcomes attention and visitors, particularly from abroad.

All the woodturners in Yamanaka are obligated to join a guild along with lacquer craftsmen and lacquerware sellers. Workshops like Nakajima's used to sell directly to customers, but now the guild is dominated by shops and wholesalers who have the power to determine the shapes and prices of goods. For a kijishi to be an artist is frowned upon by sellers, who want them to stay in their lane and simply be producers. Nakajima is both. *I am a difficult person for them*, he says.

ON MY THIRD PIECE, a larger bowl, Nakajima taught me how to turn the inside. (It's a lot harder.) I was pleased with my effort, but Nakajima couldn't have something come out of his studio that was not up to his standards. He took over the lathe and made a second pass, taking away layers of the interior until it was as thin as one of his.

That day, as we took a break and sipped coffee in front of the stove, he mused that perhaps next I could learn to finish the bowl with urushi, lacquer made from the sap of *Toxicodendron vernicifluum*, a tree in the same family as poison ivy. Then he promptly rescinded the offer, worried that my husband would be mad at him if I hurt my skin. Urushi contains urushiol, the same irritant as poison ivy and oak (to which I am severely allergic, but I didn't mention that). Once it hardens, the danger is gone, but I've seen the scabbed arms of the wood-turning students.

The students are surprised and awed that I'm friends with this master. *Isn't he scary?* they ask. To me, he's always kind and patient, but to his apprentices he can be strict and harsh. I suspect that at first he saw me only as a foreign guest to whom he was promoting his craft; later, he respected me as a professional in another field. Though he's teaching me, I'm a friend, not a student. Shikki, wooden lacquerware, is not my chosen profession. I am an outsider, and I can skirt the rules of hierarchy.

But Nakajima too is an outlier. He's direct and doesn't soften his opinions. If someone's work doesn't reflect an innate sense of grace, if they've cut corners, if they've overlooked details, he doesn't hesitate to point it out. This frankness and confidence, in a culture that values subtlety and modesty, doesn't win many friends. Nor does his ambition to be an artist in a craft that has rigid parameters. *If a craftsman becomes an artist, this tiny town condemns it*, he gripes. Still, his dedication and skill earn him respect. He's narrowly focused on being the best he can be, and he's stubborn as hell.

Eventually I did persuade Nakajima to teach me fuki-urushi, the technique that literally translates to wiped urushi. We needed a new project together. When common language fails us, the act of making something is our way to communicate.

When we open the mysterious plywood door at the back of the studio—the door that is always closed to visitors—he tells me, only half-joking, that it's "top secret." No woodturner does fuki-urushi, this smooth transparent finish, better than Nakajima. We take off our shoes and step over the threshold onto a mauve carpet. The small room is lit by a few bright lamps, and the walls are lined with finished work, some his, some his father's. In the middle of the room is a high workbench, covered in newspaper, with racks of works in progress curing underneath in a makeshift muro, a climate-controlled cabinet.

He hands me a pair of cotton gloves and a pair of white rubber dish-washing gloves to wear over them. Even at-your-own-risk Nakajima protects his skin from urushi. Using a handmade applicator called a tanpo, meaning drumstick—fashioned from a wad of pillow stuffing wrapped in saran and then a square of silky pink rayon secured over it with a rubber band—I rub thinned black urushi onto the bowl. This first layer soaks into the dry wood, seeping through its pores and beading on the opposite side. I spread it around in little circles the way he shows me, careful not to miss a spot. It saturates more or less depending on the angle of the cut and part of the wood grain, bringing out patterns that look like tiger stripes and river rapids. We leave it to dry for a few days before sanding it down on the lathe to reveal more variation in the wood grain.

The mirrorlike finish that he insists on takes up to fifteen ultra-thin layers. He looks down on quick work with thick layers as tactless cheating, and overdoing it as gaudy. Each coat is rubbed on and then buffed off, so the gloss builds up slowly—very slowly in Nakajima's case. Between each application, probably six to eight for my bowl, we'll need to wait a day or two for the urushi to harden.

Every few evenings I go to Nakajima's studio, after his assistants have left. I arrive by bicycle in the dark, and I can hear the motor of the lathe and the sound of a blade making contact with wood. I consider it a sign of real friendship that now he lets me come without a chaperone or translator, and we get right to work without coffee.

After the first coat of urushi dries, our next job is wet sanding, to further smooth the surface, reveal the grain, and remove dust. Nakajima blows the sawdust off his jumpsuit with compressed air before we step into the secret urushi room. We set up my bowl on something like a potter's wheel, with vacuum suction to secure the work in place. With a small dish of water and fine sandpaper I polish the bowl, working from 800 to 1300 grit (so fine I could buff my nails with it). Nakajima checks my work and nods his approval, barely hiding a grin. Then we head out for okonomiyaki and highballs.

Over late-night sushi one time, I hear him tell the chef that I learn more quickly and understand better than his apprentices. I wonder if they might do better if he showed them the same kindness and encouragement? Under constant criticism, I would make mistakes too. Even with his gentle guidance, I've broken two tools and am afraid to make anything on my own.

With wet sanding finished, my next lessons are dedicated to applying urushi. Nakajima lets me practice on some of his bowls, not just mine. I watch him work, trying to memorize the steps. Starting with the outside of the bowl, he uses the homemade tanpo applicator to rub urushi on in circles, turning the wheel by hand. He presses the pedal to spin the bowl and slowly spread the sticky urushi from top to bottom. With a folded paper shop towel, he wipes off the excess, then buffs in little circles. He inspects for any smudges, then repeats the process on the inside. He removes the bowl from the wheel with clean paper shop towels and gently buffs one more time before setting it on a board to dry. Then it's my turn to try.

With persistence, and the help of smartphone translations, we teach each other the vocabulary we need for these sessions. *Usui*, thin. *Sofuto tachi*, soft touch, gently. *Tsuya*, gloss. *Okay*, okay. I work studiously while he snaps pictures of his novelty pupil. When I think I'm done, I cock my head and ask, *Okay? Okay*, he says and nods, intently double-checking my work.

On these evening visits, Nakajima shows me what he's been working on (and will often return to after I go home, working late into the night). One day it's two dozen tea containers, with lids that fit so perfectly they glide on, making an airtight seal. Another day it's a handful of tiny netsuke boxes. Or it's a stack of three hundred identical owan (soup bowls). Many of these started with a rough form hewn by another craftsman (those towers downstairs) and will be sent off to yet another to be finished with urushi; each has his own specific job. Kijishi, Nakajima's job title, all make the same things: the details set them apart. Extreme precision, flawless finishes, thin edges, and a graceful but hard beauty identify Nakajima's work.

You can see his touch most in his sakuhin, the things he makes for galleries and competitions. These large bowls intended to sit on a pedestal—though he says he'd be as happy to have them used as displayed—release him from the confines of predetermined shapes. He asks me to take off my ring before handling them, and I feel a solemn hush as he passes me each work. They're made of horse chestnut, with streaks of wood grain gleaming through dark urushi like the aurora borealis.

I didn't know a bowl could thrill me like one of Cy Twombly's paintings or Pina Bausch's dances. Somehow, contained in the curves of these thin walls is the tenderness of making such a refined thing contrasted by the feeling that they are cold and impenetrable, held together with the sweet tension of a silhouette that arcs as if it might topple, but it won't. He's the first to admit that some pieces are more successful than others, explaining that when he overthinks, the feeling doesn't come through.

He shows me his father's work too, and his own early work that looks like it or like Kawakita's. As time passes, they diverge. Takehito Nakajima found his own voice. He favors cool translucent black or clear varnishes over warm browns. He selects wood with beautiful eyes, knots, and burls, emphasizing them with his painstaking method of applying urushi. And the shapes he makes are almost voluptuous compared with the stiff but masterful work of other kijishi. Even in standard forms, a saké cup or a miso soup bowl, I can immediately identify something made by Takehito Nakajima when I see it in a restaurant or ryokan.

Why—when his skill is so refined, his best work so moving—is Takehito Nakajima not yet designated as a Living National Treasure? There are politics involved, and Nakajima plays by his own rules socially and creatively. Living National Treasure is a colloquial term for a designation that translates more accurately as Intangible Cultural Property, and it's meant to protect important crafts that might be endangered—to preserve a static tradition, more than to honor the brilliance or innovation of the craftsman. But tradition, as Nakajima says, is dynamic. A century or more from now, the work still talked about and admired will reveal who was the real treasure.

My third bowl is finished; we've applied the eighth and final glossy layer of urushi. Nakajima sends me to his friend Yamazaki's studio so I can sign the bottom in golden maki-e. It looks like an imitation of a Nakajima bowl, I notice when I place it next to the ones he's given me—the ones I use every time I make miso soup, then wash and dry with more care than any other tableware I own.

My happiest moment, says Nakajima, *is to meet someone who understands my work and wants to use it for a long time.*

Midnight Fried Chicken

TIME: *1 hour, plus 24–48 hours for marinating*
Serves 4 as a snack, 2 as a meal (with rice)

The ramen shop around the corner from Engawa stays open until 2:00 A.M., or whenever the last customer leaves. The karaage chicken there is firm and flavorful with sweetened soy and garlic, coated in a fox-colored crust of potato starch that stays crisp on the table through a second round of highballs. I have yet to persuade the shop's surly "mama" to give me a hint at how she makes it so good. (She warms more quickly to the men I come in with, especially Nakajima.) But by cooking it again and again until it tasted right, I might have outdone her.

1½ teaspoons grated fresh ginger, with its juice

2 teaspoons grated or pressed garlic (about 3 cloves)

2 tablespoons dry-tasting saké

3 tablespoons soy sauce

2 teaspoons granulated sugar

4 skin-on chicken thighs (680–900 grams/1½–2 pounds), deboned (do it yourself or ask your butcher; see note)

Peanut oil, or a mixture of peanut and canola or safflower, for frying

150 grams (1 cup) katakuriko (potato starch)

¼ teaspoon fine sea salt

½ teaspoon black pepper

Lemon wedges, for serving

Lettuce leaves and cucumber slices, for serving

Note: Japanese chicken is often fattier and more flavorful than most of what's sold in America. The best approximation is chicken from a farmers' market. You'll probably have to debone it yourself, but there are plenty of video tutorials for that online. Don't worry about doing it cleanly, because you're going to batter and fry the chicken anyway. Bonus: you'll have bones for making stock.

1. In a shallow container big enough to hold the chicken, combine the ginger, garlic, saké, soy sauce, and sugar. Cut the chicken into roughly 8 cm (3-inch) chunks. Toss the pieces in the marinade to coat them. Cover and refrigerate for 24–48 hours to brine the chicken so it becomes firm and flavorful.
2. Pour peanut oil into an aluminum or stainless steel pot to a depth of about 8 cm (3 inches). (The pot should be tall enough so that the sides are at least 5 cm [2 inches] higher than the surface of the oil.) Heat the oil to 175°C (350°F). Place several layers of newsprint or paper towels on a sheet pan.
3. Meanwhile, place a wire rack over a second sheet pan. In a bowl, combine the potato starch, salt, and pepper. Remove one piece of chicken at a time from the marinade, tuck in any jagged bits or skin as you roll it in the starch to form a coating around the outside; rest it on the rack. Repeat with all the chicken.
4. Fry 2 to 3 pieces at a time, gently shaking off excess starch before lowering each one into the pot with a spider or long chopsticks. Keep the oil temperature around 165°C (325°F)—it will drop when you add the chicken—and no lower than 150°C (300°F). Fry 3–4 minutes, until golden; remove from the oil using the spider or chopsticks, and cool on the prepared newsprint or paper towels.
5. When all the chicken has been fried once, heat the oil to 190°C (375°F). Fry the chicken pieces a second time, keeping the oil be-

tween 175° and 190°C (350° and 375°F), until the crust is deep golden brown, about 1 minute. Transfer to a fresh layer of newsprint or paper towels. This second frying makes the coating stay extra crisp, even if you don't serve the chicken immediately.

6. Cut the chicken pieces into 2 cm (1-inch) slices that are easy to pick up with chopsticks. Serve hot, with lemon wedges to squeeze over the chicken, and lettuce leaves and cucumber slices for a cool, fresh contrast.

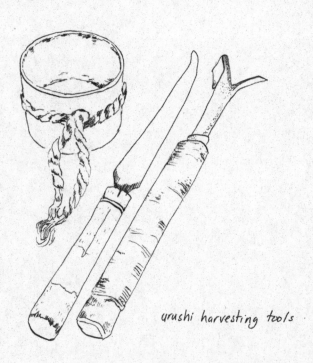

urushi harvesting tools

Six

The Lacquer Tree

Yamanaka is a hazardous place for someone who's allergic to urushiol, the allergen in both poison ivy and the urushi tree, *Toxicodendron vernicifluum*, from which Japanese lacquer is made. Most people who choose urushi painting as a profession are blessed with immunity or only a mild itch. I break out in a bubbling rash with the slightest contact. Sometimes I notice the telltale cluster of blisters on my neck or the back of my hand when I haven't been anywhere near a lacquer studio or urushi tree. In a town where nearly 20 percent of the population is involved with the lacquerware trade, there are probably traces of the potent oil on the door to the convenience store and the menus at my favorite izakaya.

My friend Murai says urushi residue from craftsmen's bodies taints the onsen water, so local children build resistance from the time they are babies. When they brush against the leaves of an

urushi tree while playing in the woods, they don't get the bubbling red allergic rash. Craftsmen tell of putting a drop of urushi
in the baby's first bathwater. Students at the wood-turning school
claim to gradually become used to urushi, until their skin no longer reacts.

It was with some trepidation that I went to watch an urushi
harvest. There are about eight hundred trees on a southeast-facing
slope above a bend in the Daishōji River, planted about fifteen
years ago. The same kinds of trees grow wild in the woods, but
Yamanaka is a bit too warm to be an ideal climate for producing
high-quality urushi. Students from the Ishikawa Prefectural Institute for Yamanaka Lacquerware (locally known as the rokuro
kenshujō, the wood-turning training center) harvest sap from the
trees to gain a deeper understanding of their materials.

These students have come from all over Japan to learn how to
make Yamanaka shikki (lacquerware). Most shikki craftsmen specialize in one part of the process. There are craftsmen who cut
rough blanks. Craftsmen—like Nakajima—who turn those blanks
into table- and teaware. Craftsmen who finish them with a smooth
lacquer of urushi. And maki-e artists who decorate those wares
with illustrations and patterns. During their two- to four-year
course, the students will practice every part of the process.

Colloquially, lacquer has come to mean any shiny finish, and
the Japanese objects finished with urushi are advertised in English
as lacquerware. But the word "lacquer" (like "shellac") is related to
the finish made of secretions from lac insects, and urushi is made
from tree sap. Urushi doesn't coat wood like synthetic finishes; it
bonds and becomes part of it, one tree material strengthening another.

I MET UP with four students—two young women and two young men—in the parking lot of the rokuro kenshujō one morning during their summer break. One of them, named Naiki, is hoping to become Nakajima's apprentice next year. She'd invited me to watch them collect urushi.

We were all dressed in long pants, long sleeves, and hats to protect us from urushiol and from the harsh sun. The towels or tenugui each of us had slung around our necks were already catching beads of sweat. A man wearing an old Yamanaka firefighter hat—a teacher—and a woman with a friendly round face—an administrator—drove us past the two-thousand-year-old Kayano Ōsugi and its shrine and up toward the nearly abandoned village of Kazetani. We pulled over above the slope where the urushi trees are planted.

Before beginning the harvest, we drank water from paper cups that smelled like turpentine from being stored with the harvesting materials. We put on gloves and cloth sleeve covers. I lowered the mesh on my hat—like a beekeeper or a jungle explorer—to protect my face from splatters and drips.

I watched a student named Raku tap an urushi tree. The trunk was straight and slim, no thicker than a runner's thigh. He cut away a horizontal strip of bark with a tool like the channel knife a bartender uses to make coils of citrus peel. The pale wood was exposed. He sliced into the wood with a sharp blade, to release the sap running between the bark and the inner core of the tree. Milky fluid beaded in the incision, and he scraped it into a bamboo cup. A tree can tolerate five incisions in a session.

The trunks are tagged with numbers and nicknames; each student is responsible for their own group of trees. They moved from one to the next, making fresh cuts above where the last incisions had scabbed over and turned black. From July through August, the students harvest urushi every five days (allowing the trees time for recovery in between). There are fewer than thirty mature trees ready to collect urushi from this year.

The sparse canopy of pinnate leaves did little to break the heat. Sweat dripped down my forehead, but I was afraid to wipe it, in case there were irritating oils on my sleeve or hand. Cicadas buzzed and a ruddy kingfisher sang from the taller, denser forest uphill.

The white urushi sap turned tan in the bamboo collection cups, and by the time we brought it all back to the school in one big bowl, it had turned nut-brown and frothy. They weighed it: fifty-six grams. Usually they get eighty, and occasionally as much as two hundred grams from one session. A few hot weeks with no rain had strained the trees.

It was before noon, and the two young women gave me a tour of the school. They showed me the lacquer rooms where they'll squeeze the urushi through a paper filter to remove sediment and paint or rub it onto woodenware. There's a big wooden muro, a humid cabinet for curing urushi-painted wares. Urushi doesn't actually dry, it hardens, undergoing a chemical change that neutralizes its skin-aggravating properties. It bonds with the wood into a strong and flexible finish. Like skin, it's durable and resilient, but vulnerable to deterioration from UV light.

We walked through the hand-carving room, the forging room for making tools, and the big workshop full of lathes where they spend most of their time learning to turn tableware and teaware from keyaki, an indigenous elm. Their soup bowls and tea boxes, saké cups and sweets trays, are on display in the gallery, all glossed in smooth coats of urushi. They showed me the maki-e room, where they practice painting intricate illustrations with urushi that they dust with glittering mineral powders. Maki-e literally means sprinkled design.

The school provides the first few years of training in place of a traditional apprenticeship, but most of the students hope to spend another five years working under a master craftsman as a deshi, an apprentice. In the year leading up to graduation, they court the mentors they hope will take them on. Once they enter a master's workshop, they will help with production in exchange for guidance and experience.

MY FRIEND "Jessica" Ching Ho came to Yamanaka from Taiwan to study maki-e as an apprentice to Mushū Yamazaki. She tells me no one's skill can equal his. *You see his perfectionism in the details*, she says. *He has talent, but he puts 120 percent into everything he makes.* His work, she says, is on the level of the best pieces from the Edo period, when maki-e artisans were employed by military rulers to decorate their household items in exquisite designs. Urushi artwork originated in China, but the Japanese made it their own with maki-e.

Yamazaki decorates limited-edition timepieces for the Swiss watchmaker Speake-Marin and fountain pens for the German company Pelikan. The Erik Thomsen gallery and the Museum of Arts and Design in New York have exhibited his luxuriously ornamented work—a phoenix flying across the top of a natsume (tea container), an incense box shaped like a chestnut with lifelike ants painted in relief. A rich brown natsume that he decorated with pine needles and fuki buds is in the Arthur M. Sackler Museum collection at Harvard.

Jessica's favorite of Yamazaki's works is a platter shaped like a flatfish called a karei. Its gills and fins are built up in high relief with layers of urushi, and each scale is a constellation of tiny gold dots. The name of this piece is written in characters that translate to "glorious," karei, a homophone of the name of the fish.

Jessica was twenty-five when she arrived in Yamanaka to join Yamazaki's studio. She'd already studied design in Taiwan and worked as a product designer, but she wanted to distinguish herself in a competitive field, and she was drawn to decorative arts—especially the surface designs of William Morris. When she met Mushū Yamazaki at a workshop he taught in Taipei, she realized maki-e was what she wanted to do.

As an apprentice to a maki-e master, Jessica is treated like a teenage daughter. Because she's so far from her own family, Yamazaki feels a duty to protect her as well as teach her. The way his family has taken her in seems to me at once remarkably kind and suffocating. Even to meet me for dinner, she first asks for permission.

It's rare Jessica has free time, but when she does, we meet to have a cozy dinner at Eimi or share a bottle of Japanese sparkling wine at Rin, a jazz bar that looks charmingly like a low-budget movie set. Jessica is my only foreign friend in Yamanaka (though I once chatted with a Ukrainian girl who worked at the convenience store, there's a good-looking South Asian man I see greeting guests in front of one ryokan, and I sometimes see non-Japanese-looking laborers working on construction crews). Jessica and I didn't come to Japan because of husbands, or to teach English, or because a company sent us. Both of us came here because there was something we wanted to learn. But with each other, it's safe to vent about the parts of Yamanaka life that are confounding.

In America and Taiwan, both of us grew up in homes open to visitors—kids who came to play, grown-ups who joined the family for dinner, neighbors who came over to help fix something—but we've learned in Yamanaka to be more private about our personal space, if only for appearances. Most of the men I'm friends with have never seen the inside of my apartment.

Jessica is a friendly and curious person. When we go out to eat, she easily engages other customers in conversation, but when they offer to pay for our drinks, she refuses, worried what her teacher would think. In Yamanaka other women have scolded her for being too talkative, especially after a glass of wine. (Her teacher and his friends are forgiven for speaking freely when they imbibe.) No one had to tell her to leave her short shorts in Taiwan; she knew she needed to dress modestly in rural Japan.

I struggle to meet social expectations in Yamanaka—or even to know what they are—but if I fail, I fail only myself. There's not the reputation of a master craftsman at stake. I belong to no one.

Once during an event I attended with Nakajima, a man named Ieda, head of the Lacquerware Association, kept pressing me, *What's your relationship to Nakajima?* If I wasn't his student, or his girlfriend, then what was it? I took offense that my answer—*tomodachi*, friend—didn't satisfy him.

A few days later, I received an email from Ieda asking me to have coffee. I texted Nakajima to see what he thought about this, and he already knew all about it. Ieda wanted to ask for my help with an English voice-over for some promotional materials about Yamanaka shikki, and he'd called Nakajima first to see if it was okay to ask me.

I realized then why Ieda had pushed so hard to know my relationship to Nakajima: he needed to know for etiquette reasons. If I was Nakajima's student, guest, or girlfriend, he would need Nakajima's permission to approach me. Just to be safe, Ieda had checked with him first anyway. If someone wants to talk to Jessica, they have to go through her teacher.

Every day, Jessica goes to the studio early in the morning to prepare before Yamazaki arrives, and every evening she takes notes on what she has learned. How to outline a design using a fine brush made from a few strands of hair. How to build up thin layers of urushi to create an image in relief. How to sprinkle gold powder evenly onto wet urushi, and whether to use a fine dust or one glittering with distinct pieces. How to buff the gold with charcoal powder to increase its sheen, and seal it with a clear top coat, free from imperfections. How to make tiny mosaics of iridescent beetle wings or eggshell shards. What kinds of flowers and birds are suitable for teaware in each season, and the style of drawing that best shows off maki-e technique.

She applies stripes of gold leaf and paper-thin pearlescent abalone shell to fountain pens that are shipped off to Europe. Her teacher pays her a small stipend for helping with his work and gives her materials to practice with. She's painted a golden spider mum on a red saké cup, green gourds on a black platter flecked with gold, a brown-gold persimmon on a persimmon-wood incense box, and a bag of treasure sinking beneath the sea on a natsume. Yamazaki Sensei points out every flaw in her work, concerned to impart as much as he can before she goes out on her own. He's proud of her—his family jokes that the only person he loves more than Jessica is his dog.

For Jessica, the gratitude and admiration she feels for her teacher far outweigh the inconvenience of muting her personal life for a while. Some of the rokuro kenshujō students leave Yamanaka without completing apprenticeships. A few prefer to make their own way. But mostly, it's because there are fewer shikki workshops than there used to be, and many don't have the time or money to train a deshi.

Apprenticeships used to last a decade, but Jessica's will end in three years. Yamazaki teaches her at an accelerated pace. She'll go home to Taiwan soon to start her own studio, but visit Japan often to gather materials and get advice from Yamazaki. She's befriended students from the rokuro kenshujō and plans to commission objects from these young craftsmen on which to build her maki-e designs.

This fall, when the urushi trees are completely tapped out, the students will cut them down. From the cut tree, a new one will grow, at a rate of fifty centimeters per year. The new trees grow fast because of the strong roots, already established to support them.

Wild Herb Dango

TIME: *1 hour*
Makes about 10 pieces

Across the street from the two-thousand-year-old Kayano Ōsugi in Yamanaka, on the way to where the urushi trees grow, a tiny shop sells kusa dango, bouncy-soft green oblongs with a mild perfume of medicinal herbs, served with or without adzuki jam and a sprinkle of sweet toasted soybean powder. If you eat there, sitting on the benches outside, next to a bucket of lacy cosmos flowers, they bring you wild herb tea made with sasa (a kind of bamboo) leaf and other plants gathered in these mountains.

"Kusa" refers to grasses, weeds, or wild herbs; in this case, it's yomogi, mugwort. Kusa dango is sometimes called yomogi mochi. In Japan and abroad, the word "mochi" can describe various mochi-textured snacks. True mochi is made from pounded sticky rice. Dango (as in this recipe) is made from rice flour—much easier for the home cook. They look nice served on a lacquered dish or a grooved wooden tray called a wagatabon.

yomogi

YOMOGI (*ARTEMISIA PRINCEPS*), known as Japanese or Korean mugwort, and European mugwort (*Artemisia vulgaris*) grow wild all over the world (we have native species of artemisia in the United States too). Mugwort pops up in flowerpots and gardens, spread by pieces of its persistent rhizome that end up in nursery pots, and its seeds blow to roadsides and fields. In Brooklyn—where they are invasive species—I see the plants pushing through sidewalk cracks and covering old lots in place of demolished buildings, and I wish I could use them, but leafy plants growing in soil contaminated with heavy metals aren't particularly safe to eat. If you must have real Japanese yomogi, you can order *Artemisia princeps* seeds (grow it in pots so it doesn't spread out of control).

Pick tender young plants in spring or the new growth at the top during any season. Rinse the yomogi leaves well, and remove any woody bits of stem.

FOR THE DANGO

30 grams (3 tablespoons) shiratamako (see note)

150 grams (1 cup) jōshinko (see note)

20 grams (1 tablespoon plus one teaspoon) granulated sugar

Katakuriko (potato starch), arrowroot, or cornstarch

1 tablespoon kinako (toasted soybean powder, optional)

1 tablespoon kibi-zatō (fine-granule semi-unrefined sugar) or organic confectioners' sugar (for sweetening kinako, if using)

FOR THE YOMOGI PASTE

About ⅛ teaspoon baking soda

20 grams (about one handful) fresh yomogi leaves or other mugwort leaves

Generous pinch of fine sea salt

Note: In place of the shiratamako (a kind of mochi-rice flour) and jōshinko (highest-quality *japonica* rice flour)—which can be found at a Japanese grocery or ordered online—you can use 180 grams (1 cup plus 3 tablespoons) mochiko (mochi or "sweet" rice flour), which is available at many supermarkets. The texture of the dango will be a little less smooth and bouncy, but still very good.

This can be made as plain dango, without the yomogi.

1. Prepare the dough. In a small bowl, mix the shiratamako with 2 tablespoons cool water; stir to dissolve. Put the jōshinko in a sturdy large bowl. Add 100 mL (scant ½ cup) warm water, a little at a time, mixing it into the jōshinko with your hand until it forms a thick paste, like putty. Add the shiratamako mixture to the jōshinko mixture and knead together. (If using mochiko instead, mix it with 175 mL [¾ cup] lukewarm water.) Cover the dough with plastic wrap or a damp towel, and set aside to hydrate for about 15 minutes.

2. Make the yomogi paste. Fill a large pot with 2 liters (2 quarts) water, add the baking soda, and bring to a rolling boil. Meanwhile, prepare a large bowl of ice water. Add the yomogi to the boiling water for about 30 seconds, until it's bright green and tender. Drain the yomogi, and immediately plunge it into the ice water. Once cool, drain the yomogi again, and squeeze out excess water (this should yield about 15 grams cooked yomogi). Roughly chop it; then grind it together with the salt, using a suribachi or mortar and pestle. Keep grinding it, adding up to a teaspoon of water little by little, to make a thick but soft paste; set aside.

3. To cook the dough, you will need a bamboo or metal steamer with a lid that fits over a pot or inside a deep wok. Line the steamer with baking parchment or muslin. Fill the pot with water up to the second knuckle on your index finger (enough that it won't boil off, but not so much that it touches the steamer); place the steamer on top. Bring the water to a boil over high heat. When steam is coming steadily through the steamer, it's ready to go. Remove the dough from the bowl and break it into 3 pieces, flattened about 2.5 cm

(1 inch) thick, and place them into the steamer. Lower the heat to keep the pot from scorching, but keep it high enough to steam steadily. Cover and steam for 30–40 minutes, until the dough is translucent all the way through and no longer tastes grainy and raw (break off a small piece to test).

4. Meanwhile, rinse out the large bowl you used to make the dough, and leave it wet. You will need a pounding stick: a pestle, French rolling pin, or rolling dowel. When the dough is cooked, wet the pounding stick. Transfer the dough to the wet bowl, add the sugar, and begin pounding. At first, the dough will just break apart. After a minute or so, when the sugar has dissolved and the dough is cool enough to touch, add the yomogi paste. Continue pounding— dipping the stick in water from time to time so it doesn't stick and periodically flipping the dough over—until the green color is evenly distributed, the dough comes together into one big sticky mass, and it's slightly glossy.

5. Lightly dust a work surface with katakuriko. Wet your hands. Squeeze off a piece of dough a little smaller than a Ping-Pong ball, shape it into an oblong, and set it on the dusted surface. Continue until you've used up all the dough; you should have about 10 dango. Dry your hands and dust them with katakurito. Gently roll each dango between your hands to give it a light, even coating of starch.

6. If using kinako, mix it together with the kibi-zatō (or confectioners' sugar); sprinkle over the dango just before serving. These taste best the day they are made.

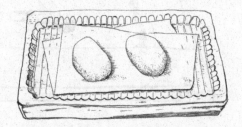

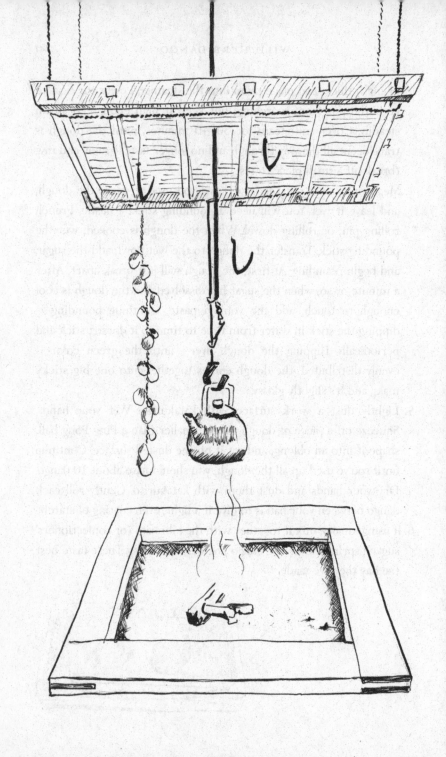

Seven

A Forest Hearth

The first time I went to Ōzuchi, on a cold November night, I wondered where on earth my new friends were taking me. We drove through terrifying darkness with sugi boughs and rocks littering the wet, and possibly icy, mountain road. The shoulder dropped off steeply on the left toward a river I could hear but not see. On the right, a narrow drainage ditch looked as if it could trap a wheel, were you to swerve to accommodate a passing car. We navigated seemingly endless switchbacks, climbing farther from the ravine and deeper into the forest. No other cars passed.

That night we arrived to a spectacular show of stars visible from a clearing with ten wooden houses arranged in a crescent, only one of which emanated a warm glow. All I knew was that we were there to celebrate a successful rice harvest—the previous year's had been ravaged by wild boars—and that only one man lived in the village, Noboru Nimaida. Ōzuchi (I would later learn) had been headed the way of about eight hundred depopulated villages around Japan—some so far gone that boars roam the empty streets and vines curl through window frames toward holes in collapsing roofs. Nimaida's return to his hometown altered its course.

We followed a footpath to a house with wood-slat siding and a tiered red-tiled roof. It was like a romantic version of Japan I'd only imagined from books or seen in samurai movies. We entered through a set of sliding wooden doors and left our boots in the wide genkan, the entryway that physically and symbolically separates outside from inside. We stepped up and crossed the threshold through another set of sliding doors, and Nimaida welcomed us into a vast, sparsely furnished room, its high rafters blackened with soot. I shuffled shyly across creaky floorboards so wide my feet didn't touch the cracks. At the center, the irori gave off a faint woodsy perfume as a wisp of charcoal smoke snaked up to hover in the darkness above.

Eight of us congregated around the irori, an open hearth about a meter square and slightly sunken into the floor, with slender logs of homemade charcoal radiating heat. We crowded close for warmth in the drafty old house, resting small dishes and cups of tea on the irori's wooden frame. Among the guests were some wood-turning students, a beekeeper, an egg farmer, and my friend Mika the papermaker—all of them drawn to Nimaida's easygoing warmth and avuncular teasing as much as to the ideal he embodies, of living in harmony with the seasons and the land. It's an ideal tightly wound up with Japanese national identity, but for most citizens more myth than reality.

Someone dished up bowls of the steaming-hot rice that we were there to celebrate. The young farmer, who raises his hens by the sea, handed out eggs to crack into the bowls with freshly grated wasabi from a mountain stream behind Nimaida's house. We tasted the rice first by itself before adding anything: the plump little grains seemed almost bouncy, so pleasing I could eat a whole bowl with no embellishment. I didn't know plain rice could taste that good.

Nimaida, his face illuminated by the fire, served wild-boar miso soup from a cauldron suspended on an iron hook above the embers. Smile lines radiating from the corners of his eyes expressed delight and youthful energy. He passed around pieces of carrot and daikon nuka-zuke. He had grown the vegetables and pickled them in bran, a by-product of milling the rice in our bowls.

In that dimly lit room the kind of glossy tableware that seems tacky under bright light gleamed subtly against the velvety darkness (even if they were plastic facsimiles). The architecture explained so much about Japanese arts that I hadn't understood until I felt what it was like to be in this kind of space (later, I'd read *In Praise of Shadows*, in which Junichirō Tanizaki extolls darkness as essential to his country's aesthetics). In Nimaida's home, I could imagine the dim rooms where geigi entertained, their pale faces glowing as they strummed their shamisen, looking not the least bit clownish in the flickering kerosene light. But we were in a simple farmhouse—not a fancy ryokan—illuminated by electric lamps. As I watched the charcoal smolder, my newest dream, however unrealistic, was to one day live in a house like this, with its own iori.

I RETURNED TO Nimaida's iori again and again. I was always welcomed with tea kept warm in a kettle at its edge, sweet potatoes roasted in the embers, or ginkgo nuts toasted in an iron pan as we talked, while a cat purred in Nimaida's lap.

It's hard to picture him—these days always dressed practically in work boots, old jeans, and fleece smelling of wood smoke— wearing a suit and tie, but until a few years ago he was a regular salaryman. When Nimaida left Ōzuchi at twenty years old—to find work, marry, and settle down nearby, in Yamashiro—there were still about twenty people living in Ōzuchi. Over time all the young people left for work and to raise their children near schools (Nimaida had literally hiked over a mountain to get to his middle school). The old people became too frail to live on their own in the isolated village, with its harsh winters and bears visiting from the forest to shake the persimmon trees. Most families come back just once a year to clean their ancestors' graves.

Nimaida never really had a plan to save Ōzuchi. He started making charcoal there again about fifteen years ago, as sort of a hobby, using his father's old kiln. The next year, a relative from Ōsaka (about a four-hour drive away) came and planted a small rice paddy on a lark. It had been a long time since anyone had grown rice there, and it piqued Nimaida's curiosity. The relative gave up, but Nimaida was captivated. *Growing rice naturally without any chemicals produces this amazing color in the fields. And it's so delicious*, he tells me. *Rice is our most important culture*, he'll say with uncharacteristic solemnity.

He was spending more and more time in Ōzuchi, about a twenty-minute drive from the town of Yamashiro, where he and his wife lived. He built a bigger kiln so he could make more charcoal at one time, about two hundred kilos, double the capacity of his dad's.

I was making charcoal, growing rice and vegetables. It takes a lot of time and it's more interesting than working in a company, so I quit, he told me, his eyes sparkling with mischief. *My wife was mad.*

By then, the last three families had left Ōzuchi. Nimaida's mother was tumbling into dementia, but in her lucid moments she talked about how much she missed their old life in the village. Nimaida missed it too. He decided to move back there and bring his mother so she could live out her last years there. (His wife, who is not a fan of bugs and wild animals, stays in their house in Yamashiro.) Nimaida's friends worry whether he has enough money, whether he has a plan. But he appears perpetually cheerful and untroubled, if sometimes a little tired.

I've often bicycled to his house, an hour's ride from the center of town. I love the feeling of riding into cooler air as I climb higher into the forest, the sounds changing as the rush of the river drops farther below. Even birdcalls seem softened by the damp earth and tufts of ferns. You don't get all that from the car. Once I saw a kamoshika (*Capricornis crispus*), a mystical-looking deerlike creature, with short legs like a pygmy goat, a shaggy mane, and small horns. Nimaida worries that I'll encounter a bear. I assure him that I put a bear bell on my bike, but he shakes his head with a fatherly look of concern and says I'm crazy.

The houses in Ōzuchi look like part of the landscape, not something imposed on it. After a rain, steam rises off the mountain ridges like a Chinese landscape painting. I feel I've arrived somewhere separate from the rest of the world and its sense of time.

Sitting at the irori's edge one afternoon, I learned to twist rice straw into ropes. Another day, I helped peel persimmons to hang on those ropes from the wood and bamboo rack above the irori (for suspending pots above the fire or for drying fish). Weeks later, we ate the dried persimmons, their sweet sticky flesh perfumed with charcoal smoke.

When I asked about his charcoal making, Nimaida brought out a box of paper cranes, singed carbon-black in the kiln, yet somehow still intact. He showed me a clock made from a piece of charcoal, resonant and hard like obsidian. Around the house there are other experiments, bamboo and gourd vases, small paintings on pieces of blackened wood. But mostly he makes charcoal for the irori that warms his home—jet-black lengths of combusted wood that burn much hotter and longer than the American briquettes we pour from paper bags onto backyard grills.

Old houses like Nimaida's are designed around the irori and its charcoal. An irori is a natural gathering place, drawing you in toward heat and light. Wide-spaced slats in the second floor let heat and smoke rise, and openings in the roof vent the smoke. Burning wood in the open hearth makes too much smoke: charcoal burns cleaner.

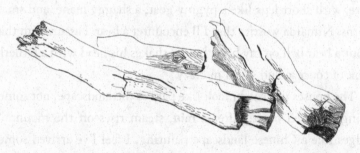

Charcoal, "sumi" in Japanese, heats the water for chanoyu, melts the iron for forging craftsmen's tools, and polishes lacquerware to a mirrorlike finish. Long ago, it was used to make malleable the steel hammered into samurai swords. For two thousand years it heated homes—in open hearths and clay pots (the original hiba-chi). It warmed kettles for tea, and charred fish and vegetables set on hand-woven wire grates. And then, under American occupation and rapid industrialization in the wake of World War II, electric-ity and gas replaced it in all but the most isolated villages.

When Nimaida was young, nearly sixty people lived in Ōzuchi—sixteen households who grew their own rice and vegeta-bles and sold charcoal to people in Yamanaka. For centuries, they'd built a series of kilns in the woods where they cut hardwood for firing. After using the wood in one area, they'd let the trees regrow and move their kiln to a different part of the forest, continuing the cycle. Nimaida tells me that when the gas lines finally came to Yamanaka in the 1960s, Ōzuchi people lost the only job they had up in those mountains.

There is still a market for specialty charcoal. Yakitori chefs prize ash-whitened binchōtan, made from ubame oak in Kishū and Tosa, in western Japan. Kanazawa tea masters favor rounds with a cross section like a chrysanthemum blossom, made from the straight trunks of sawtooth oak by a family on Noto, the peninsula that reaches into the Sea of Japan above Kaga. Recently, industri-ally produced activated carbon has become a trendy ingredient in beauty products and wellness drinks.

But no one wants to pay a premium for utilitarian charcoal, when they can fuel their cookouts with cheap imported stuff from the hardware store for as little as ¥100 (less than $1) per kilo. Ni-maida tells me he uses nara trees, a general term for the various species of oak dotting the hillsides around Yamanaka that make a good but unremarkable product.

Nimaida says each year that it might be his last. Transforming

wood into stable, long-burning fuel is so time consuming and labor intensive that nearly everyone else in Yamanaka and its surrounding villages has given it up. I asked Nimaida if I could see
how it's done. He explained to me that the three-day process starts
with an all-nighter, which he usually passes drinking with his
brother. *I'll bring the beer*, I promised.

IN LATE AUGUST, Nimaida messages me to say that charcoal making will start the next day. It's his third and last time of the season.
His schedule is subject to the whims of the weather, and there's a
typhoon about three days away, leaving just enough time to transform a kiln full of logs into two hundred kilos of carbon. I pack a
small bag with a change of clothes and a toothbrush, unsure how
long I'll stay in Ōzuchi.

I'm ready with a six-pack and a bag of junky snacks when Nimaida picks me up in his minivan on an overcast but sticky morning. He thinks I'm crazy to be interested in the dirty hard work of
making charcoal. *Crazy!* he repeats, chuckling and shaking his
head as a grin lights up his face.

When we arrive in Ōzuchi, there are twenty-two volunteers
from Taiwan, Russia, and Japan helping with farming. The terraced rice fields behind the cluster of houses climb like golden
stairs up to curtains of blue evergreens. Glossy eggplants hang
from deep purple plants in the vegetable plots at the center of the
tiny village, and fat overripe cucumbers fill a blue wheelbarrow
under a clothesline fluttering with towels.

As Nimaida and I walk up the hill toward the charcoal kiln at
the edge of the woods, we pass a sixteen-year-old girl pushing a

rototiller and a group of college boys starting a weed whacker. With a daily rotation of chores, and new farming skills, these volunteers are largely independent. But Nimaida tends to them as though they were his children, placing ice packs on fevered foreheads, driving them to and from the train station, and worrying over their heartbreaks.

When the first six college-age volunteers came to Ōzuchi, five years ago, it was supposed to be a onetime thing. It was a friend's idea. But after their two-week stay ended, Nimaida recalls, *Ōzuchi felt lonely, and I kept thinking about how fun it was.* He invited more volunteers and was happy when Ōzuchi filled again with languages and foods he didn't know. By now, young volunteers from twenty-three different countries and all over Japan have come to Ōzuchi to steward the land and experience a fading way of life.

Now, even in winter, Nimaida is rarely alone; volunteers help him shovel snow and care for empty houses. His home is full of gushing thank-you notes from young adults whose hearts he—and Ōzuchi—have touched. Some come back year after year, to spend their days tending fields and walking in the woods and their nights watching stars and talking around the fire. One couple who met there even got married.

I want them to learn the full life of Ōzuchi—the rice fields and vegetable plots, making an irori fire in the morning, river swimming and outdoor baths—the things I enjoyed as a child, says Nimaida. *I hope they'll choose their life with an understanding of the options.*

NIMAIDA'S KILN IS built into a hillside where the farmland meets the forest. Tree roots and ferns come through the dirt wall at the back. It's protected by a shed with a high steep-pitched roof, extending past the kiln to shelter a couple of ratty old couches and stacks of cardboard boxes full of charcoal from the first two batches this summer. After this third batch he'll have enough to warm his house all winter.

The kiln is essentially a man-made cave with a domed top, a stone wall across the front, and a hobbit-size door. Nimaida ducks inside, and some volunteers and I pass him wood through the low opening. The logs are about as thick as my arm and tall enough to reach my chest or chin; they're not light. Nimaida packs the wood in vertically, tightly as a fresh jar of Red Vines. Close to the mouth he places a row of fatter logs and then a piece of corrugated metal to shield the hardwood from direct contact with flames.

THERE ARE TUBS of red clay soil that he brought from the mountainside. He wets the red dirt with a watering can and gives me a pickax to turn over the heavy mud. He stacks blocks of stone and brick in the mouth of the kiln, mortaring them with this red mud, until only the top third is open. Between this wall and the corrugated metal shield is a gap that we fill with firewood.

The aim is to get the vertical hardwood logs extremely hot in a low-oxygen environment, burning off the moisture and volatile compounds so what remains is nearly pure carbon. It's a process, like cooking, that requires both precision and improvisation. Even if you follow the recipe, the moisture or density of this year's wood, the air temperature, or humidity can alter the results.

It's late afternoon by the time we make the fire. I'm dusty and

tired from the morning's labor, my arms scratched by tree bark. Nimaida adds a handful of dry sugi brush and lights it with a wooden match. Smoke and kicked-up dust fills the shed, stinging my eyes and making it hard to breathe. Nimaida fans the flames with an uchiwa, a paddle-like paper fan, heart shaped and pink with a Minnie Mouse design. A yellow towel wrapped around his head catches beads of sweat.

By six, the fire is coming along, and we sit outside drinking beer and eating pizza-flavored potato chips while some of the volunteers prepare dinner down at the house. Another group of them furiously fans the fire (it's hard to tell if this is actually productive, but they're having fun). The cicadas that dominate the soundscape of humid summer days give way to a gentler chorus of crickets and frogs.

As evening turns to night, Nimaida climbs on top of the kiln and uncovers a chimney near the back, which he fits with a tall metal pipe. The high-metabolism fire is ravenous now, and we're feeding it logs every half hour. When I step outside for air, the thick smoke obscures a half-moon overhead. We take another break to watch the moon set behind the mountain. The wind picks up, pleasantly cool in contrast to the hot shed but portending the incoming typhoon.

A woman my age named Yōko drives up to join us after a day of studying maki-e. She enthusiastically takes over piling wood on the fire and fanning it attentively. Gen, a young architect, joins us for a while, playing recordings of sweet mellow jazz from his iPhone. All of us are drawn to the wildness of Ōzuchi, the tenuous link to a romantic past, and Nimaida's warmth.

The walk back to the house takes only a few minutes, but at night it's long enough to get a little scared of what spirits or animals might be lurking in the dark. When Nimaida was a child, the kilns were much deeper in the woods. His face bathed in the orange glow of the fire, he reminisces.

Once, before he was in elementary school, he begged to go with his father to a kiln three kilometers into the forest. His father agreed. When it got dark, little Nimaida got scared and wanted to go home, but he was stuck there with his dad all night. He laughs at the memory now. His father's last kiln is a stone's throw down the hill from this one, at the edge of the village.

Around 1:00 A.M. the fire starts singing in a low whine, and pale violet flames lick the outside of the kiln. Smoke spills out of every crevice, like small creatures trying to escape. A few wisps creep out of the chimney—a sign that the fire is finally getting hot enough. We take turns fanning and stoking to maintain the heat.

My eyelids feel heavy, but I don't want to miss anything. What if this year really is the last time he makes charcoal? Even if I wanted to sleep, vague fear and discomfort keep me awake. It's not so much the stick bug crawling up my ankle or the large beetle that landed on my shoulder that gives me the creeps, it's the thought of more dangerous bugs lurking in the shadows. At least the smoke keeps mosquitoes away. But what if I doze off and then die of smoke inhalation? I do eventually drift to sleep on a dirty

old couch around 4:00 A.M., waking again with the first light as
Yōko is leaving for work.

BY NINE IN the morning I'm already sweating from the humidity.
In the daylight, the bugs and filth seem less threatening, and the
smoke isn't so stiflingly thick anymore. I ask Nimaida why he
doesn't do this in the autumn when the days aren't so hot. He says
it's too hard to get the kiln up to temperature and keep it there
when the weather is cold. And you can get a chill sleeping outside.

As the second day of charcoal making commences, Nimaida
climbs above the kiln to measure the temperature of the smoke
coming steadily from the chimney now. When it reaches around
80 degrees Celsius, he'll know it's 500 to 600 inside the kiln—hot
enough for good charcoal (though only half as hot as the kiln for
fancy binchōtan). Haze no longer fills the shed. Nimaida starts
building the wall higher at the mouth of the kiln, adding bricks
and red mud to hold back the fire and choke off oxygen.

He leaves me in charge of the kiln for the afternoon while he
goes to do errands and take care of the volunteers. I stay nearby—
read a book, listen to the cicadas and birds, and nap on the dirty
old couch—adding logs to keep the flames steady and smoke
pouring from the chimney.

THAT EVENING, another visitor joins us for dinner. Sakura, in her
early forties, is one of the few hunters in this area under seventy

and the only woman. As we talk and drink around the irori—still a gathering place even when it's too hot for a fire—she promises to bring me bear meat when the hunting season starts in November. (I can't say I'm excited about eating such a magnificent animal, but I am grateful for the gesture of friendship.)

Sakura leaves around 1:00 A.M.; in a few hours she'll be out checking boar traps. Nimaida and I tend the kiln one last time before bed. The wind is rushing through the treetops, making an unsettling sound like a river pouring down the mountain. He adds another layer of bricks to the wall and puts logs on the fire, then leaves it to burn. Tonight we will sleep.

ON THE THIRD DAY of charcoal making, it's barely dawn when I hear Nimaida calling to me, *Wild boar coming!* Half-awake, I think he means there's one running around, and I leap out of the hammock where I'd slept, excited and nervous. But moments later Sakura and a white-haired man, her hunting teacher, pull up in a car and unload a freshly killed young boar. They butcher it there by a cold stream, as the morning sun comes up over the mountain, cutting across the valley in hot golden beams. We pack the meat into coolers and carry it up to the house, where Nimaida asks me to cut it into smaller pieces to pack into the freezer.

The fire needs less tending on the third day. After a dinner of boar curry, the temperature of the kiln is finally high enough. Our job now is to seal it off in order to extinguish the ultrahot fire. We carry watering cans up from the house again and again to moisten tubs of soil mixed with ash. Nimaida fastens boards across the front of the kiln. The boards hold in place a thick wall of soil-ash mixture that we will build up layer by layer over the course of several hours. Outside, it starts to rain.

Some time past midnight, we finish making the wall. Nimaida seals the chimney, cutting off all air supply to the fire. After three days tending the kiln (and barely sleeping), my work is done.

That night, I sleep on the floor in the big room next to the irori. The typhoon rattles the roof and shakes the walls, but it isn't the first storm this house has weathered, and I feel secure boxed inside its thick beams. When I wake after sunrise, the rain has stopped, and Nimaida is already up and about. I trail after him blearily, coffee in hand, stepping over persimmon branches torn down by the wind, green fruit still clinging to them. I find him at the kiln, surveying our work in the light of day. If he'd sealed it perfectly, he says, we could open it today. But you could still feel heat radiating from its walls. He'll wait a week or two to make sure there are no embers still burning inside.

The typhoon has passed, and Nimaida will turn his attention to preparing for the rice harvest and planting fall vegetables, until the next storm comes. Because of his efforts, Ōzuchi is now registered as a historic landmark. *But that only protects the houses, not the way of life*, he says. That, he feels, is his job, and he wants to do his best in his lifetime. Because he has no children, Nimaida hopes one of the volunteers will inherit his caretaking of Ōzuchi. *Even if I had children, there's no guarantee they'd want to do this*, he says.

Nimaida takes his mother, riding piggyback, down to the car, to deliver her to the nursing home where she stays during the day so he can work and look after the volunteers. He'll deliver me back to Yamanaka too.

The road to town is glistening wet and littered with small sugi branches, like the first time I came to Ōzuchi. I spend nearly two hours in the onsen that morning, scrubbing and soaking away the smoke and dust from my skin and hair, until finally I feel ready to rejoin modern life in town.

Hunter's Stew

TIME: *2 hours*
Makes about 6.5 liters (7 quarts), 25 small servings

This is shishi nabe, game stew. Nabe is the Japanese word for a pot and for a soup or stew you make in it. Shishi is usually inoshishi, wild boar, but it can include other game. Nimaida makes shishi nabe in the huge iron pot hanging over his irori—with carrot and sato-imo (taro) from his garden, homemade miso, and thinly sliced boar meat that his hunter friends drop off. He tells me there's no recipe, you can add whatever you like. But if I ask him, teasing, whether broccoli or tomato would be acceptable, he says no, absolutely not.

Kawamoto, who hunts boars, makes his shishi nabe like tonjiru, country pork stew, adding burdock and torn pieces of konnyaku. He says it's important to start with starchy root vegetables that thicken the broth, and to use a variety of mushrooms—their rich earthiness complements the gamy meat. (To be honest, this stew is satisfying even without the meat!)

Use this recipe as a guide, but make it your own. Serve shishi nabe alongside a bowl of rice and a few pieces of Japanese pickles to make a complete meal. This makes enough to feed a small army of volunteers or a large party of friends. If you don't have a big enough pot, divide the ingredients between two, or halve the recipe.

> *Note:* To slice the boar meat very thinly, freeze it for an hour or two first so it's firm but not rock hard. Other game meat, or pork, may be substituted.

1 piece konbu, about 35 cm (14 inches) long

2 kilograms (4½ pounds) root vegetables, any or all of the following:

>   Japanese (or Korean) sweet potato
>
>   Yellow potato
>
>   Sato-imo (taro), peeled
>
>   Renkon (lotus root)
>
>   Burdock, scrubbed

1 medium onion

1 large carrot

1 block (about 200–300 grams) konnyaku (optional)

500 grams (1 pound) mushrooms, any or all of the following:

>   Shiitake
>
>   Maitake
>
>   Buna shimeji
>
>   Enoki
>
>   Nameko

100 mL (scant ½ cup) mirin, or more to taste

300 grams (1 cup) miso, or more to taste

500 grams (1 pound) wild boar, preferably fatty cuts, sliced very thin (see note)

1 package (about 100 grams) abura-age (thin fried tofu)

1 large negi or 3 fat scallions

Shichi-mi tōgarashi or yuzu-koshō (optional), for serving

1. Put the konbu in a very large pot with about 2 liters (8 cups) water. Steep it over low heat while you cut the root vegetables.

2. Cut the sweet potato, yellow potato, and peeled sato-imo into chunks just small enough to fit in a spoon. Halve or quarter the

renkon lengthwise, and cut into 1 cm (½-inch) slices. Cut the burdock into sasagaki (the same way you would sharpen a pencil with a
knife) or julienne. Add these vegetables to the pot. Increase the heat
to high and bring to a boil, then fish out the konbu and discard or
save it for another use. Lower the heat to keep the broth at a steady
simmer, skimming the foam occasionally.

3. Cut the onion into large dice. Cut the carrot into ran-giri: roll it
quarter turns as you slice across it at a diagonal, to make irregular
multifaceted pieces. Add the onion and carrot to the pot. If using
the konnyaku, rinse it in hot water, then tear it into bite-size pieces
and add to the pot. Add more water, if necessary, to cover the vegetables; keep simmering.

4. Cut or break the mushrooms into large bite-size pieces and add to
the pot. Add more water, if necessary, to cover the vegetables.

5. Continue to simmer the soup until all the vegetables are soft enough
to eat, 10–15 minutes after the last addition, then add the mirin
and miso. Taste and adjust the seasoning, adding more mirin for
sweetness or miso for salt and umami if necessary.

6. If the meat smells particularly gamy, blanch it for 30 seconds in boiling water before adding it to the pot. If not, add the thinly sliced
meat directly to the soup.

7. While the meat cooks for a few minutes, place the abura-age in a
sieve, and pour hot water over it to rinse off excess oil. Cut it into
bite-size pieces, and add it to the pot. While the abura-age heats
through, thinly slice the negi or scallions, and add them to the pot.
The stew is now ready to eat (but can be kept warm over low heat
for up to an hour).

8. Ladle steaming-hot shishi nabe into small bowls. If you like, pass
shichi-mi tōgarashi or yuzu-koshō for spice. The stew tastes even
better reheated the next day.

Eight

Lost and Found

T here's a picture of me and Shinichi Moriguchi that I love. We're standing next to a pile of logs, in front of the sheer indigo noren (the curtains that hang above entryways in Japan) the same color as his loose workman's pants and my denim jacket, which is embroidered with red camellias. The sixty-five-year-old craftsman wears red basketball shoes and an enormous puffy down vest. His gaze is sharp, but his bristly gray push-broom mustache nearly curves into a smile. I'm at least a head taller, and yet his presence is larger.

I've just made my first wagatabon, a carved wooden tray named for Wagatani, a tiny village upstream from central Yamanaka that has been underwater since 1965. I'm holding my wagatabon in the photo, grinning. When Moriguchi first came to Yamanaka looking for wagatabon nearly twenty years ago, he couldn't find a single one. People say that when Wagatani was submerged by a dam, the small wooden trays could be seen floating on the water: they were not among the things people took with them.

Up the valley, Moriguchi has revived the craft that drowned with Wagatani. His is the only occupied house in Kazetani, Village of the Wind, and only on weekends, when he comes from Kyōto to make his wagatabon. Kazetani, once a stop on the trade route running from the mountain hamlets of Kutani and Wagatani out to coastal Fukui, had lain dormant until he arrived. Tanuki (raccoon dogs) played freely around its overgrown shrine as moss crept over the bridge leading to the four remaining houses.

The narrow road to Kazetani winds through the forest southwest of Kakusenkei—past the urushi plantation that wood-turning students tap each summer to collect sap, and a defunct gravel pit—converging with a stream glistening over blue and gold volcanic rock. Ecru turtle doves take off from low-hanging branches, and in the evening chipmunk-striped uribō (baby boars) and soft brown bunnies dart across the road. I've seen Moriguchi stop his car to remove a large toad from harm's way. During the winter, he disregards a DO NOT ENTER sign posted by the city for the safety of drivers and clears rocks and branches from the road himself.

The house, which he hasn't particularly bothered to renovate, is a decade or two older than he is. Beyond the indigo noren, he's made the dusty main room into a gallery. There are still tattered folding screens and mildewed tansu from the previous occupant.

Each of the dozens of trays on display is carved from a single piece of wood, with its own idiosyncrasies. What they have in common is a rectangular shape, split vertically from a log, and ridges corrugating the inside, across the grain. Some are nut-brown with almost iridescent swirls of wood grain running perpendicular to the gouged ridges. Others are singed matte black. Most have the cool gray luster of weathered siding. My favorites show a path of wormholes along one edge, or a brass staple reinforcing them where the wood has split. A few have chevron patterns carved into their outer edges. Their unvarnished surface feels smooth but porous, the way a well-worn wooden spoon does.

Moriguchi's workshop, attached to the side of the house, is scantly separated from the outdoors by mud plaster walls and a cement floor. It's filled with piles of logs, both for the cast-iron stove that heats the space and for making wagatabon. Finished work cures on shelves along the left wall, and to the right are bags of wood chips piled up against a workbench littered with postcards and catalogs for art shows (Moriguchi's and his friends') past, present, and future. A few of his small sculptural wooden vases hold wildflowers. A low table and folding stools at the front half of the room accommodate visitors.

Moriguchi presides over the atelier from the back, where he sits on a short stump with a cushion stapled to the top. He works at a low bench, really a section of solid beam, surrounded by curved and flat chisels, and hand planes of all sizes. Piles of wood chips collect at his feet. He periodically stands up to sharpen his tools on an electric wheel. The space is filled with the steady tap, tap, tap of a mallet driving a chisel across the green (unseasoned) chestnut slabs that will become wagatabon. He wields his tools with a peculiar stiffness that would be easy to mistake for arthritis.

The day that photo of me and Moriguchi was taken was the first time I visited his atelier, on the cusp between winter and spring just over a year ago. My friend Kohagi, a shy but fearless woodturning student, had asked me to come meet a sculptor. When she said *sculptor*, I worried about wasting my day looking at the half-baked work of some sheltered young artist with more confidence than craftsmanship, but I agreed anyway, because you never know. The moment I arrived at Moriguchi's woodland atelier, I was enchanted.

I thought we were coming for only a little visit, but Moriguchi gave me and Kohagi small slabs of wood to make our own wagatabon. He presented us each with a mallet and two chisels—one flat and one curved—with which to hollow the slab and carve the grooves. He coached us while he hammered away at his own work. He made it look easy, but as I gripped the round chisel, it sometimes dug too deep or veered out of parallel with the previous line. *Don't think; feel*, he said in English, just as Nakajima had.

He cracked jokes with Kohagi about my long spider legs, splayed out awkwardly in impractical heeled boots as I crouched on a too-low stool. We took breaks for coffee and sweets. He smoked cigarettes and restarted the CD player whenever silence fell over the workshop. I was fixated on finishing my tray, and the hours melted together as the same sentimental pop played over and over.

When we got to the last few steps, he let me in on a *top-secret technique* (which I will not disclose here, but which he would likely teach you too if you came to his studio) for cutting grooves into the vertical ends of the tray. Then he showed us how to level the back, its imperfections smoothed but not erased by the blade of a big sturdy wooden hand plane. We softened the edges with a tiny plane no bigger than a matchbox. A Moriguchi wagatabon looks rough-hewn, but there's not a single sharp edge or splinter to catch on your hands.

It was dark by the time we swept up the wood shavings. I left thinking that I liked carving wagatabon even more than turning cups and bowls. Each one is different, based on the way the wood splits. They're often asymmetrical, preserving a natural edge or an interesting knot or burl. Their sturdy unpolished form invites use, unlike fine lacquerware that sometimes seems too precious to touch.

BY THE TIME I work up the courage to ask Moriguchi if I can be his assistant, I've made two more wagatabon. It's August; the noren from that photo has faded to a weathered pale blue, and Moriguchi calls me Hannah-chan, a term of endearment you might use for a niece.

My job is to lightly sand and stain his finished pieces and help with other small tasks like putting price stickers on work for upcoming exhibitions. He wants me to teach him English, and though my Japanese is still shaky, I translate terms for his tools and techniques. There aren't so many chores for me to do: mostly, he teaches me to make wagatabon.

There is no cell phone service in Kazetani, and never for a moment do I feel bored or lonely enough to miss it. When my hands and forearms ache from gripping the chisel and mallet (probably too hard in my beginner's anxiety), I step outside to take in the color of the sky, the wind through the treetops, and the wildflowers that change daily. I collect flat blue stones from the stream to use as chopstick rests and coasters.

We share the workshop with grasshoppers, spiders, and the occasional mouse, who come and go as they please through the porous walls. *Are you afraid of snakes?* Moriguchi asks me one afternoon. I'm not. He points to the rafters where a silvery skin has been shed in coils, perfectly intact. He says it's good luck: it means money will come.

A cast of old woodsmen rotate through. They gossip and devise improvement projects, like the plywood bulletin board I helped three grandpas install. They assume I don't understand their rambling Japanese, and mostly they're right, but I pick out familiar names and infer from their tone that the gossip isn't mean-spirited; its purpose is to share local news and the pleasant patter of conversation.

Gato-san, who runs a stylish modern lacquerware shop with his elder brother, drops by every few weeks for advice on the wagatabon he's making as a hobby. Ishiguchi-san, a well-groomed and friendly retired ironworker, comes most weekends, bringing some nice fish or fruit, and stays at least long enough for a cup of coffee. The most frequent visitor is Hirata-san, a wiry eighty-something craftsman, with white hair and dark triangular eyebrows that look painted on. He uses Yamanaka wood-turning techniques to make intricate incense boxes that look like miniature temples, with tiny rings around the spire that spin freely, turned from the same piece of wood. He can turn plates thin enough to see through.

Shūhei Hirata was born in Wagatani (the origin of *wagata*bon), to a family who carried charcoal by horseback from their remote village down into Yamanaka. They were one of only two or three families who owned horses in the village of about two hundred people. The rest made their living cutting timber and firing charcoal and grew their own vegetables and rice.

Before that, many Wagatanians were in the shingle business, splitting thin rectangles from freshly felled trees. December to March, when they couldn't work outside, they made useful things from small pieces of wood, such as bowls and trays—wagatabon. There were wagatabon with deep sides for offering grains to spirits, wide shallow ones for carrying tea and sweets, and ones made for presenting tobacco to guests. At least a few trays ended up a half day's horse ride away in Daishōji, where presumably they'd been traded for other goods.

Some say Wagatani people used the shingle-making scraps for their trays. Others will tell you they saved the most beautiful pieces. Either way, they lost their closest shingle market after Yamanaka burned in 1931, a few years before Hirata was born: the town rebuilt with ceramic tile roofs. Hirata told me his family used wagatabon to feed their cats.

Hirata remembers the dark road, too narrow for cars, that he traveled by bicycle or motorbike to get to Yamanaka for middle school and then to apprentice to a woodturner there for seven years. He worried about bears on his commute.

By the time construction began on the Wagatani Dam in 1961, Hirata was a bachelor in his mid-twenties. Some people fought its construction, but the price of charcoal was dropping, and mountain life was hard. When they left to make way for hydroelectric power and flood control, they lost the land where they could grow their own food, but they gained the conveniences of town life. Hirata saw an opportunity to make his own workshop. He designed the house that he lives and works in now and helped build the joinery himself.

THERE IS NO mention of wagatabon in a history of Yamanaka that was published in 1959. But in 1963, as the Wagatani Dam was being constructed, a craftsman named Tatsuaki Kuroda wrote about wagatabon in a periodical called *Mingei Techō*. Kuroda—a woodworker and lacquer artist designated a Living National Treasure—was a proponent of a folk-craft revival called mingei that started in the 1920s. The cultural activists of the mingei movement extolled the beauty of things crafted for everyday use, and argued for the value of a purely Japanese aesthetic. They sought out rustic and rural objects made by anonymous craftsmen.

A century before Kuroda wrote about wagatabon, a craftsman named Tasuke Nakasuji did make a name for himself carving the trays, and his work became known as Tasuke-bon. The next craftsman to be remembered for his wagatabon was Hatsujirō Hiraoka, working from about 1890 through 1940. But by the early 1960s no one was making wagatabon, so Tatsundo Hayashi revived the craft with the encouragement of Tatsuaki Kuroda.

Moriguchi knew none of this. He had studied sculpture and in the 1980s was building sets for samurai movies. He loved wood and exploring ways to use it—making wooden key chains and toys. He started learning urushi from Tatsuaki Kuroda's son, Kenkichi, and lacquering his own grooved sculptures and kōgei, high crafts, with up to twenty coats of flawlessly smooth urushi. When

Kenkichi Kuroda's wife saw a tray Moriguchi had made, she said it reminded her of wagatabon. It was the first Moriguchi had heard of the wooden trays from Wagatani. (He says now that his work hardly looked like wagatabon at all, but he's lucky she said so.)

When Moriguchi first came to Yamanaka searching for wagatabon, around 2000, they weren't in the woodenware shops, in the museums, or at the wood-turning school. The craft had nearly disappeared. He found something like a wagatabon that had originally been a signboard above the entrance to a shrine, and the owner of an antiques shop in Daishōji directed him to someone who owned a few trays. Over the next few years he tracked down as many wagatabon as he could, photographed them, and began teaching himself from the photos.

Looking back, he says that making formal kōgei with urushi was stressful and didn't suit his personality. Kōgei uses precious wood, but he was more interested in ordinary, often-overlooked materials, like the chestnut that wagatabon are made from. Their raw surface appealed to him, and he abandoned lacquer. That brought him closer to the kind of woodworking he was searching for in his early experiments. Lacquer, he realized, kills the natural quality of the wood—its ability to change color and texture. Glossy kōgei loses its luster over time, but folk crafts become more appealing as age and use add character.

Along the way he befriended Hirata, who'd thought nothing of leaving cat dishes (wagatabon) behind in Wagatani, until he met Moriguchi. Hirata gave Moriguchi some advice on his wagatabon. Moriguchi gave him a few trays (which he uses to display small sculptures and things from his grandkids). Hirata made Moriguchi some hand planes.

Hirata tells me it's too late for him to learn a new craft—he has his own work to make—but he wants to support Moriguchi as much as he can. In rokuro, wood turning, if you make two hundred bowls, each one must be identical. But wagatabon are infinitely varied, and *Anyone who wants to learn can make one*, says Hirata. One afternoon, as the two friends coach me on using the big hand plane, I hear Hirata teasing Moriguchi that his work has become too good; it's lost the amateur's charm.

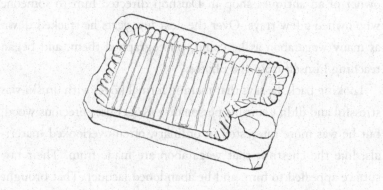

A FEW YEARS before I met Moriguchi, he was hospitalized for a stroke. He'd been making wagatabon for more than a decade at his Kyōto studio. He had an exhibition coming up, so he asked someone to bring his tools to the hospital, and he worked while he recovered. He could no longer open his right hand, but he could grip a mallet.

He kept hammering away. The stroke only strengthened his resolve to establish wagatabon as a legitimate and lasting craft. If he was going to teach people about wagatabon, he decided, he needed to be in Yamanaka, close to its origin. After a false start in a house with a leaky roof, Moriguchi found his Kazetani atelier. He says he's made plenty of wagatabon, and his main purpose now is to make sure the craft won't be lost again.

Moriguchi tells me he likes Yamanaka because there are lots of strange people. *Like me and you, Hannah-chan*, he says. Outside the atelier, the piles of old wood and broken tools that may be garbage or material for future projects, and the old garden overgrown with weeds, remind me of the crumbling homesteads around where I grew up—another small town in the woods that was conservative and yet a good place for anyone who didn't quite fit into mainstream modern society to occupy a cabin in the woods.

I love being in Moriguchi's workshop, and I too am more suited to making wagatabon than shiny flawless bowls. Really, I'm more his student than his assistant. He has taught me to shape staples from brass nails. I hold the small nails with pliers in the flame of a blowtorch, hammer them flat on an anvil, then bend them and trim the ends to a point. If a wagatabon cracks while you're making it, you hammer in one of these staples to reinforce it. The damage becomes an upgrade, like kintsugi, golden repair.

He has taught me how to make kuri-shibu, chestnut tannin, by boiling wood shavings with iron nails until the mixture turns black and the shavings are tinted gray. I paint this on his finished trays, and it reacts with the tannins in the wood to make it look instantly weathered. When I work too hastily, he patiently teaches me to paint one side with care, let it dry, and then paint the other.

He's taught me to drive iron wedges into the top of a short log, splitting the wood into slabs. Some pieces split too small or not flat enough to make wagatabon. Instead of throwing them away, he uses all these scraps to make other things: vases, dishes, small sculptural objects. He tells me he even has an idea for using the bark (what it is, he hasn't revealed).

My Japanese is getting better—I can understand much more than I can speak—and occasionally I even catch humor. (Like when Moriguchi tells me, conspiratorially, that Hirata cut his hand with a chain saw but was more afraid of young Kohagi driving him to the hospital than of the injury itself.) But for most of what we do, language isn't really necessary.

If you pay attention, tools and materials tell you how they want to be used, but often we get preoccupied with words, thinking too much about what we've been told instead of what is right in front of our eyes. It's frustrating not being able to ask a complex question, but I can almost always figure out what I need to know by closely watching what Moriguchi does.

The wagatabon I've made are piling up in my apartment. One, on the floor next to my futon, holds my glasses, a necklace my husband gave me, and a gold pencil for journaling. On my desk, my collection of pretty and useless things—a yellow silk moth, some duck feathers, and a pinecone—rests on a small gray wagatabon with a big knot in one corner. I put a larger one by the door for my keys, a pocket-size memo pad, and my gray silk wallet filled with the things I need for tea lessons.

Now that I've made all these, Moriguchi is teaching me something new. He gives me pieces of split wood that are too warped, too uneven, or too small for wagatabon and asks me to carve plates of my own design. He lets me use the good mallet, the hard rubber one he usually keeps for himself. He tells me he wants me to learn to have a conversation with the wood, instead of imposing my own idea on it.

Maika-san, a woman in her forties who works as a delivery driver in Kanazawa, is there every Sunday, even when Moriguchi isn't. Kami-san, a gallery owner, also comes often to make her own wagatabon and keeps a set of tools at home. Others come for a onetime workshop: ladies who drive up for the day with fancy bentō lunches and chic clothes, or students from the forestry school in Gifu who camp out for the weekend.

They are all making wagatabon; the plates are a special challenge given to me. I wonder if it's because I'm especially good at it or because I'm especially bad at it. *You have a sense for making things*, Moriguchi says.

Moriguchi is a strict but gentle teacher. He's easy on the first-time students, but for me, Maika, and Kami he corrects small details, pushing us to improve our technique each time. He learned through trial and error, by looking at the work of deceased craftsmen and making hundreds—maybe thousands—of wagatabon, but he wants to make it easier for us by telling us the right way.

On a recent afternoon, I was helping load his car. Hirata arrived more restless than usual because he'd quit smoking and all but did my job for me, grabbing the heaviest boxes before I could get to them.

Moriguchi drives all over the country, unloading logs, mallets, chisels, and planes into galleries and workshops to teach new students. He hopes that if he shows enough people how to make wagatabon, it can become a tradition like the wooden bowls and cups that Yamanaka is famous for. But the administration of Yamanaka's wood-turning school have rejected adding Moriguchi's wagatabon class to their curriculum. To some, wagatabon still carries the stigma of folk craft, lacking the sparkly prestige of lacquerware.

Over the past twenty years, Moriguchi has built up wagatabon's reputation. Television shows and magazine articles have told his story. His wagatabon are for sale in Gato's shop on Yamanaka's main street for hundreds of dollars apiece, and they are in the prestigious collection of Kayōtei ryokan. It seems as though half the businesses in town use small wagatabon as money trays (for accepting payments and giving change). But still, the craft's future is precarious.

I take for granted that I can go up to Kazetani anytime and make wagatabon with Moriguchi. It feels as though he has always been in that rustic atelier and always will be. But he's worried that he could have another stroke at any time and die or become paralyzed. *My atelier will collapse without me*, he frets, *but bigger schools will carry on*. He wants to teach wagatabon in public institutions. He wants to teach the teachers.

Moriguchi will never tire of making wagatabon, he says, because each piece of wood is different. But now his focus is on spreading the craft and keeping its integrity. As he taps away at another new wagatabon, he tells me, *I have to teach quickly and take care of my students while I still have energy to do so.*

There are 2,820 river systems in Japan. On 746 of those river systems, there are 2,755 dams. People have been building them here since 600 C.E. to store water for irrigating rice fields. Later, in the postwar rush to modernize, dams were constructed for flood control and hydroelectric power. In the decades since the Wagatani Dam was built, environmentalists have drawn attention to the devastating effects that damming rivers has on wildlife. The life cycles of fish and fireflies have been disrupted. What else might we have lost, without even knowing it was worth saving?

Pickled Wasabi Greens

TIME: *45 minutes, plus overnight pickling*
Makes 1 small jar (200 mL or 8-ounce size)

The wasabi root that's grated to serve with sushi only grows well in very clean, cold streams, but the stems and leaves of wasabi can flourish on shady hillsides, and even in gardens. I gathered armfuls of the greens along the river outside Moriguchi's wood-carving atelier in Kazetani—as a deerlike kamoshika watched me from farther up the mountain—to make wasabi shoyu-zuke (pickled in soy sauce) the way Noboru Nimaida, caretaker of Ōzuchi village, taught me. Nimaida uses the sweet soy sauce typical of Ishikawa, so no sugar is necessary. But if you're not using amakuchi shoyu (sweet soy sauce), a little sugar helps balance the sharp bite of the greens.

Pick the flower stalks of wasabi before they bloom, when the buds are plump and the stems and leaves are tender. Their spicy flavor is concentrated in the stems (not so much the leaves), but once the flowers bloom, the stems become fibrous.

1 bunch wasabi leaves and stems (about 200 grams)
Fine sea salt
2 tablespoons soy sauce, or more to taste
1–2 teaspoons sugar, to taste (optional)

1. Rinse the greens and shake off the water. Cut the leaves and stems into roughly 5 cm (2-inch) lengths. Place them in a small pot or heatproof container with a lid. Sprinkle them with a few big pinches of salt, and gently massage it in for a few seconds. While the salt draws water from the greens, bring a kettle of water to a full boil.

2. Pour boiling water over the greens for a few seconds, until they barely begin to wilt. Count to three, and then immediately pour off the water, using the lid to keep the greens in while the last of the water drips out. Cover the pot or container, and let stand for 30 minutes.

3. Transfer the greens to a small jar with a lid; discard any remaining liquid. Add the soy sauce and sugar (if using). (Nimaida doesn't measure the soy sauce; he just pours it about halfway up the greens in the jar.) Cover and refrigerate overnight. The greens will give off more liquid as they pickle.

4. By the next day, they're ready to eat. Taste and adjust the seasoning with more soy sauce or sugar if necessary. If you'd like to keep them longer than a month, add enough soy sauce to cover the greens— submerged in brine they will last until next spring's harvest. Store in the refrigerator.

Wild Things

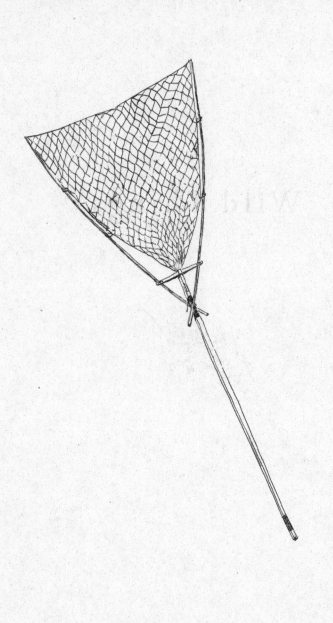

Nine

Samurai at the Duck Pond

Entering the saka-ami clubhouse at the edge of Katano Kamoike (Katano Duck Pond) feels like stepping back in time fifty years, but the sport of netting ducks is much older. On the evening of the year's first hunt, November 15, vintage sumo footage happens to be playing on the TV in the corner of a tatami mat room, enhancing the time-warp effect. A picture window with a small telescope looks out on the bird preserve, where noisy ducks loaf on the pond and swans take off in formation as the sky shades pink. Of the dozen or so men gathered around a kerosene heater, sipping small cups of green tea, only a few are under sixty. *We're not used to having a beauty like you here*, one of them says to me in Japanese, and then some other things it's probably better I didn't catch.

The sun drops behind the hillside, still golden with autumn leaves, and the men head into the woods carrying handmade nets that look, for now, like bundles of wooden spears. They climb the short steep trail to their lookouts at a brisk pace. The hilltop where they hunt is called a saka-ba (a sloped place). In a clearing where the pine trees have been cropped short, each of them assembles five or six Y-shaped nets. The stem of the Y is a sturdy wooden pole. The arms are bamboo, braced at the crotch, and secured to the pole by cotton cord. Between the arms, they string a fishing net. All together, this Y-shaped ami (net) stands about twice as tall as the man who holds it.

I came today with Kazuo Kawamoto, a lacquerware manufacturer with posture as sturdy as a tree trunk, a shiny shaved head resembling the Buddha statues sold to Western tourists, a friendly face that looks younger than his fifty-five years, and meaty paint-stained hands. I don't know him well, but we often cross paths at the small Sunday morning farmers' market in front of the onsen, where I go to have coffee with my favorite old ladies and he stops by after his morning bath to pick up local gossip or drop off boar meat. At Engawa bar one evening, Kawamoto agreed to let me watch saka-ami hunting because I'm Shimoki's friend. He talks to me in slow, clearly enunciated Japanese that's easy to understand.

He's asked me to wear dark clothing and keep my phone and notebook in my pocket. Ducks are particularly sensitive to light and movement and can pick up UV rays that are invisible to humans and other predators.

The hunt begins when the sky is still light, but the human eye can no longer detect color in the evergreen branches. The men take their positions, seated on crates atop wooden platforms called kamae-ba at the crest of a hill above the pond, camouflaged by a stand of pines and sun-bleached plumes of tall susuki grass.

The ducks get louder and the men get quieter. Silhouetted against the fading sunset, each hunter crouches with his net held out horizontally in front of him, like a tennis racket ready for a serve. Wigeons, teals, and mallards begin their flight east to the fields where they feed on gleanings overnight.

You hear the whistle of their wings before you see the first formation fly in overhead. Then the whoosh of nets as hunters thrust them up vertically into the air, throwing them two or three lengths directly overhead. The nets fall to the ground with a heavy thud if they've caught a duck, a light clatter if not. The soft needles of stubby pines in the clearing break their fall.

One hunter times it perfectly: his net soars up to intercept a duck from the narrow gap in its field of vision, and the duck has no time to change course. The hunter runs to his net to find a northern shoveler stunned from its fall, like a bird that's flown into a window (or a football player whose head has hit the ground too hard). Before the shoveler has a chance to come to, the hunter wraps a string tightly around its neck.

The duck dies quietly in the dark. There's none of the brutality of death by gun or barnyard slaughter—no blood, no squawking. Perhaps a slight rustling, a last flap of the wings, and then silence. Wood clacks together as the hunter picks up a new net.

I've never killed an animal, even though my parents raised sheep, partly for meat. They had some traumatic experiences early in their back-to-the-land days with amateur chicken killing and left it to professionals thereafter (except when it was necessary to eliminate the occasional attack rooster). The closest I have come was sneaking into the garden when I was about eight or nine and hiding in the raspberry bushes to see how the lambs were slaughtered. The woolly eight-month-old animal stood beside the slaughter truck one moment, and the next moment it was headless on the ground.

I expected to be disturbed by the sight of a freshly killed duck, but instead I'm overtaken with fascination and childlike wonder. Look at this incredible being! Its intricate feathers, its cleanly webbed feet, the serrated lamellae of its bill like a whale's baleens!

After thirty minutes, darkness has fallen. Flashlights and headlamps come on, and the hunters collect their nets. Twenty men caught three ducks—a good day. On a great day, they might bring back ten. This is not an efficient way to hunt. Instead, it is a game of concentration, patience, and precision and a direct link to Kaga's samurai past.

Kaga had one of the largest samurai classes of any domain. They were a military order who abided by a strict code of conduct. In Inazō Nitobe's *Bushidō: The Soul of Japan*, he likens bushidō, the way of the warrior, to chivalry. Nitobe helped create the modern idea that samurai were required to be fearless of death, unwaveringly loyal to their lords, stoic, educated but not erudite, and unflinchingly honest.

In the late seventeenth century, there lived a samurai named Genemon Murata, said to be so agile he could catch a sparrow with his bare hands. One evening, he was returning from fishing at Katano Beach, west of Kamoike. As he crested the hill heading inland, a flock of ducks approached. He thrust his fishing net into the air and caught one—or so the story goes. Genemon Murata refined the net for catching ducks, and the sport caught on with other samurai as a way to hone agility and focus during relatively peaceful times.

For nearly two hundred years—through the final centuries of military rule and the flourishing arts of the Edo period—the sport was restricted to samurai. It opened to civilians only after the Meiji Restoration, when the loosely affiliated sovereignties that had made up Japan were united under centralized rule from Tōkyō and the feudal system was abolished. Samurai were stripped of their titles and swords, but bushidō persisted in their hearts—and hobbies.

This year, at least a dozen men will hunt at Kamoike every evening, unfazed by rain, sleet, or snow, until February 15, when the season ends. In the late nineteenth and early twentieth centuries—when there were more hunters, more birds, and fewer regulations—they could catch more than five thousand ducks in a year. Now, due to a complex web of environmental and cultural factors, they capture two to three hundred.

To participate, you need a net-hunting license from the city and membership in the club. You can't buy these nets at a hardware store, so you'll need to persuade a senior hunter to give you one or teach you how to make them. Protective of their community and the ecosystem around the pond, the hunters rarely admit visitors (besides the occasional family member or close friend). I was lucky to get a glimpse into their world, but I want to learn what keeps these men out in the cold all winter, catching hardly any ducks. One day with them is not enough.

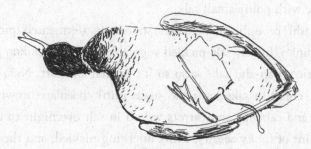

Back at the club, Kawamoto asks me to join a group dinner at Bantei, one of two restaurants in Kaga where the hunters bring their saka-ami-gamo, net-caught ducks.

Kawamoto's little white Subaru van reminds me of the old VW my cousin used to drive—which was always charmingly broken, seemingly held together by duct tape, and a little musty smelling. The back is full of hunting and fishing gear. There are rolls of electrical tape and string on the dashboard for repairing nets. The defroster doesn't work, so he has me wipe the inside of the windshield with a rag as he drives. He explains happily that he can't afford a new van because he has too many hobbies—fishing, mushrooming, hunting, and jūdō—and this car is nostalgic because he's driven it up into the mountains so many times.

In the party room at Bantei, Kawamoto tries to seat me at a table with a few of the senior hunters. They grumble that there is room for only one, so Kawamoto gives me his spot and leaves me to fend for myself. Yūji Higashi, a seventy-year-old hunter, gruffly welcomes me with a flurry of inappropriate jokes and assumptions, delivered with eyes slightly averted. He reminds me of an uncomfortable middle school boy—obnoxious, but not threatening. Seated across from Higashi, mild-mannered Norio Yamashita (who will catch the second-largest number of ducks this year) rescues me with polite small talk.

Higashi brought homemade tsukemono (fermented pickles) and oshinko (lightly salt-pickled vegetables). There's daikon pickled in rice bran and saké kasu so it's golden and tart; Nara-zuke daikon, cured in saké kasu and sugar until chocolate brown and meaty; and cabbage and carrots wilted in salt overnight to bring out a hint of funky acidity. I love anything pickled, and these are some of the best pickles I have ever had! I take seconds and thirds. My enthusiasm softens Higashi.

I learn that he harvests wakame and uni (it is my dream to eat an urchin straight from the sea, my feet still in the water as I crack it open and slurp the sweet flesh), and that he has several vintages of umeboshi at any given time, made with ume fruit from his garden. Some feminists will think me a traitor, but there's a certain amount of sexism I'm willing to tolerate for a good pickle. I'm determined to befriend Higashi and get him to teach me how to make tsukemono like this.

We're served sashimi of sweet prawns and silvery aji on lavishly colorful kutaniyaki dishes, skewers of duck (hunted by gun, not net) with sections of fat green onion, oily slices of charred duck breast served with crisp butter lettuce, and sticky-sweet bones with the tiniest bit of meat from one small saka-ami-gamo caught today. Glasses accumulate on the table, filling endlessly with saké, wine, and beer. The chef joins us, ladling out bowls of kani nabe (snow crab hot pot) and talking warmly with the hunters who will bring him their precious saka-ami ducks.

I'm at the edge of drunkenness by the time we leave (most of them are far past that point). Kawamoto delivers me home by daiko (a taxi service that also drives your car home for you). Boldly, I ask if I can come back to watch them hunt again. He says yes.

A FEW DAYS LATER, Kawamoto picks me up a little after 4:00 P.M. He drives as only a born-and-raised local can, taking scenic back roads to avoid traffic lights and turning down terrifyingly narrow side streets without hesitation. Our route loosely follows the Daishōji River, which originates in the mountains above Yamanaka, toward its outlet into the Sea of Japan. The duck pond is tucked into the hills that divide farmland from Katano Beach.

On the way, Kawamoto tells me he's been doing saka-ami hunting for thirty years and that it takes one or two decades to get good
at it.

Some of the men I trail to the saka-ba today look like war vet-
erans, with flower-shaped hunting badges pinned to their hats like
medals. Many of them have on workwear in muted shades of sea
foam and aqua. Some dress in camouflage, and a few wear hunting
vests with an inexplicable number of pockets. (In my mind, the
fashion award goes to the cool grandpa in a heavily pinned burgundy hunting cap, with a salt-and-pepper lampshade mustache,
angular wire-rimmed glasses, teal work pants, and rain boots with
leopard-print lining.)

One man, rushing from his job at a travel agency, pulls on rain
gear over a shirt and tie. Most of them are carpenters, fabricators,
builders, and artisans, so they can arrange their schedules to accommodate early evening hunting. Two of the hunters cook at
restaurants specializing in duck. Saka-ami-gamo is said to be most
delicious because the fowl don't bleed or release stress hormones
when they die.

In the heyday of saka-ami hunting there were 670 saka-ba. Military lords and high-ranking samurai each had their own. Today,
fewer than thirty members of the saka-ami club maintain nearly a
hundred kamae-ba (platforms) clustered at eleven shared saka-ba
around the pond. At the beginning of each season they choose
spots by drawing and rotate depending on the day. But there's always some milling around and polite negotiation before the men
settle in with their nets. The experienced hunters know the best
position for the day's conditions and will wait to see who doesn't

show up so they can take their kamae-ba if it's a better one—deferring, of course, to rank.

There is one new guy this year, a forty-something cook-turned-electrician named Hatada who drives an hour from Kanazawa every evening. He wears a pair of split-toed tabi shoes—very stylish, but not particularly warm. For three years he will be a "baby" only allowed to hunt at the baby spots, or help the other hunters.

Hatada and I watch from the back of the clearing as nets begin raining down. There's the sound of beating wings and ducks whistling to one another, then *swoosh, thud, clatter*—again and again. Hatada runs to each net that lands with a thud, pulling the string tight around the duck's neck.

They catch thirteen today, a massacre. It will turn out to be a season record.

THE SAKA-AMI CLUB is a low building at the edge of the pond, with a large tombstone beside it to honor the souls of dead ducks. Every autumn, a Buddhist monk officiates a prayer service there. Inside, each hunter has a cubby for his nets, boots, and rain gear. There's an avocado-colored refrigerator, a scale for weighing ducks, and a bulletin board where the kamae-ba assignments are posted.

It's a month into the season now. While the younger guys prepare their gear, the senior hunters gather in the tatami room to watch sumo wrestling. Takeo Yamamoto, eighty-two, presides over the kettle. He'll pour you tea if you've earned his respect (he usually ignores me and the young guys).

Yamamoto is old enough to remember the Allied occupation,

but sunspots and snow-white hair notwithstanding he looks barely seventy and spry as any of the young hunters. Today, he's passing out roasted sweet potatoes, kept warm on the kerosene heater. The sweet potato flesh is golden, the color of kabocha squash, *like the old days*, they say. Kawamoto gives me his. *Ah, nostalgic!* says Yamamoto as he eats one.

Kawamoto introduces me to Toyotaka Ikeda, a seventy-six-year-old hunter with an encyclopedic knowledge of saka-ami lore who speaks in Kaga dialect peppered with antiquated vocabulary. *Is she single?* he asks.

When Ikeda was young, families living near Katano Kamoike supplemented their income from rice by hunting ducks and selling them to fish shops and restaurants. But Ikeda's family made their living growing peaches and pears and kept most of the ducks they caught to eat themselves. Boys used to go along to keep the ducks from escaping the nets while their fathers continued to hunt. Ikeda caught his first duck when he was eleven.

Maybe I can be like those kids, helping out the hunters so I can learn the sport.

Higashi, the pickle guy, has not acknowledged me since the party, but on the way to the saka-ba I tell him how much I liked his pickles. After an uneventful hunt, he gives me three persimmons.

THE FIRST SNOW DAY comes at the end of December. Contrary to what I expected, the weather brings out more hunters. The forest is quiet, but the pond is lively. December ducks are said to be most delicious, still well fed from autumn with a thick layer of fat to protect them from the winter chill. But today they elude capture.

IT'S THE NEW YEAR, and the days are getting longer. It's been a week since anyone killed a duck.

Today's sky is periwinkle with tufts of rose. I count thirty-six swans gliding on the pond outside the clubhouse window. It's still bright at five, when we hop back in Kawamoto's car to go to Ōsuna, Big Sand, instead of walking to the nearby saka-ba favored by the older hunters.

We turn off almost immediately onto a muddy road—more of a path really—snaking up the mountain without ever straightening until we reach a pullout next to a boar trap. One more hunter pulls in, Kimihiro Nishino. At forty-four, he's one of the youngest, unpolished and sincere in his manner, with a cigarette usually dangling from the side of his mouth. He looks tough, but the other guys call him Nishi-chan, a term of endearment for somebody cute.

The three of us walk a sandy pine-needle-strewn trail through chartreuse moss and dry brown nara leaves. Spindly windswept trees signal proximity to the ocean. The path pitches steeply, so I'm breathless when we reach the summit with a clear view of Mount Haku, spectacular in its snowcapped volcanic glory, extending seamlessly into a crystalline range that reaches north as far as I can see. The mountains fade into the sky as darkness falls.

Kawamoto wants me to know what it feels like to be a hunter. Crouching in anticipation, you feel your pulse quicken *doki-doki!* he says, miming a beating heart. The net starts to feel heavy. You hear ducks flapping. Kawamoto names them, *magamo* (mallards), before they come into sight. Suddenly you have a split second to decide if one is in your range. In two swift motions, you lift your net like a flag, then thrust it into the air. Thud! Kawamoto caught one. He runs to finish it with a quick tug of the string around its neck.

I see the first star come out. Kawamoto catches another. Two more stars. And then it's quiet. As he untangles the netted ducks from the low pine trees, total darkness envelops us.

We hike down with headlamps. I can see Orion's belt from the road back to the clubhouse. Most of the other hunters have already gone, but a few are there to admire Kawamoto's catch—the only two today—breaking the dry spell. There's some jocular teasing about me being a good luck charm or a muse or some nonsense. This talk embarrasses me, but maybe they won't mind my coming back if they think I bring luck.

It's not until we're in the car that Kawamoto shows his excitement and pride. *I caught the first duck of the year!* he says, beaming. He delivers the two mallards to Bantei, entering through the back door to the kitchen and telling the tale of battling wind atop Ōsuna. *One out of three ducks served at Bantei is mine*, Kawamoto tells me. He keeps few for himself: there's more glory in being of service. He'll be out tomorrow to try again.

I desperately want to try cooking one of these ducks, but I'm already imposing, so it would be totally inappropriate to ask for one. I'm only a guest and—I suspect—to the old men, an unwelcome one.

A WEEK INTO January it's raining, and the forecast predicts wind. *There probably won't be more than one chance today*, Kawamoto says.

His route (which varies) gives us a chance to observe movement across the rice fields, in the treetops, and on the surface of the Daishōji River.

Puffy gray clouds hang low in the sky, breaking beyond the pond to let through a crack of pale orange light. The wind picks up, bowing young bamboo behind the clearing and tugging at the hunters' nets. A camellia has passed full bloom, dropping its deep pink flowers.

A plane coming in low looks like a fireball floating out of the sunset. Its engine is the only sound as hunters settle into their spots. The waterfowl—out of sight on the lake below—squawk and splash as they organize their departure.

Feeling the wind shift, Kawamoto changes his net. The ducks that pass over are too high, or too far to the left or right. Darkness falls swiftly because of the low cloud cover, and the hunt is over in fifteen minutes, with no catch.

The hunters discuss the plane: like the ducks it took an unusual route because of the wind direction. I ask Kawamoto if ducks always fly high when it's windy. He explains that it depends where in the sky the wind is; they will fly under or over it, always taking the easiest route. *Ducks are natural experts in wind.* To catch them, saka-ami hunters must be too.

WE DRIVE PAST the clubhouse to the top of the hill. Kawamoto stands in the field gauging the wind, rotating his body to face directly into it. I'm not sure if he was joking, but I've heard him say his bald head is good for detecting changes in the breeze. It's a beautiful mid-January day—almost warm. Everyone will come today.

Higashi spots me in the parking lot. *She's a strange foreigner*, he says to his friends as he hands me a package of his homemade pickles: umeboshi and Nara-zuke, neatly sliced and topped with an ornamental leaf.

This breaks the ice. Some of the old men talk to me for the first time. They're surprised I like tsukemono, and they want to know what other Japanese food I eat and how many times I've come to Japan.

The wind is low, and the excitement is palpable. Conversation turns to the crescent moon, and the clouds darken to charcoal gray. Two or three nets fly up, but land empty. Expectations soared high, but the ducks flew higher.

Kazu Yamagishi, the youngest hunter at thirty-nine, who ventured out to a more secluded spot, caught the only duck today. Most of the hunters leave deflated, but a few stay to make repairs on the trail.

In the Edo heyday of saka-ami hunting, lords and high-ranking samurai dispatched warriors to maintain their saka-ba and steward the habitat that kept the migratory ducks coming from as far as Siberia. The domain lowered the tax on rice farmers around the pond, who flooded their fields, attracting waterfowl to eat the soft grains left in the water after harvest.

After the official end of feudalism in 1871, saka-ami opened to ordinary citizens, and within a few years a newly formed saka-ami hunting association took over care of the pond. They persuaded the government to halt military drills and cannon tests at Katano Beach and ban not only gun hunting but anything that might frighten the waterfowl. According to a history published by the city of Kaga, one man was even charged for brandishing a basket (you read that correctly) near the pond.

The association planted trees on the west end of the preserve, to prevent sand blown in by ocean winds from filling the pond. They trimmed weeds and removed saplings from the water's edge. Succession, the gradual transformation of wetland to forest, is a natural process. But as more and more wild land was developed, the hunters' gentle interventions at Kamoike preserved one of the few habitats in Japan where migratory waterbirds can winter.

Tonight, three hunters are hammering stakes into the ground and leveling them to build steps in the steep trail. The high beams of a Jimny illuminate their work. Kawamoto explains they do maintenance at night so they don't disturb the birds.

You have to think like a duck, he says.

AFTER TWO MONTHS of watching Kawamoto hunt, I'm starting to check the wind instinctively. It's perfectly still when he picks me up.

The sky streaks orange as we cross the river, minutes from the pond. Kawamoto pulls over beside the fallow rice fields so we can watch Mount Haku shade salmon behind us. *In just a moment it will become more red*, he says, standing behind the van snapping pictures with his phone.

I brought homemade kimchi for Higashi, the pickle guy, and it gets him to crack a smile, however briefly. He leads me inside the clubhouse to a pile of enormous snow-white daikon from his garden and picks out a good one, handing it to me unceremoniously.

He's nice to the ladies, I hear someone say as Higashi heads out with his nets.

Kawamoto takes me to a spot called Takauchi, a short drive up the road and a quick steep hike to a hilltop on the eastern side of the lake. Young Kazu is up there already, his nets assembled. He has the good looks and slightly sullen, standoffish demeanor of a rebellious teen heartthrob (though, in fact, he's a proud father and dedicated chef).

Takauchi is quiet—the soft pines not even fluttering—with a broad view of the surrounding hills. The lake is hidden by thick trees, but I can locate it by the calls of waterfowl. A few white cranes glide across the darkening aster sky. Kawamoto says it's okay for me to sit on a kamae-ba; I climb a chest-high ladder to the one next to him.

Looking out from a hunter's perspective, I feel my pulse quicken and senses sharpen. We listen for whistling and flapping in the dusk. Kazu catches one. Kawamoto catches one. Two times a duck flies directly over my head, the missed opportunity taunting (Kawamoto will tease me about it in perpetuity).

Kawamoto lays out their two male mallards for comparison: the belly of his has brownish feathers, like the icing on a Mont Blanc chestnut cake; Kazu's is pure cream. Kawamoto hands me the brown-belly mallard to carry down the hill. I hold it by the neck the way he did, its head a knob above my fist. Through my thin gloves, I feel the warmth of its body—so recently alive—and the delicate bones in its neck. *Thank you, thank you, thank you*, I repeat in my head, feeling sadness but not guilt. I wonder if the bird in my hand has a mate who will miss him.

Back at the lodge, tough-guy Nishino comes in with a yoshi-gamo, a falcated teal. Green-black feathers crest its head, a ring of white encircles its neck, delicate gray and black stripes lace its body, and ornate curls of white and gray drape from the tips of its wings. It's extraordinary to see up close—from the smooth black webs of its little feet to the glisten of its black agate eye. Its crest, which shimmers green and copper in sunlight, is lifeless black under the fluorescent lights of the clubhouse. Its death breaks my heart, but then, these waterbirds might not even be here were it not for the dedication of saka-ami hunters.

After World War II, an American general and his companions, unconcerned with local law, began hunting at Kamoike using guns. In the years that followed, as the Americans continued to shoot waterfowl, fewer ducks gathered at the pond. The Allied forces disregarded letters from saka-ami hunters pleading with them not to use firearms at Kamoike.

Finally, the saka-ami association's leader, Yasutarō Murata, made the daylong journey to general headquarters in Tōkyō, where he found a sympathetic ear in Dr. Oliver L. Austin, an American ornithologist stationed with the natural resources department. Dr. Austin convinced the U.S. Army that the long history of saka-ami had been critical to the preservation of habitat for wild birds and that it must be protected. (Austin would later write *Birds of the World*, *The Birds of Japan*, and *The Birds of Korea*, and from Japanese hunters he adapted a method of using nets for catching birds to tag and release, which is still in use today.)

With the protected status of Kamoike restored, the fowl re-turned. Mallards (like raccoons and sparrows) have adapted to suburbs and cities all over the world, but birds of a more delicate disposition require a pristine ecosystem to thrive. Tomoe-gamo (Baikal teals), an ostentatious cousin of the yoshi-gamo worthy of a portrait by Hiroshige, travel in large flocks from Siberia each winter to feed on wild rice at Kamoike. Elsewhere they're vulnerable to pesticide-poisoned grain and overhunting, but here they need only worry about natural predators, like the ojiro-washi (white-tailed sea eagles) that follow a similar migration.

Ojiro-washi, rarely seen in Japan south of Hokkaidō, have been persecuted since the advent of agriculture for competing with humans—stealing fish from boats and sometimes picking off livestock as big as lambs. In the U.K., they were hunted to extinction. But these raptors find peace at Kamoike, where they can spread their two-meter wingspan, soaring between the coast and their lookouts above the pond.

In 1993, Kamoike was designated a Wetland of International Importance by the Ramsar Convention, a treaty protecting wetlands all over the world for "wise use." The ten-hectare (twenty-five-acre) protected area of marshland could fit inside Central Park thirty-three times. But the small preserve hosts as many as ten thousand birds annually, of more than two thousand species.

Wise use means stewarding the land, not leaving it untouched. Rangers, rice farmers, and saka-ami hunters share responsibility for managing Kamoike. You could argue that killing ducks is an odd way to protect them, but these twenty-six hunters with their quiet nets are less of a threat to wildlife than the urban, industrialized, and materialistic way that most of the first world lives. This swath of habitat has been preserved through centuries of political and social change.

WE LEAVE YAMANAKA in hail and lightning. *This is terrible!* exclaims Kawamoto cheerfully. The tunnel under the mountains takes us west into milder weather. Low clouds cast everything gray and melancholy.

Only seven men hunt today. The ducks are leaving the pond early, circling and assessing the air currents, but the hunters wait for dusk. Up on the hilltop the wind blows so loud it's hard to hear anything else, but it settles after sunset. Kawamoto gets one chance—almost. It's the only net he throws today. The ducks fly unattainably high. Soon I hear nets folding, the poles clacking together—another, and another. Kawamoto is the last to quit. The seven fanatics leave empty-handed.

I'LL DEFINITELY CATCH *a duck today if I eat these!*

Then I want to eat a whole pile of them!

Gathered around the sumo match on TV, the hunters are eating doughnuts I brought, still warm from frying. It's hard for me to express myself with any nuance in Japanese; the doughnuts are meant to convey my gratitude that they've tolerated my presence. I knew almost everyone would come today, because the conditions are perfect, and there's less than a month left to hunt.

The pond is still as glass. Wisps of clouds look like sea foam collecting on a beach. It's nearly warm as spring. Through the picture window, I watch an egret move in slow motion.

Yamamoto (tea boss, I've privately nicknamed him) pours me a cup. *I don't know her name*, he demands, reaching for a doughnut, suddenly curious.

The hunters chat in relaxed, gentle tones as they take their positions. Golden light frames the mauve hills to the west that divide the pond from the ocean. A waxing moon hangs in the eastern sky, two days from full. The dimming light softens their voices as it does the fading colors in the landscape. From his platform, Kawamoto narrates the hunt like a sportscaster.

There are some close calls, but—in spite of my doughnuts—they catch only one duck.

AT THE SAKA-BA, heart-shaped camellia petals are scattered in the mud like confetti. Carrying a large boxy red flashlight that makes me think of my grandfather, Higashi (pickle guy) climbs an aluminum ladder lashed by rope to a high-stilted kamae-ba. The platform is constructed of shipping pallets and plywood, with saplings for rails, faded by the elements to look like driftwood. Kawamoto ascends the one next to it, and I occupy the one to his right to watch. The men are so used to me now that I'm not bound to the usual rules for guests.

Kawamoto's net trembles as he considers for a split second whether a duck is in range. Higashi's net sails through the air, cutting off the flight of a mallard. For an instant, the duck's velocity stretches the net forward—like a soccer ball soaring into a goal—before gravity pulls it to the ground.

Back at the clubhouse, Kawamoto records five ducks on the daily register. Yamashita (the number two hunter who I sat beside at the opening-day party) returns the empty paper doughnut box to me, neatly folded, so I can use it again. *That means we want more,* teases a man named Inui, who is outlandishly, unrelentingly flirtatious. *It's Hannah's birthday tomorrow*, Kawamoto tells them. *Catch me a duck, please*, I ask, thinly veiling the request as a joke.

On the drive home, an impossibly big moon, the color of a ripe persimmon, hangs on the horizon. Kawamoto asks if I want to practice cooking duck. *I do want to.* We fall back into comfortable silence.

He asks me to wait while he makes a quick detour to his house. He comes back with a frozen duck, plucked clean except for its head, so I can tell it's a mallard. *Really?* I ask several times, accepting the gift. *It's from last year*, he tells me, *so it might not be good, but please try*.

Your hands must be cold from holding it, he says. *I'm happy*, I reply, smiling from ear to ear.

HIGASHI (THE PICKLE GUY) asks if New York is like Tōkyō. *It is*, I say. I've lived there about ten years, I tell him, but I grew up in the country. When I was a child, I played in the woods every day. *Me too*, he says, eyes sparkling with good memories.

The weather has been miserable all day, so there aren't many hunters. But the rain stops before sunset, and specks of peach punch through the dense clouds at the crest of the blackening horizon. Big flocks circle and circle.

Several nets fly up as the first group of ducks swoops over: only Kawamoto's makes contact. He runs to it, untangles a small duck, tucks it in his pocket, and returns to his kamae-ba. It's not long before nets start folding, but Kawamoto stays poised, gazing into the distance. He's the last to give up.

Kawamoto takes the duck out of his pocket. By the light of a headlamp, he quickly ties a band around the bird's neck, pulling one end with his teeth and the other with his free hand. *Let's go,* he says, and with few words we walk back to the clubhouse.

In the bright light, I see that it's a little kogamo, a green-winged teal—the only catch today. Most of the men left early.

He gives me the duck. *Really? Really?* I keep asking. He seems pleased to make me so happy—the only one who could do it today. He tells the guys he gave me a frozen duck yesterday too. Generosity is status.

I'm almost as excited as if I were holding a live wild animal. On the way home, I cradle the kogamo in my lap, unable to resist stroking its silky feathers (even though it seems absurd to pet a dead thing). *Poor thing, isn't it,* says Kawamoto. He tells me he's always sorry when he pulls the string around its neck, that he apologizes to the duck. *Please cook it well*, he instructs me. I tell him I will take it seriously.

He cautions me not to put it in the refrigerator or it will be hard to pluck. *Keep it for a few days in a cool place—the flavor will improve*. The hunters often keep ducks in their cars for a week at a time. *Bring it back if you want me to show you how to clean it*, he says.

I'VE SPENT A full week gazing fondly at my duck, admiring its speckled breast, iridescent green wings, and smooth black bill, and thinking about the best way to cook it. It smells only like clean cold feathers. Today, Kawamoto will teach me to pluck and butcher it.

The sun is still high when he picks me up a little after 4:30. *They'll be watching TV for another hour*, he says. It's too bright to start hunting. Not one cloud interferes with a spectacular view of

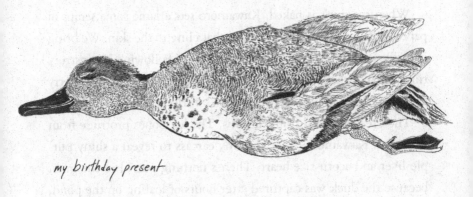

my birthday present

Mount Haku, its petal-pink snowy peaks chiseled by lavender-gray shadows. He drives past the club, not to check the wind, but to watch the sunset from Katano Beach, a few minutes up the road. The vermilion orb of the sun shoots coral beams across icy waves, gliding across golden puddles that ebb back into the sea. A surfer paddles out toward an orchid horizon. When the sun sinks, we clap with a family playing on the beach, then head to the duck pond.

Yamamoto (the tea boss) walks up to me with a smile and gives me two chocolate candies. He says he has a cat at his vegetable plot named Hana (my name in Japanese). Everyone expects to catch a duck today. No one does. Tough-guy Nishino says it's too bad, he still wants to give me a birthday present.

Hatada, the new guy, lingers to watch us defeather my kogamo. In the driveway, we work under a motion-sensor light that keeps flicking on and off. Kawamoto shows me how to pluck the big feathers one or two at a time with a swift tug (like tweezing eyebrow hairs) and rub away the down with my thumb, careful not to tear the delicate skin. It's satisfying. What would take Kawamoto twenty minutes takes me nearly an hour.

When the duck is naked, Kawamoto sets aflame some scraps of paper and singes away flecks of fuzz that cling to the skin. We bring it inside and lay it on sheets of paper towel. Following his instruction, I make shallow incisions along the breastbone with a petty knife, gradually slicing deeper into the soft flesh. It smells like meat.

The breasts unfold from the ribs. The leg bones protrude from the meat. Kawamoto opens the tiny carcass to reveal a shiny purple liver and acorn-size heart. There's nothing putrid in the guts, because the duck was captured after hours of loafing on the pond, before flying off to eat fallen grains of rice in fallow fields. There's maybe a teaspoon or two of innards to discard.

My ducky-chan—as I'd taken to calling it, as if it were a stuffed toy—is gone. In its place I have a zip-top bag of meat, bones, and organs.

The two times I've eaten saka-ami duck before, there was too much merriment for the meat itself to make a lasting impression. But tonight, it's just me and my duck.

There's no oven in a Japanese kitchen, just two burners and a fish broiler. I char the bones under the flame and make them into broth. I sprinkle salt and sugar on the bony bits of leg and wing and broil those to gnaw on—they taste like pork cracklings and sweet shrimp shells. I soak hoshi-gaki, dried persimmons, in red wine (and pour myself some in a crystal juice glass).

The breasts wait on my cutting board, salt-and-peppered, small as matchboxes, and the color of Bing cherries, with a thin layer of fat beneath the skin. I sear one (the other is for Kawamoto, and I'll bring him a take-out box next time we go hunting), rendering the skin crisp, and then rest it on a saucer. In the grease left behind, I soften minced onions and deglaze the pan with wine. I simmer the persimmons in that with spoonfuls of the broth, until it reduces to a sauce.

A lock of hair that falls in my face smells like duck fat.

Reverently, I sit down to eat. A shallow pool of wine sauce collects around the duck breast and stewed persimmon. The meat has cooked blue gray on the edges, but sliced, the center bleeds deep burgundy. It smells almost like prosciutto and tastes like dry-aged steak, with the firm but yielding texture of a juicy roast chicken. Maybe it's my imagination, but it evokes marsh grass and oak leaves and the sweetness of gleaned grain.

I don't know if it tastes different from wild duck shot by a gun. I feel differently about it. With wordless gratitude to the duck, and to Kawamoto, I sop up the juices with buttery white milk bread.

WHILE SNOW FALLS OUTSIDE, I eat liver and heart on toast, with lots of butter and caramelized onions. I am determined to use everything from this duck and to like it.

I dream of saka-ami hunting nearly every night now. I don't wonder anymore why the men go out there; I wonder when I can go with them next.

GEESE ALWAYS LEAVE the pond first, passing overhead while we walk to the saka-ba. There's patchy snow on the ground, melted by the afternoon sun. A few soft flakes fall intermittently, looking exactly like the duck down that still clings to my raincoat.

Waiting for dusk, the old guys talk to me about local foods I should try—in fast dialect that's hard to follow. I refilled the doughnut box today, and they seem pleased. Before we leave tonight, Ikeda will give me chunks of daikon and herring pickled with kōji rice. Higashi, after insulting the kimchi I gave him (he's working on a batch to show me how it's done) and remarking that the doughnuts are very sweet, brings me a soft drink from his car and offers me another daikon.

Daylight stretches later and later; the end of the season is closing in.

The moment the hunters take their positions, a thick flock of kogamo swoops over—so many that the beating of their wings sounds like freeway traffic. But they are out of reach.

THE HUNTING GETS harder as the ducks begin to migrate north.

Atop Ōsuna, we're exposed to the strong western wind. Mount Haku is invisible behind a blanket of gray clouds, but at least the rain has stopped.

Kawamoto gets one chance, and he catches one duck—a huge mallard with a glittering green head. There are no twinkling stars to light our descent, only our headlamps cutting through the nara branches on the narrow muddy path.

Kawamoto's duck is one of only four caught in the past week. It will be a gift to two of his friends in other prefectures: nabe (hot pot) sets prepared by Bantei's chef and delivered by mail. In the old days, Kaga's lords would send five saka-ami ducks to the Tokugawa shogunate each year. Until recently, a couple of mallards was a standard gift to newlyweds.

THERE ARE ONLY ten days left in the season. Kawamoto wants at least two more ducks.

Yamamoto (tea boss) greets me with a pat on the back and something along the lines of *You're becoming a hunter, aren't you!* Three years of training doesn't sound so long on a beautiful day like today. Yamamoto says he'll retire in a few years. He has about seventy-five nets at home that he's inherited from other hunters over the years. Like a samurai who always leaves his home as if he may never come back to it, he's repaired all seventy-five nets so another hunter can use them when he dies.

Kawamoto climbs a stilted platform in a row of five, divided by pine trees; I watch from the back of the clearing. The men remind me of birds, perched on their kamae-ba, calling to one another across a cantaloupe sunset.

The first flight of nets clatter to the ground empty. But then I watch Kawamoto's soar up to intercept a mallard; it nearly falls on my head. I check that the bird can't get loose. More ducks are coming in fast and high, and I look up in time to see Kawamoto capture another that sails down to my feet. My heart is in my throat, like watching a tense game: neither team has a clear advantage, and the outcome is uncertain. He throws his net, and up, up, up it goes—YESSSS! A third mallard falls, and I run to it.

None of the three are dead. I want to kill them quickly the way Kawamoto does, but I don't know how. Hesitantly, I tuck the female's wings together, as I've seen the hunters do, so she can't flap, but I feel sorry for her as she regains consciousness. I'm glad when Kawamoto comes to finish them.

Thank you, he says. *One is for Hannah-san.*

Carry them, please, he directs me. I follow him back to the club-house, grinning in the dark.

He tells the others he was relieved that I was there, and so he's rewarding me with a duck. He was happy he could keep hunting while I watched the ducks in his nets (it's a story he will continue to tell anytime someone worries saka-ami hunting might be too upsetting for a girl to watch).

TEN DAYS LEFT. Papaya-pink clouds and blue sky reflect on the rice paddies we drive past.

Only Yamashita and Nishino catch ducks today.

I ask Kawamoto how to tie the string around a duck's neck. Using Nishino's lifeless mallard, he shows me how to fold its neck backward and tie the string tightly so the duck dies quickly. If you don't do it right, he explained, it takes time. I'm not afraid to kill something, but I'm afraid to kill it badly.

INSTEAD OF HIS usual paint-splattered tracksuit and rubber boots, Kawamoto is dressed nicely today, in sage-green canvas pants and a green stadium jacket, with tan leather lace-up Vans; Sunday is date day with his wife, and this afternoon they went to a nearby town for sushi. At the clubhouse, he pulls on waders and a camou-flage raincoat.

Clouds hide the sunset, but break overhead. There's snow on the ground and a crescent moon. My fingers feel frozen. While we wait for the light to fade, Ikeda (the saka-ami history expert) and Higashi (the pickle guy) clip branches of sakaki (*Cleyera japonica*), a waxy-leafed sacred evergreen, to place on the altars in their homes.

Six ducks are captured between four men. I tease Inui (the flirt) about catching me a duck, and he seems genuinely disappointed that he couldn't yet. Only five days left.

It's a funny thing, but the duck in my entryway gets more dead as the days pass. I decide to dispatch with it myself. I've watched Bantei's chef do it (in less than fifteen minutes) and practiced once with Kawamoto. For reassurance, I search for videos online, but the way most American hunters clean and butcher a duck seems sloppy and wasteful compared with the precision and care I learned from my teachers here.

Alone, the work is intimate and intense. I worry I'll hurt the poor thing if I handle it wrong, even though it's been dead for a week. It takes me an hour to fill a cardboard box with down and feathers, leaving the duck bare except the tips of its wings and a hood of shiny green on its head. I singe the clean skin over the flame of my gas cooktop.

As I slice into the flesh, following the lines of bones and muscle groups, my curiosity is more powerful than any squeamishness. I manage to disassemble the bird with little waste: carcass and feet for soup, legs and wings for confit, organs to sear in butter and eat on toast, and breasts that I've decided to cure in salt and hang for another week. I even cleaned up the gizzard this time and cut out the tongue—I'll figure out how to cook them later.

I'm still ambivalent about killing and eating animals, but I want to be a saka-ami hunter.

WAY UP HERE who would know if Kawamoto gave me a net? We hiked up behind a small cemetery, to a ridge above the highway with a sweeping view of the mountains, back into the woods on a path lined with ferns and sasa, to a clearing where five precariously high kamae-ba look very Swiss Family Robinson. The saka-ba is called Sarukosue, Monkey's Playground. No one else is here. Light snowflakes fall, disappearing by the time they land.

What if I climbed the kamae-ba, with a view of the ocean to the west and the pond somewhere in between, and held a net? I would tremble with excitement, listening for beating wings, my arms growing tired from holding the long wooden pole, my whole body tuned to any movement in the darkening sky. I might even throw the net, recklessly, at a flock of kogamo.

Kawamoto nets two ducks, but they escape.

Afterward, as he's putting away the teacups, Yamamoto says (not directly to me, but so I can hear) that he will miss my face. Tomorrow is the last day.

SOON WE'LL BE saying goodbyes, but while everyone prepares their gear one last time, it feels like a party. Even the ducks gliding on the pond seem extra energetic. Kazu, the young chef, greets me in English: he's been holding out on me this whole time! We talk a little and I learn that he's a surfer and a DJ—I hope we'll still have a chance to become friends. Inui lays on the heavy-handed charm, as usual. Higashi gives me an envelope. Inside are two of his pickle recipes, handwritten on a sheet of printer paper: a treasure.

Kawamoto and I end where it all started (according to legend) with a samurai on his way home from fishing—on Ōsuna. A misty half-moon glows through a veil of pale gray clouds that drape to the midline of Mount Haku. The lights of modern life speckle the valley below, a world apart from this samurai sport. Kawamoto and I watch the sky in companionable quiet, but few ducks fly over. When it's time to give up, Kawamoto tosses his net into the air in salute to the end of the season, and I toss one up too.

For the darkest months of the year, when I usually feel melancholy and reluctant to go outside, I spent evenings watching the sunset at the edge of the duck pond and days in anticipation of what the next hunt would bring. I noticed the landscape change day to day as the camellias bloomed and dropped their flowers and the long sasa leaves dried to look like goose feathers scattered on the trail. I learned to track the direction and strength of the wind. As light faded from the sky, I meditated on the sound of beating wings.

I'm going to miss these guys. There's a party tomorrow for all the hunters, but after all I'm not one of them. We're pulling out of the parking lot when Yamamoto calls out to me and Kawamoto. He comes up to the car window and hands me the empty doughnut boxes—a request, and invitation. I know where to find them next November.

Duck and Scallion Skewers

TIME: *20 minutes*
Makes 12 skewers

K azu Yamagishi is a saka-ami hunter and adopted heir to Yamagishi, one of two restaurants to serve net-caught duck in Kaga. He showed me that you don't need fancy charcoal or complicated seasoning to make perfect skewers of duck and scallion, only a hot cast-iron pan and salt and pepper. We used wild duck, but the recipe works for farmed duck or even chicken (especially a flavorful heritage variety).

Kamo negi is a phrase implying a duck carrying green onion (negi) for you to cook it with. It means a stroke of luck, one good thing bringing another, or easy prey: kamo and negi are a sublime combination of flavors.

12 bamboo or wooden skewers (preferably 15 cm/6-inch teppō-gushi)

225 grams (8 ounces) duck breast, skin on and boned

225 grams (8 ounces) duck thigh, skin on and boned

4 negi, or 8 of the fattest scallions you can find

Fine sea salt and freshly ground pepper

1. While you prepare your ingredients, soak the skewers in water. Trim any cartilage or yucky-looking bits off the duck but leave the fat. Score the fatty side of the breast and thigh, making shallow diagonal cuts through the skin and fat (but not the meat) at 5 mm (¼-inch) intervals; this helps the fat melt and the skin crisp.
2. Cut the breast into 5 mm (¼-inch) slices. Cut the thigh into triangular or irregular 4 cm (1½-inch) pieces. Cut the white and pale

green part of the negi or scallions into 4 cm (1½-inch) lengths (save the dark green part for another use).

3. To make the skewers, thread a piece of scallion, thigh, scallion, and breast (in that order) on a skewer. For the breast, make two loose accordion folds and skewer the meat through the middle of the folds. Switch the order on the next skewer: scallion, breast, scallion, thigh. Continue until you've made 12 skewers. Sprinkle each skewer generously with salt and pepper on both sides.

4. Preheat a large cast-iron skillet over medium high; do not add any oil. When you can feel the heat rising from the skillet, place 4 skewers of meat and scallion in the pan. Use a large spatula to press them into the skillet. Shift the pressure so each part of the meat gets pressed into the pan, paying special attention to the fatty bits.

5. When the meat is kissed brown, about 1 minute, flip the skewers to the other side. Cook, pressing into the pan, until browned, about 1 minute. You want the pan hot enough so that the meat browns on the outside and is still a little pink on the inside, but not so hot that the pan is smoking.

6. Pour the fat out of the pan. Repeat steps 4 and 5 with the remaining skewers. Serve hot—with saké or something cold and fizzy to drink.

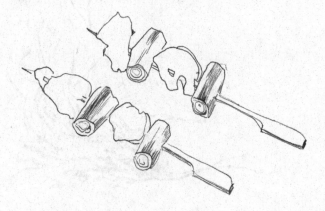

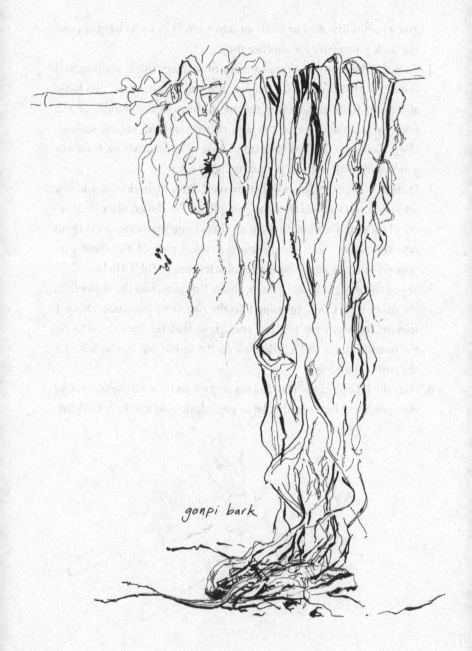

ganpi bark

Ten

On Paper

O n Mika Horie's handmade paper, landscapes exposed in gradients of cyan interplay with the textures of ganpi fibers. Yamanaka is not a papermaking town, and for Mika that was part of its draw; she can make her work without the pressure to join an artisans' association and conform to their standards. *I'm not a craftsman; I'm an artist*, says Mika. She earned her photography MA in London before returning to Japan to learn papermaking, then followed the opposite path of most young people who flee the countryside for better jobs and a more convenient life in the city. Mika moved from Kyōto to Yamanaka not long before her thirtieth birthday.

You would never know it from her polite response, but it irks Mika when people ask if her artwork is made with rice paper, as we call it in the West. There is no such thing as paper made of rice. Mika patiently explains that Japanese paper, washi, is made from the inner bark of kozo, mitsumata, or ganpi shrubs. There are contemporary Japanese papers made from hemp, bamboo, or cotton.

Rice straw is only rarely used as filler in cheap papers—never the main component.

Washi is often more translucent than industrial Western paper made of wood pulp, and it's more durable. Screens and doors that divide rooms; lanterns that illuminate homes and festivals; paddle fans for cooling off in the humid summer; folding fans to use as props in tea ceremony and folk dance; scrolls for calligraphy and painting; umbrellas to protect from rain and sun; gift wrapping; and origami—all these are made from washi.

Among the varieties of washi, ganpi is the most delicate in appearance. During the Heian period (794–1185), when Kyōto was the capital of Japan, ladies wrote poetry on tissue-thin sheets of ganpi paper. It's also strong. Mika tells me her paper could last a thousand years. The oldest printed text in the world is on washi, some of it ganpi: the Hyakumantō Darani, one million prayers encased in miniature wooden pagodas between 767 and 769 C.E. Not far from here, in Fukui prefecture, Japan's oldest existing paper money was printed on ganpi in 1661. Ganpi, which is naturally pest-resistant, was the paper of choice for government documents, textbooks, and stamps in the Edo period, until cheap industrial paper replaced it in the nineteenth century.

Unlike other washi materials—such as kozo and mitsumata—ganpi shrubs (*Wikstroemia sikokiana*) are difficult to cultivate. Boys in Yamanaka and neighboring Yamashiro used to collect ganpi in the mountains as an after-school job and sell the raw fibers to papermakers just south, in Fukui prefecture.

Fukui's Echizen villages have more than a millennium of washi-making history. According to the *Nihon Shoki*, an exhaustive chronicle of Japanese history and mythology compiled in 720 C.E., a

Korean monk brought Chinese papermaking technology to Japan in the seventh century. Echizen artisans claim papermaking started there as early as the fourth or fifth century, perhaps brought by explorers on boats carried by ocean currents from Korea to Fukui. Legend has it that a goddess came up the river to Echizen and—feeling sorry that they could not grow rice on their land—taught the villagers how to make paper using their abundant clean water (scholars speculate that she was actually a Chinese or Korean woman).

When Mika moved to Yamanaka, it had probably been fifty years since anyone had harvested ganpi. Her artwork has revived the harvest, if only on a minuscule scale.

I've known Mika since the first day I arrived in Yamanaka. She pulled up to Engawa bar in a drab green vintage Land Cruiser (she needs the big car, she explained, for going up into the mountains to collect materials) and stepped out wearing John Lennon sunglasses and drapey linen clothes, her wavy hair falling to her shoulders. Shimoki had arranged for her to be my Japanese teacher while I worked at his bar, and she introduced herself in careful English.

She taught me useful Japanese words and phrases, but more than that she helped decode the nuances of indirect communication. It took me a while to realize that in Japan when someone says *that might be difficult*, what they mean is *no*. Kyōto, Mika's hometown, is known for manners so subtle that even other Japanese people find Kyōto speech infuriatingly unclear. (For example, if someone offers you tea, it can mean you've overstayed your welcome.)

By local standards, Mika is almost as much of a foreigner as I am in Yamanaka. This community tends toward suspicion of outsiders, but she puts her elderly neighbors at ease by making daily small talk and joining neighborhood cleanup days and festivals for the local shrine. Her careful propriety obscures the fact that her life is unconventional: a single lady, living alone, pursuing an art career.

In the beginning, Mika would pick me up twice a week and drive me to her studio, an old farmhouse beside a brook. She'd turn up the kerosene heater and make coffee, dripping the water from a slender brown enameled kettle onto artisanal beans (from Kyōto, Amsterdam, San Francisco—wherever her most recent travels had taken her). While I waited for her to bring the coffee in matte gray ceramic cups, I gazed through a wall of sliding glass doors at rice fields across the street or looked at her latest work pinned to the wall: cyanotypes of the surrounding landscape, printed on washi made from shrubs that grow on the mountain behind her studio.

It's hard to imagine Mika doing anything sudden or impulsive. She drives the same cautious, deliberate way she speaks. She sets up her large-format 1970s Deardorff camera (which she saved for two years to buy) in the field to compose each shot. And she exposes the images onto her handmade paper in natural light, which can take up to two hours, depending on the weather and time of year.

But when a real estate agent showed her this house on the outskirts of Yamanaka, she knew instantly it was the one. It had been empty for more than twenty years, so neighbors were surprised to see two men in suits and a young woman going inside. An old man came over to see what was going on, and Mika introduced herself; she explained she was a photographer and paper artist. The man told her that when he was in grade school, he used to harvest ganpi shrubs and sell them for pocket money.

At the studio in Nara where Mika had learned papermaking,

she couldn't afford ganpi fibers. Four kilos cost ¥10,000 (that's nearly $100 for a few pounds). Listening to the old man, she realized that in Yamanaka she could harvest ganpi for free! She took note of the brook and the well. Making ganpi into paper requires nothing more than cold clean water—no binder or stabilizer.

There was no bus to this area, and it was too far to walk to town, she calculated, so she'd need a driver's license and a car if she lived there. The agent said another family was also interested in the house. Mika signed a rental contract that day. As soon as she got home to Kyōto, she went online to find the nearest driving school and started the next day.

Two and a half months later, in February, she drove to Yamanaka to move in. *It was my first time to see beautiful snowscapes*, she says. The house was full of musty furniture, ugly dishes, outdated appliances, and broken old tatami mats. She spent her first day cleaning and setting up camp in one room with the few things she'd brought with her: a sofa bed, a small desk, and a kerosene heater.

Three days later, Mika was dusting cobwebs when Nimaida, passing by on his way to Ōzuchi, walked right into her genkan and introduced himself. He told her about his village where he was making charcoal. He'd been curious about the car—with Kyōto plates and a new driver sticker—parked in front of a house that had been empty for decades. Nimaida told Mika he'd harvested ganpi as a kid—one year he earned enough money selling the fibers to buy a new bicycle. He promised to teach her to identify the shrubs when spring came.

With the help of a carpenter named Kuniharu Murai, whose father and grandfather specialized in temple and shrine carpentry, Mika renovated her downstairs into a studio and the upstairs into a bedroom. She had glass doors installed across the engawa (the porch running along the front of the house) to let in light, but kept the torn paper shoji in the entryway, beautiful in a way that can only be created by the passing of time—*wabi-sabi*, Mika explains.

She got rid of the tatami mats and put in a dark wooden floor that's easier to sweep. Cracks in the mud plaster walls still let drafts through, but the new toilet has a heated seat and bidet (she tells me it was the simplest she could buy). She didn't mind investing in the rental property, because she intended to stay a long time.

Mika lives among nests of shredded ganpi bark that hang from bamboo poles to dry—like art installations themselves. The ribbons of fiber drape from near the ceiling down to the floor, which is stained blue here and there with iron salts from her photographs. Minimal furnishings reflect her love of simple design and natural materials. Bottles of soy sauce and vinegar on the shelf between her studio and kitchen are wrapped in newspaper, so that their loud colorful typography won't disrupt the serene aesthetic. Even her clothes tend toward the same indigos, grays, and ivories of her artwork.

Over the years, our formal lessons shifted to an easygoing friendship. Sometimes, while we talked in her studio, I helped peel off and discard the brown outer layer of ganpi bark, piling up the pale velvety ribbons of inner bark for her to make paper from. It's tedious work and I never made much progress. She drops off bags of the bark to friends who help with this process for a small fee.

Mika invited me to make my own paper one overcast day. She'd already boiled the fuzzy ribbons of fiber in a cauldron of well water for four hours, drained the fiber in a large sieve, and placed the sieve in the brook overnight to remove impurities and acids so the paper would be of archival quality.

When I arrived, she pulled the sieve out of the brook; the fiber was the creamy flaxen color and soft matted texture of wet wool. A breeze rustled the persimmon trees.

She placed a handful of fibers on a large flattish rock half-buried beside the stream and showed me how to pound the fibers into pulp with a large wooden mallet. My arm tired quickly from swinging the mallet, and I realized how strong Mika must be, though she appears lithe.

It would be faster, of course, to process the pulp by machine, but she likes the variation that results from breaking it up by hand. The uneven pieces add character to her paper and create a mesh that doesn't rip easily. She tells me that after a storm the pulp picks up bits of plant matter and debris from the rock and they become part of her artwork.

Before Mika began making paper, she bought washi to print her photos on. She thought, *It's a shame that this paper is handmade but every sheet is the same.* Artisans strive for uniformity, but Mika wants to see individuality in each sheet.

I watched Mika fill a black tub with fresh water and mix in the cottony pulp. The slurry looked like an overcast night sky, with wispy clouds moving across the moon. She picked up a wooden frame with a screen stretched across it. Her face reflected on the water as she leaned down and slid the frame through the clouds of pulp. A thin deposit settled on the screen. She watched the water drain and then scooped two or three more times, until she was satisfied. She gave me a

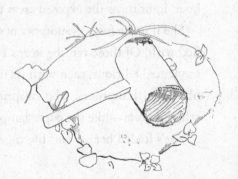

postcard-size screen to try, and I dipped it into the silky water and lifted it out, watching the pulp settle into an organic latticework.

Mika makes around ten sheets of paper in a session. After they've dried for an hour, she transfers them from the screens to a smooth board to finish drying. Professional artisans use a wide brush to smooth any wrinkles out of tissue-thin sheets of ganpi paper, but Mika flattens hers—made sturdier to support photographs—with a baker's rolling pin.

Her paper, she says, is thick. When it dries, it has no more heft than a sheet of printer paper. It looks matte gray white at first glance but has a subtle luster. *No other paper is as luminous as ganpi*, says Mika.

When there are clouds, Mika makes paper so that when the sky is clear she can print. Mika tells me she wishes for a partner and children, but the expectations most men have of their wives in Japan are incompatible with her artist's life. *I need freedom to travel and see new things*, she says. *I can't have dinner ready at a set time every day. If the weather is good, I need to print.*

On sunny days she brushes the paper with iron salts and exposes the images in the front yard. She places negatives on the treated paper, or arranges bits of plants, or makes polka dots from umeboshi, the salty-sour pickled ume fruit she loves. Over the course of half an hour, light turns the exposed areas the color of Japanese indigo dye.

She'll make forty cyanotypes of one image to get ten she's satisfied with. Of those ten she keeps two or three and sells the rest as numbered editions, each with its own unique interaction of ganpi fibers and blue tones. The misprints she saves to repurpose into other projects—like the paper lamp shade hanging in her entryway.

She's folded her art and life together so that the aesthetic experience is unfragmented, flowing from one activity to the next. Her art doesn't need to be conceptually complex to be compelling.

The processes of papermaking and cyanotype printing are simple enough that she can teach them to beginners in one-day workshops. Two high-end ryokan in the area send their guests to Mika's studio for these experiences. Kayōtei added her to their curated list of artisans soon after she moved to Yamanaka. Through them, gallerists, curators, and collectors from around the world find their way to Mika's studio and fall for everything about the place. They buy her artwork as mementos of their time with her—the straightforward beauty of the blue landscapes on ganpi paper signifying a dreamy Japanese country life.

Through these connections Mika has found gallery representation in Belgium and New York and traveled to art fairs in Amsterdam, Basel, and Arles to show her work and gather inspiration from other artists. Mika has what most artists only dream of: a big studio in the peaceful countryside, and at the same time the kind of creative community and audience for her work that usually requires living in a big city.

BESIDES MIKA, most of the people I spend time with in Yamanaka are men a decade or two older than me. It's mostly men—not women—who have time to make new friends. The women of Yamanaka run businesses, cook three meals a day for their families, and volunteer for community events. The few in their thirties, like Mika and I, are primarily at home raising children, while their husbands work long hours and fulfill their own set of social expectations: drinking with colleagues and former classmates.

Mika doesn't find my friendships with men odd. *It's natural for creative people like us to be friends with craftsmen and artisans*, she says. But she's learned to navigate the antiquated social norms and suspicions of small-town life. Talking about her romantic prospects, we count on one hand the single men within a decade of our age. To keep her distance from Yamanaka social politics, she looks for romance elsewhere—when she goes home to Kyōto or travels abroad.

I turn to Mika often for advice—like when Nakajima (my woodturner friend) texted to see if I'd like to go to a shakuhachi (Japanese bamboo flute) performance at Kayōtei. I was thrilled to be invited to this rare concert, but concerned that it might look as though we were on a date if Nakajima and I arrived together to a formal event.

Can I just say we don't want gossip, and ask if a friend can arrive with us? I asked Mika, knowing that Nakajima hates petty small-town gossip more than anyone. *Oh no*, she said, *that's too direct!*

Ask him if Kano-san is going too, she instructed. I worried that Nakajima might not get the point, but I followed her advice. Nakajima texted back: *I will pick Kano-san up at 6:45 and pick you up at 6:50.* Not only did he understand exactly what I was really asking, but he'd already thought of that concern and taken care of it. Mika expected it to go like that, but I was amazed by the invisible conversation that happened between what was actually said.

THE TIME TO harvest ganpi is after the last snow and before the shrubs leaf out. I went with Mika, Nimaida, and two other friends to gather ganpi on an April morning. The cherry trees bloomed in big puffs of pinkish white, echoed by fluffy clouds in the bright blue sky. Green was beginning to come back into the landscape along the river that we followed toward Kurakake Mountain.

Mika had dressed for the outing in tall birding boots, a safari hat, and her John Lennon sunglasses. Our guide was an old man named Yamashita who wore a Komatsu tractor hat and matching work jacket. We met him at an elementary school that had been turned into a community center. When there were still enough children in the area to fill this school, those kids might have collected ganpi, but now only Mika and one couple on the Komatsu side of the mountain use the ganpi here.

Yamashita drove us to the trailhead in his kei truck, with Mika, Nimaida, and two other friends riding under the green canvas canopy. I rode in the cab, listening to Yamashita enthusiastically list off American cities he knew of and tell stories about the woods, while we rattled along a gravel road, past egrets standing in rice paddies, and into the woods.

We parked at a dead end and hiked into the mountain carrying small handsaws. The ascent was steep, and I quickly got winded. Yamashita (who later told me he holds a sixth-degree black belt in jūdō) and Nimaida trotted up without hesitation. Most of the underbrush was still bare, but fiddlehead ferns were emerging and violets bloomed at our feet. The white flowers of wild magnolia dotted mountains in the distance.

Yamashita and Nimaida explained briefly how to identify ganpi among the other leafless shrubs by the sheen of its bronze bark. The biggest ones are fat as a silver dollar in diameter, while some are as thin as a finger, and none reach more than two meters high. Once you cut it, you see a ring of green between the bark and the woody white center. It has a vegetal fragrance, like a mix of adzuki

beans and cut grass. The wood looks fuzzy and pulpy; I can imagine how someone more than a millennium ago thought it might
be a useful fiber.

The older men went bushwhacking across the mountainside
while the rest of us stayed near the trail. We spent all morning
wandering up Kurakake Mountain, scanning the brush for the
telltale bronze sheen of ganpi. The search is fun, but Mika warned
us not to gather too much, because the real work was yet to come.

It seemed easy enough to find ganpi, and I was proud to collect
a few dozen branches. Nimaida and Yamashita emerged with big
bundles. They looked at mine and laughed: all but a few pieces
were the wrong kind of shrub. I hiked down with only a bouquet
of violets. Identifying bare ganpi isn't a skill that's easily learned
in a day. I realized how lucky Mika was to arrive in Yamanaka
while there were still people who could teach her.

With five years of practice, Mika had only a few misidentified
branches in her armful. Nimaida showed us how to wrap one of
the flexible twigs around a bundle of ganpi to tie it together.
When he was a kid, he would have stripped the bark in the mountain to lighten his load, but we hauled the whole branches down
to the truck. Mika, Nimaida, and the others rode on top of the pile
of brush, while I chatted with Yamashita up front.

We took a break for onigiri and vending machine drinks outside the community center. The air was chilly, but the sun was
warm. After lunch we began to strip the ganpi. Nimaida showed
me how to crack each branch to loosen the bark, then peel it in
wide strips. The bark comes off in ribbons, velvety linen white on
the inside, with a skin of avocado green between the white fiber

and the bronze outer bark. I worked gloveless so I could grip it more easily, and as the afternoon wore on, my hands became raw.

I understood viscerally why handcrafted ganpi paper isn't going to make a comeback for postage stamps or paperwork. But art making doesn't need to be practical or efficient. Mika's work creates a link to Yamanaka's past and makes relevant a skill that would otherwise have vanished from this area.

When we had finished peeling every branch, the stripped-bare wood looked like a pile of sun-bleached bones. We each kept a few sticks as souvenirs, and loaded the tangles of fibers into the back of Mika's car.

THE RIBBONS OF ganpi we harvested hang in Mika's studio window. Daylight filters between the strands onto the blue landscapes and abstractions pinned to the plaster wall. This house belongs to Mika now. She bought it after a few years of renting. She confides in me that it might intimidate some potential romantic partners— who feel the societal expectation that men should financially care for their families—that she owns property and makes a good living from her work. But she has created a beautiful life, with or without someone to share it with.

While she transforms the fiber into paper with the alchemy of water, ganpi is growing in the mountains for next year's harvest. Its silky oval leaves open in late spring, and in early summer its pale yellow flowers bloom; when autumn frost arrives, the leaves drop and the shrubs go dormant until spring. *I have everything I need*, Mika says, *to make my art: sunlight, water, and ganpi.*

Umeboshi

TIME: *4 hours (partly inactive), plus 4–6 weeks pickling and 1–2 days drying*
Makes about 4 liters (4 quarts)

Pink pickled ume fruit, *Prunus mume*, always make me think of Mika Horie, who loves to eat them and uses them as a motif in her art-work. The timing of making umeboshi is built around the seasons in Japan: when the ume trees fruit, when the red shiso grows lush and leafy, and when the rainy season ends and days become sunny. This recipe comes from Yūji Higashi, a duck hunter I call "the pickle guy." His umeboshi are wonderfully complex and subtle; my mouth waters just thinking of them.

The best ume for pickling are yellow green and not quite ripe (when they turn golden, they're ready for jam). I've made umeboshi with hard green ume (better for cordial), and sour American plums, but they weren't quite as good. Though usually translated as plum, ume is botanically close to apricot, and unripe apricots can be substituted. Look for ume in Japanese markets in the late spring, or check with local Japanese cultural societies or online pickling communities about where you can buy ume directly from a farm.

EQUIPMENT
Kitchen scale
Large enameled pot or food-safe bucket
Large fermenting crock or glass container (at least 6 liters/quarts)
Drop lid or plate to fit inside the crock/container
Pickling weights or large freezer bags filled with water

WEEK 1

3 kilograms (6½ pounds) ume (*Prunus mume*), ripened to
greenish yellow

Fine sea salt, for rinsing and cleaning

240–300 grams (8½–10½ ounces) sea salt (8–10 percent of the
ume's weight)

WEEK 2 OR 3

3 handfuls red shiso leaves (optional, for color)

Fine sea salt (if you are using the shiso)

> *Note:* If you use equipment not specifically designed for
> pickling and fermenting, make sure it is nonreactive and won't
> be corroded by acid or salt. Metal is out of the question unless
> coated in glass enamel. Be wary of glazed ceramics not ex-
> pressly for pickling. Glass is the safest. My personal preference
> is to limit use of plastics to processes that last a few weeks or
> less and not use plastic for long-term storage.

1. As soon as you get your ume, rinse them and place them in a large
   food-safe bucket or nonreactive pot. Add three handfuls of fine sea
   salt and enough water to just cover the plums. Mix gently, and leave
   the plums to soak for 2–4 hours. Meanwhile, wash any equipment
   that will touch the plums and rinse with very hot water. It's a good
   idea to sanitize it with a spray of high-proof alcohol, white vinegar,
   or boiling water, then air-dry.
2. Rub a few pinches of the measured salt around the inside of the
   fermenting crock to prevent mold. Remove the plums from the salt
   water one by one. Pick out the stem using the point of a wooden
   skewer (this is important to prevent mold), and place the plum in
   the fermenting crock. Once you've placed one-third of the plums

in the crock, sprinkle with one-third of the measured salt. Repeat until you've used all the plums and all the salt.

3. Place a drop lid (or plate) on top of the ume, then add weights on top of the drop lid equal to one and a half times the plums' weight (4.5 kilograms, or about 10 pounds). Alternatively, you can place one or two freezer bags full of water (1 liter/1 quart of water weighs 1 kilogram/2 pounds) on top of the drop lid or directly on the fruit so the bags conform to the shape of the crock. The important thing is to weight all the plums somewhat equally. Cover the crock with a lid, or if using a jar, wrap the whole thing with a clean garbage bag to keep out dust and daylight.

4. A WEEK OR TWO LATER, when the *umesu*, ume "vinegar" (technically not vinegar since it's citric, not acetic, acid), has covered all the ume, it's time to reduce the weight and add the shiso (if using). (Higashi describes the quantity of shiso as 3 large onigiri's worth.) Rinse and dry the shiso. Place a mesh strainer over a bowl, and put one handful of shiso in the strainer. Sprinkle generously with salt, and massage until the leaves wilt and release purple juice. Squeeze out and discard the juice, and set the wilted leaves aside. Repeat until you've used all the shiso.

5. Return all the shiso leaves to the strainer. Salt and massage the leaves again, but keep the juice this time. Put all the leaves in a small food-safe mesh bag, or tie them in cheesecloth or muslin. Uncover the crock, and remove the weights and drop lid. Tuck the shiso bundle in with the ume, so it's submerged in umesu. Add the reserved shiso juice. Replace the drop lid (if using) and reduce the weight on top to equal the starting weight of the ume, 3 kilograms; cover.

6. ABOUT 2 WEEKS LATER, when the forecast predicts 3 days of sun, it's time to dry the ume. In Japan, it's typical to spread them out on a big flat woven basket placed on a balcony or in a field. In New York, I hang them on my fire escape in a mesh box with a zipper (from a

Korean market, intended for drying fish) to keep out curious squir-rels. You could even put them on baking sheets lined with dish tow-els in a sunny window and aim a fan at them. The important thing is good airflow all around the ume and as much dappled or indirect sunlight as possible (to prevent mold). Make sure the ume are not touching one another, and rotate them once or twice as they dry. Reserve the salty-sour umesu.

7. If you used shiso leaves, spread them out to dry too. Later, store them with the umeboshi, or continue to dry until crisp, and grind into a powder to sprinkle on rice.

8. AFTER 2 OR 3 DAYS, when the ume have shriveled slightly and feel dry to the touch but still soft, gently return them to the crock or transfer to glass jars for storage. You can store them in umesu for soft umeboshi, or pack them dry (with the partly dried shiso leaves) if you like firmer umeboshi. They are ready to eat now, but will only improve in concentration and complexity of flavor (for up to about 5 years).

Eleven

Year of the Boars

It's hard to wash away the stink of wild boar. Even after I scrub, shower, and soak, it lingers in my hair for days. I've been tagging along with a hunter named Sakura Yoshida as she makes early morning rounds, checking boar traps placed off side roads at the edges of town, where the forest presses against small villages in varying states of abandonment. Japan has a murky relationship with meat, but a long history of game hunting.

Hunting was popular where I grew up, but I loved animals, and I had the impression that the hunters—with their rifles and four-wheelers—didn't. Sakura would show me otherwise. To be a good hunter, you need to understand the behavior of your prey, and getting to know an animal like that tends to make you respect it.

Sakura is friendly without being talkative, which put me at ease when we met through common friends while picking apricots. Her short haircut reveals cauliflower ears from her years on the national jūdō team, before middle age and motherhood softened her. Sturdy in both temperament and build, she identifies more with the boars she hunts than with the delicate flower she's named for. A faint gamy smell clings to her clothes—the way shepherds smell like lanolin, or cowboys smell like horse.

It's the year of the boar in the zodiac calendar, and people born under its sign are said to possess determination and courage. Shops offer adorable boar-shaped trinkets and sweets, and restaurants have illustrated boar-themed calendars on their walls. To the men and women who hunt inoshishi, the animal represents physical strength and cleverness. (Boars have been known to elude hunting dogs by running in a circle to leave their scent, then tiptoeing off in another direction, as the dog circles endlessly.) Sometimes the beasts are even credited with chivalrous bravery for defending their families. Boys are given names that contain the character for inoshishi: Inosuke, Isaburō, Isuke. But wherever there is agriculture, real-life boars have a reputation for being ill-tempered, destructive, and dangerous. They make news for charging at old ladies, breaking into schools, and doing millions of dollars in crop damage every year.

Unlike in parts of America and Europe where wild pigs are an invasive species, *Sus scrofa* Linnaeus is indigenous to Japan. They presumably have a useful role in the ecosystem, but no one around here can tell me what it is. Perhaps their rooting for nuts, roots, bugs, and worms turns over the soil so new vegetation can grow? Like us, once they get a taste for cultivated grains and sweet potatoes, they prefer the convenience and flavor.

In this part of Ishikawa, it was rare to see boars until about ten years ago. With their short legs, they can't survive the winter where thirty centimeters of accumulated snow lasts more than seventy days. But as the winters become milder, the boars expand their territory.

In populated areas, they adjust their schedule to work the night shift. Overnight, they can plow through a rice field, eating the grain and knocking over stone walls. Once they've feasted and frolicked, they wallow in the cool mud. By morning, it looks as though a drunk driver tore through on an out-of-control tractor. My friend Nimaida has lost his entire rice crop to boars at least three times. When they raid vegetable gardens, upturning crops in search of grubs and tubers, a season's labor can be undone while the farmer sleeps.

Fencing might seem like an obvious solution, but it's socially complicated. Vegetable plots and rice paddies are typically clustered together on open land. If you fence your own, you endanger your neighbor. You'd need to fence the whole area, or even the whole village, and it's hard to find the political will or the financing when the population is declining, or there are strict historic preservation guidelines that limit what's aesthetically acceptable.

There was a time in Japan when residents took turns guarding fields at night. They shared patrol duties with wolves, revered in folklore as gods of the mountain. Now emboldened boars often outnumber elderly residents, many of whom have given up in their battle against wild raiders. Their land is overtaken by weeds that provide cover for marauding animals. The risk of attack, once spread over many cultivated fields, is now focused on the few that remain—vulnerable targets bordering enemy territory.

In the battle to control unruly wildlife, even potential allies were exterminated. Japanese wolves were persecuted to extinction at the turn of the last century. Now humans are the boars' only predator.

Sakura had heard stories of devastated crops from her friends and neighbors, and she wanted to do something about it. Three years

ago, in her early forties, she got her hunting license. Most of the
men who hunt in Kaga are over seventy. She was the only woman.

At first, there was some grumbling about it being inappropriate for a man and a woman to go out into the woods alone (and
concern about how a lady could pee without a toilet). But she
found a seventy-year-old mentor, Hoshiba-san, who didn't care
about that nonsense and was happy to have a strong young helper.
Under his tutelage—and with her own fierce determination—she
became a skilled hunter.

She has arranged her whole life around hunting. She works
nights at a convenience store so she can patrol at dawn. It takes
about an hour to circle all the traps. If there's a boar to butcher,
that's easily another three hours in the field from slaughter to
cleanup. And that doesn't count processing the meat and cleaning
gear at home. Most hunters here spend more on licensing fees and
equipment than they bring in from selling meat (if they sell any at
all) or killing pest animals for the city.

The back of Sakura's boxy compact van is outfitted for butchering in the field: royal blue heavy-duty rubber gloves hang from
clothespins, two sawhorses and a sheet of plywood sealed with
glossy mustard-yellow paint (a standard-issue hardware store item
in Japan) slide under a platform, on which is set a bin big enough
to hold a whole animal's worth of meat, a powder-blue plastic basket for organs, various knives with bright-colored electrical tape
marking their handles, and disposal bags. (Her teenage daughters
complain about the car's animal odor.)

Sakura and Kawamoto (my duck hunter friend) are on the same
boar-hunting team this winter, with one other man, Seki-san
(Grandpa Seki they call him, though maybe not to his face). They

rotate weeks doing patrol: driving before dawn each morning to eight or ten traps at the south and east edges of Yamanaka. (Other teams cover their own territory.) If they've caught a boar, the patrol person calls the others to help dispatch it.

IT WAS KAWAMOTO who showed me the picture of Sakura's car, flipped sideways on the curve of a snowy road in late December. He'd received the photo that morning at 2:00 A.M., along with the rest of the hunters in their group, with a message that said, *Yabai!* meaning roughly, *Oh shit!* She was out checking traps after her night shift at the convenience store when the car lost traction and skidded toward the ravine. The other hunters rushed to the scene. They found Sakura unscathed but too shaken to deal with the two young boars she'd captured. They pushed her car upright and left the animals huddled together in their metal cage as snow continued to fall on and off.

A day later, I went with Sakura to retrieve the young boars. She drove a rental car cautiously into the snow-covered forest, retracing her tracks toward the site of the accident. Our friends Sakai, an engineer-turned-farmer, and Ohkubo, a park ranger, followed in a pickup with most of her hunting gear—one of those narrow-wheeled white kei trucks that every farmer, craftsman, or manual laborer in this town seems to own. More accustomed to oversize American SUVs with four-wheel drive, I'd wondered what people do with their kei trucks when it snows: they drive them.

The two small boars became frantic when they saw us, charging at the sides of the cage, biting at the heavy-gauge wire, splattering muddy slush toward us with remarkable fury. They'd spent the night and day exposed to the elements, but they put up a strong final fight.

Sakura carried a high-voltage battery, in a custom-made wooden box with a handle, up the short slope to the trap, several paces from the road. She clamped two cables to the wire box trap to make a circuit and switched on a charged spear connected to the battery by a cord. The spike at the end of the spear is not so much to puncture the boar as to conduct the current. She stepped toward the charging boar and pierced a tender spot below its ear, sending an electric shock through its body. Instantly, the boar stiffened and collapsed in the mud, lifeless. And then it was the second boar's turn to die.

With a rope hooked to its snout, we slid each dead beast across the snow like a grotesque sled, into the stream on the opposite side of the road. A few clumps of sedge grass in the blue-gray stream-bed remained defiantly bright green. Sakura washed the mud from the boars' coarse winter coats and with it some of the smell. She punctured an artery in each one's neck to let out blood; the river turned bright red around her yellow rain boots.

In milder weather she'll butcher boars right here by the river, but that day we loaded them into the bed of Ohkubo's kei truck. Curled together in a plastic bin, the two little boars looked as if they were sleeping. *They look cute*, everyone said.

We drove farther into the mountain, past the Wagatani and Kutani dams, up toward the uninhabited village of Suginomizu. There's a soba restaurant and a café that open on summer week-ends, but in the middle of the winter no one is there. We shoveled shin-deep snow off a narrow bridge with a NO CARS sign, and then drove across it to park near a work shed beside a fierce icy-cold river. Feathery wet flakes were still falling—the kind of snow that's terrible for skiing but perfect for snowballs.

Against the quiet backdrop of frosted evergreens, Sakura began gutting the animals in a shallow spot at the river's edge. Her first cut was around the anus, which she tied off with a piece of string to keep the contents of the intestines from contaminating the meat. She sawed open the belly, pulled out the warm innards, and cut the spongy pink lungs away from the ribs.

The heart and liver she kept in a powder-blue plastic basket, letting the river water clean and chill them. (If Kawamoto was here, he'd take the gallbladder home to dry and pack into gel capsules that he claims cure a hangover.) The rest of the organs she left for the crows, already watching and calling out, and other scavengers that will come after we've gone, leaving the riverbank clean by morning.

The first time I watched Sakura butcher a boar—in Ōzuchi while I was helping Nimaida make charcoal—I thought to myself, *I couldn't do that.* I know it's cowardly, but I still don't want to touch the dead beast. I can cut up whole poultry and I can gut fish, but a big furry mammal is both more repulsive and more sympathetic.

Inside the shed, we'd set up Sakura's butchering table: glossy mustard-yellow plywood balanced on sawhorses. Sakai and Ohkubo hoisted the carcass onto the table with its legs pointing skyward like a cartoon of death, the open cavity of its belly gaping. Sakura handed me rubber gloves and a small sharp knife.

My hesitancy to participate was quickly subsumed by my drive to master a new skill—to be better than the boys. I'd watched her teach Sakai how to make small light incisions, gradually peeling back the skin, and I emulated the way she aimed her honed blade slightly toward the skin so as not to cut away the soft fat that wraps the muscle. Better to shave as close to the inside of the skin as possible; if a little stubble ends up on the fat, you can scrape it away with your knife like toast crumbs off butter.

We sliced off the trotters, and the leg skin flopped down onto the table. Sakura rolled the boar on its side to cut the skin away from the spine. With a well-aimed sturdy knife, she severed the spinal cord from the skull, then folded the head and feet into the skin, and slid the whole pelt into a bag for disposal. What remained on the table looked and smelled like something you'd see hanging in a butcher shop. The animal had become meat.

We slid a knife into each hip joint, and unzipped the ribs from the spine by cutting in a zigzag motion. Sakura broke the backbone into manageable lengths for me to take home and make into stock—I hate to see anything go to waste. There were eight sections of meat to divvy up—front legs, rear legs, loins, and sides of ribs—and still a second boar to butcher.

I went home that day with a garbage bag full of muscular legs, meaty ribs and sturdy bones, and a big purple liver. I was exhausted, but my work was not done: in my little kitchen, I rinsed the meat and cut it into manageable pieces. I followed Sakura's instructions to age it in the refrigerator for a few days, uncovered, before wrapping each section in plastic, then foil, and freezing it in zip-top bags. I blanched and simmered the bones, and my apartment began to smell like a ramen shop.

All winter and spring the meat kept coming. I cooked and gave it away as fast as I could, but still it overwhelmed my apartment refrigerator and freezer (not half the size of an American appliance). In my ovenless Japanese kitchen, roasting was out of the question. I cooked stew and curry, Bolognese and ragout, gyōza and sausage patties, mapo tofu, and beans braised in bone broth. I made flour tortillas and boar carnitas for my friends who'd never had a real taco. I prepared liver pâté and rillettes and threw a dinner party. But there was always more boar meat.

I swapped recipes and photos with Sakura, who was making ham and chashu. She never buys meat from the supermarket: she doesn't need to, and she worries about hormones and antibiotics from industrial agriculture.

I asked my friends and neighbors how they prepare boar meat, or shishi niku as it's called. If it was something they cooked at all, the answer was almost always shishi nabe, a hearty miso-seasoned stew of meat and vegetables—carrot, napa cabbage, sato-imo (taro), or whatever is on hand. The nabe is good, especially when Sakai slices a particularly fatty cut ultrathin on his deli slicer. The iron-rich meat is more flavorful than buttery grain-fed beef or pallid pork from the supermarket, and the snow-white winter fat melts into the stew. But I want to eat the same recipe only so many times.

I ran into a dead end looking for local recipes, because boars were rare in this part of Japan until the last decade. In general, meat cookery in Japan is not as refined as the sophisticated fish and vegetable cuisine. The meat people cook at home is simple and quick: thin-sliced pork stir-fried with ginger; bits of beef simmered with potatoes; diced chicken sauced in dashi and beaten egg. They buy farm-raised chicken, beef, or pork from the butcher or supermarket, already cleaned and boned, then sliced or cubed and even pre-seasoned (the butcher shop kitty-corner from where I'm living will even cook it for you). Most people don't have ovens for roasting chickens or beef tenderloins, and hardly anyone is cutting up and braising an entire boar shank or rack of ribs.

In Yamanaka boar is not on the menu at local restaurants, ex-cept when Kawamoto drops some off and they run it as a special—most likely kushi-yaki, salted meat grilled on skewers. But boar is tough and pungent unless cooked gently for a long time or sliced very thinly. I can see why some people find it revolting. When they hear I'm cooking boar, they say, *Isn't it smelly?*

The thing is, Japan didn't have a widespread meat-eating cul-ture until relatively recently. That didn't mean people ate no meat. What it means is, meat eating was mostly pragmatic and a little secretive until the late nineteenth century. And the cuisine around it didn't develop into something venerable like French charcuterie or shōjin ryōri, vegan temple cooking.

Japan's mountainous, densely forested main island isn't suited to large-scale livestock production. Before globalization it was more practical to subsist on plants, grains, and seafood. Shintō, a belief system in which all things have a spirit, cultivates respect for nature. Buddhism, which came by way of Korea in the sixth century, discourages killing animals; it was for centuries the reli-gion of the elite, but certain values seeped into (or were imposed on) daily life for all classes.

A peasant family may have kept half a dozen hens for eggs and a cow for pulling their plow, and in 675 the emperor Tenmu en-acted a law against killing those animals during the cultivating season (what happened in the off-season was, I suppose, a farmer's private business). Game animals, however, were excluded from the law. Over the centuries that followed, the strength of the rules and taboos against meat consumption (which varied by region and class) waxed and waned. They were eroded by Christian missionar-ies in southern Japan during the mid-sixteenth and seventeenth centuries (who according to *The Jesuit Mission Press in Japan* pro-cured a cow for an Easter feast to feed four hundred, featuring a dish that sounds like an enormous paella).

Even when the Tokugawa shogunate kicked out the missionar-ies in 1615 and proclaimed a total ban on meat eating and hunting in 1687 (ostensibly for religious reasons, but likely to keep weap-ons out of the hands of the masses), the law made exceptions for agricultural pests, and meat as medicine. A farmer could own a weapon to protect his crops from raiding wildlife, and one in two did. Boar meat eaten medicinally was discreetly called botan (pe-ony) or yama kujira (mountain whale). Even the shōgun ate meat, often gifted by placating domains (for example, the saka-ami ducks sent from Kaga).

Still, when Commodore Matthew C. Perry arrived from Amer-ica in 1853 to force the opening of Japanese ports, his request for a cow to eat was refused. He was told by the government that people owed it to their cows to take care of them in exchange for the animals' work pulling plows on their farms.

Things changed from the Meiji period forward, beginning in 1868. Japan opened its ports and embraced, among other foreign customs, meat eating—promoted as a way to increase stature and strength. Ramen from China became mainstream. There were an estimated fifteen hundred Western-style restaurants—serving the likes of katsu (cutlets) and hanbāgu (hamburger steak)—in Tōkyō by the end of the nineteenth century. The rise in livestock agricul-ture shifted the dynamic between people and wild animals. Wolves were no longer helpers; they were a threat—one that was elimi-nated permanently early in the twentieth century.

Yaki-niku, grilled meat, took hold after World War II, when

two million Koreans who'd been conscripted during the war remained in Japan (along with protein-hungry Allied forces). Now all-you-can-eat beef and cheap hamburgers proliferate. A free trade agreement in 1991 opened the cattle chute, and a stampede of cheap American beef trampled the already precarious traditional diet of vegetables and fish. Japan's best-known meat culture—ramen, katsu, yaki-niku—is borrowed and relatively new (in the last hundred years or so).

The Japanized word "jibie," from the French *gibier* (game), first appeared in a Japanese newspaper in 1985. In recent years, it has all but replaced other Japanese words for wild meat. It sounds fancier than "shishi niku." When meat eating was embraced as modern and worldly, boar was sidelined as something backward, old-fashioned. But now, out of both pragmatism and fashion, shishi niku—and jibie in general—is having a moment.

At a game butcher in Hakusan City, not an hour's drive from Yamanaka, the most prized cuts of boar sell for ¥8,000 per kilo (about $34 a pound). At the Michelin-starred Les Saisons in Tōkyō's Imperial Hotel, a jibie tasting menu costs ¥35,700 (about $330). But here in the countryside, if you know a hunter, you can get an endless supply of boar meat for free. In fact, when open hunting season ends and the cultivation season begins, the government pays people a bounty for each boar they trap and kill.

AFTER A MONTH of joining Sakura on patrol, I've lost my squeamishness about butchering. There's one more light snow, and

Sakura picks me up at 6:00 A.M. *It looks like powdered sugar,* she says as the sun comes up over snow-dusted forests. *I want to eat it.*

Near the spot where her car flipped, a kamoshika (Japanese serow) watches us from the far bank of the river. It looks magical, neither goat nor deer, with a humanlike stare. We watch it—and it watches us—until it climbs out of sight over the hilltop. We hope for it to appear again next time.

The traps are empty that day, but tanuki (raccoon dogs) or uribō—baby boars, too small to trip the wire—have eaten the nuka (rice bran, which is plentiful and free) that she leaves as bait. Sakura tells me that boars give birth in the spring and fall. The autumn babies usually don't survive the winter. With so little snow, this year is different.

Most people were grateful for the mild winter. Last year they had to shovel two meters of accumulation off their roofs and driveways, the heaviest snowfall since 1963, they say. But if a mild winter means an increased boar population, that's bad news for agriculture.

Sakura was hoping for snow so she could practice tracking footprints, chasing down boars with a team, and shooting her prey with a rifle. Owning a gun in Japan requires a lengthy licensing process and storage either at a gun shop, or in an expensive locker at home with unannounced visits from the police to make sure the gun is stored correctly.

One morning, we find a sow in the trap and her mate waiting beside her, outside the trap. He runs into the woods when we approach, and she rattles the cage in desperation. *Poor things*, we say, and there's a heavy silence.

That day Sakura's teacher, Hoshiba, wants her to practice using her gun. While we wait for him to arrive, Sakura puts on her orange Japan Hunters cap and vest and steps into rain pants. She tells me she prefers killing trapped boars with electricity because it's faster. *It looks like the gun hurts them*, she says.

When Hoshiba, Kawamoto, and Seki have all gathered, I follow Sakura up the hill to the trap while the others wait by the road. I cover my ears as she takes aim. Poised among sugi trees with the rifle on her shoulder, Sakura waits for the boar to look at her, then shoots it between the ear and the eye. It wails and writhes in agony before going still. No matter how destructive boars can be, or how fearsome they look, it's sad seeing an animal die.

BY THE END of February, Sakura has a new car, outfitted with all her gear. Ume trees are starting to bloom. The mountains at dawn look like paper cutouts in shades of blue, paler the farther away they are. Subtle pink gradually brightens the colorless sky. When we pull over to check traps hidden from the road, she points out boar and tanuki prints on the frosty ground, and the spiky trunks of tara-no-me shrubs; their young leaves will be delicious for tempura, she says.

Sakura is at ease with the contradiction of both admiring and killing animals. She has the tanned pelt of an unborn baby boar she once found inside a pregnant mother that she slaughtered; it's soft, beautiful, and unsettling. I watch her kill one boar whose belly looks slightly swollen. When we gut it, she cuts open the uterus. Inside are three embryos, small enough to fit in my gloved palm, their tiny hooves still soft and pink, remarkable to behold. We leave them for scavengers.

The day our friend Aya joins us, there's a big sow in the trap. An uribō, no bigger than a teacup pig and still striped like a chipmunk, anxiously paces in the brush nearby. (Baby boars are called uribō, melon boy, because they are round and striated like a melon.) We chase away the baby. When we butcher the mother, I notice her skin is loose from the piglets she carried, and I wonder what will become of them.

Aya is studying for her hunting license so she can defend her organic vegetable garden. She and her husband raise chickens for eggs and for meat that they sell as yakitori at their seasonal beach café. When she gets her license, the number of woman hunters in Kaga will double.

Nationwide, the overall number of hunters is less than half what it was fifty years ago, but the number of women hunters is growing. I suspect there have always been women like Sakura and Aya who wanted to hunt, but custom dictated that it was a men's activity. Now, like the keepers of many traditions, hunters are beginning to welcome women because they are desperate to slow the decline of something they hold dear. And farmers are grateful to anyone helping them battle intruders from the forest.

There is a week in late March when Sakura and her team catch a boar five days in a row. If I'm not out with her before dawn, making the rounds as the birds wake up, then I'm sleeping lightly, checking my phone around 5:00 A.M. to see if they want help with butchering.

By day four of the streak, we are hoping for a break, but in the lowlands east of town there's a big one, angry and full of fight. Sakura calls Seki and Kawamoto. It's all hands on deck. The fur along the beast's back bristles like armor. He charges his full weight against the cage, splattering us meters away with pungent mud, reeking of shit and pheromones.

The first shock of electricity doesn't kill him. With the second stab, his body stiffens. He lets out a final groan before collapsing into the mud. Kawamoto strains to drag the body out of the cage; it must weigh at least as much as he does, and both of them are built for power.

Sakura pierces the artery in its neck with such accuracy that the blood spurts like a Tarantino murder scene, a gurgling fountain of red soaking the forest floor. Kawamoto and Seki haul the dead boar into the back of a truck and drive it to a nearby river.

While we butcher the boar, they chat about the bell-shaped pale yellow flowers on the bank that were unopen buds a day or two ago. Uguisu, the little green birds that are harbingers of spring, call from the brush. Two hawks circle overhead, waiting for us to finish and leave them lunch.

Most hunters would throw away a big male like this. Young boars and females flush with winter fat are best to eat. But instead of taking it to the dump or burying it in the woods, Sakura and Kawamoto will feed this boar to their dogs. They say it makes their coats gleam.

On the fifth day, Kawamoto and Seki have obligations in the morning. I will help Sakura. Kawamoto comes briefly for the slaughter so he can help us hoist the carcass into the car. Before he leaves, he gives us provisions: convenience store sandwiches, onigiri, and a drink called Hot Lemon, which reminds me of the hot Tang my dad made on backpacking trips when I was a kid. We drive to Ōzuchi and set up at the spot where I first saw Sakura butcher a boar last August. I remember thinking at the time that I could never—would never want to—butcher a boar. But now I'm good at it—better than Seki, and not as fast as Kawamoto but possibly more precise.

It's the last boar I butcher with Sakura. We toss some scraps to the crows overhead, trying to befriend them. Open hunting season ends in another week. After that Sakura will take a few weeks off before beginning pest management for the city. From April through October, citizens can file complaints about problem animals, and neighborhood teams are dispatched to set up traps. The city pays a bounty for each boar killed.

Sakura's going to quit the convenience store soon and start a new job, when the Jibie Base opens thirty minutes away in Komatsu. It will be a place for butchering and selling game meat and teaching people how to cook it. The first jibie butcher in Ishikawa prefecture opened in Hakusan City in 2011. A similar place opened in Shizuoka prefecture in 2015. Locally and nationally, government agencies are streamlining the rules that help bring meat from hunters to restaurants and consumers.

Even in the unlikely event that hunters take back the front of rural farmland, that win alone would not reverse the decline of village agriculture. But there's a hope that interest in game meat could help revitalize rural economies, bringing gastro-tourism to areas where agriculture and forestry have lost their vitality. For Sakura, at least, the Jibie Base will provide an income doing what she loves.

In summer, when it's light before five, Sakura is out making rounds at 4:00 A.M. (while I sleep in). I'm still using the meat from that last boar. I have washed the beastly scent of pheromones and fur from my hair and clothes, but the battle between humans and boars will continue indefinitely. It's a war of our own making, exacerbated by killing off wolves and warming the planet. The boars, too, will continue their struggle for survival, for dominance over the landscape. We're not so different.

Ramen Bolognese

TIME: *4–5 hours*
Serves 6

Yamanaka does not have its own traditional recipes for wild boar, so when my freezer filled up with boar meat, I looked to European peasant food for inspiration (as many Japanese chefs do too). Every time I cooked Bolognese, the cut and fat content of the meat I had were a little different, and I used whatever wine I wanted to drink, pouring a splash for myself and the rest in the pot. Every time the long-simmered sauce turned out silky and rich.

The fresh ramen noodles at Yamanaka's supermarket are excellent (while the dried Italian pasta is mediocre), so instead of spaghetti I used the thickest, curliest ramen I could find. The sauce clung to the bouncy yellow noodles, reminding me of tantan-men. I liked it even better than spaghetti—even with powdered Parmesan cheese shaken from a green can.

> *Note:* If you don't have a meat grinder, cut the meat into chunks and freeze it for an hour or two so it's firm but not rock hard. Pulse the semi-frozen chunks in a food processor, or mince with a knife as small as you reasonably can.
>
> Other game meat, pork, or beef can be substituted for the boar. If it's lean, double the butter.

1 kilogram (2¼ pounds) fatty wild-boar meat, ground or minced
(see note)

60 grams (3 tablespoons) butter, plus more for serving

1 large onion, diced very small

1 large carrot, diced very small

2 ribs celery, diced very small

Kosher salt or sea salt

Freshly ground pepper

2 tablespoons tomato paste

600 mL (2½ cups) wine (red or white, but high acidity is good)

500 mL (2 cups) whole milk

½ teaspoon freshly grated nutmeg

500 mL (2 cups) stock or water, plus more as needed

6 servings fresh ramen noodles (about 120–140 grams each)

Chili flakes, for serving (optional)

Grated Parmesan cheese, for serving

1. Heat a large Dutch oven over medium-high heat. Without adding oil,
   cook the meat, breaking it up with a wooden spoon, just until the
   pink is gone, about 5 minutes; transfer it to a bowl. Lower the heat
   to medium.

2. In the same pot, melt the butter and sweat the onion, carrot, and
   celery until the onion is translucent but not browned, 2–3 minutes.
   Season with two or three pinches of salt and a pinch of pepper. Add
   the tomato paste and cook, stirring, until it coats the vegetables and
   turns brick red, 5–7 minutes.

3. Add the wine and raise the heat to high. As soon as it boils, reduce
   the heat to keep the sauce at a simmer, stirring occasionally, until
   the wine reduces by half, about 30 minutes. Add the meat with another pinch of salt, and a pinch of pepper.

4. Add the milk (don't worry if it curdles) and nutmeg, and cook at a gentle simmer, stirring occasionally, until the liquid has mostly evaporated, 1½–2 hours. Add the broth or water, and continue to cook at a low simmer for 1½–2 more hours, stirring more frequently as the sauce thickens, and adding a little more broth or water as necessary to keep it from scorching. It's done when the meat is meltingly tender, and the gloss of rust-colored fat disperses through the almost gelatinous sauce. It should be thick, with almost no liquid left. Season generously with salt and pepper. Keep warm, or store in the refrigerator for up to 5 days (or in the freezer for a few months) and reheat before serving.

5. Bring a large pot of lightly salted water to a rolling boil, and add the ramen noodles. Boil until al dente, according to the cooking time on the package; drain. (I don't recommend adding the cooking water to the sauce, as you would with Italian pasta, because of the alkalinity of ramen.) Toss the noodles with butter to taste, and the warm sauce; serve with chili flakes (if using) and lots of grated Parmesan cheese.

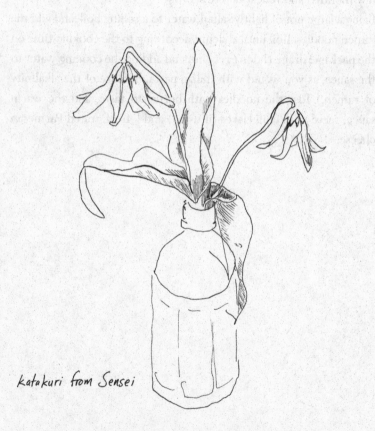

katakuri from Sensei

Twelve

Mountain Meijin

Everyone talks about Japan's iconic cherry blossoms, but after their pale petals fall to the ground in April, a rainbow of wildflowers light up the mountains. It's the best time to pick sansai, mountain vegetables.

The character for san in "sansai" can also be read as yama (山), meaning mountain. "Yama" is interchangeable with "forest" in the way people use it. You go into the yama. Spirits dwell in the yama. The yama is dangerous. Satoyama is the village forest used for raw materials and foraged foods, and okuyama is the interior forest rarely traveled except by brave hunters and master foragers.

Sansai season starts in the slow quiet period between the last snow and the burst of spring color. Cars pull over suddenly, and people jump out to hunch by the side of the road looking intently at the dirt. I wondered what they were doing until I learned about fuki-no-tō—dots of neon green that push through dead leaves in the brown landscape of late winter—the shoots of fuki (butterbur or coltsfoot in English). As February melts into March, amateur foragers fill plastic shopping bags with the bitter buds to make into tempura and fuki-no-tō miso.

I started searching for fuki-no-tō as I jogged through Yamanaka's quiet neighborhoods, stuffing the pockets of my windbreaker. I spotted it through car windows, like an I Spy game. I eyed it in neighbors' untended gardens. The general shapes and colors of the Yamanaka landscape were familiar to me, but most of the flora and fauna were still foreign; learning to identify even one useful thing made me feel more at home.

I SPENT MY early childhood either in the woods or in my mother's garden, asking her questions while she weeded. I knew the scientific names of plants before I knew how to read. And it seemed like a cruel irony when I had to go to school, pulled away from a place where there were limitless things to learn and forced to sit in a classroom with twenty-four other kids, filling out worksheets.

Much of our five-acre farm was uncultivated meadow. Some years, button mushrooms emerged in the part of the pasture grazed by our sheep. In the way-back, where the grass grew tall enough for a small child or resting deer to hide, there were blackberries in late summer that stained my lips, hands, and clothes. Garter snakes coiled on the thorny branches to soak up the sun.

One Sitka spruce in the pasture must have been two or three hundred years old. Our family of four, holding hands, still couldn't circle its girth. Beside it was the wild cherry tree with the best fruit. I would wedge myself between the two trunks in a pike and walk my way up to where I could climb into the cherry tree and pick its fruit or bend its branches down to my younger brother, waiting below.

The field extended back along a wetland that sang with a chorus of frogs in early spring. Evenings, we canoed on the slough, listening to red-winged blackbirds, looking for beaver dams, and watching the mountain turn red. I plucked stiff dark green bulrush shoots and nibbled their sweet white ends.

A band of woods—forested with maple, alder, wild cherry, second-growth redcedar, and a few Christmassy bushes sprouted from berries carried by birds from a nearby holly farm—divided our farm from the North Fork of the Snoqualmie River. In the woods, I picked translucent jewel-toned salmon berries and velvety thimbleberries that fit on my fingertips and made my mouth pucker. I pulled licorice ferns from moss-covered maples and chewed them until the sweet roots tasted bitter.

I WANT TO KNOW Yamanaka like that, but I need a teacher. A meijin is an expert. "Meijin" can be applied more liberally than "shokunin," a word for a master of their craft. Meijin can specialize in something that may or may not be their trade, and it need not produce a product. It implies significant time invested in accumulating knowledge and skill.

The mountain meijin are mostly men in their sixties and older, who walk with their gaze fixed on the ground, or lingering into the trees, reading the landscape. They know the names and uses of hundreds of plants and not only which mountain to find them on but which bank of the river, which particular grove of trees they'll be sheltered among. They can take you off trail and walk directly to the spot where a rare flower is in peak bloom.

They drive rugged cars that look like miniature Jeeps, for navigating narrow rutted mountain roads. Sturdy knives hang in holsters from their belt loops, ready to dig roots and slice stalks. They carry folding handsaws for clearing trails. Bear bells clipped to their backpacks chime as they walk.

They're elusive, everyone said. Those guys will never share their secrets, they warned me.

But a friend introduced me to Yoshiharu Nishiyama. Nishiyama Sensei, I call him, or just Sensei. A gentle man with graying caterpillar eyebrows and long thick eyelashes, he's a tree doctor, jumokui. When a sacred tree becomes sick, the shrine or municipality can call on him to diagnose and treat it. Kayano Ōsugi, the two-thousand-year-old tree draped in shrine rope and lightning-shaped paper amulets, at the south end of Yamanaka, is one of his patients. He's also a biotope planner, a consultant on restoring ecosystems: if a town loses its fireflies, he'll help them create a holistic plan for bringing the land back into balance. His business card says *Building a society that coexists with nature so future generations can live happily*. His work is for the children's children, he says.

The first time I met him, I brought an antique illustrated guide to Japanese plants that I'd found in a used-book store. We flipped through it together, and I told him in my broken Japanese which plants we also had at home, like the plantain leaves that could soothe a nettle sting. Nishiyama Sensei was eager to share delight in the natural world, and from that day he was my teacher.

First, he showed me how to harvest low-growing sasa bamboo leaves for tea, and yomogi (mugwort, *Artemisia princeps*) for pounding into mochi. As the weather softened into spring, he taught me to recognize katakuri (*Erythronium japonicum*), a rare wildflower with graceful purple-pink petals that curl open in the afternoon. I recognized its name from katakuriko, the potato starch I use to make fried chicken; I learned that katakuriko used to be made from the bulbs of this plant. Its ephemeral flowers are prized for tea ceremony, but when I found them on walks in the woods, I left the blooms to go to seed. The leaves I sometimes picked to blanch, and steep in cold dashi and soy sauce.

Nishiyama Sensei said he wanted to show me everything he could, since I might stay only another year. We never talked much on our nature walks, but I could tell he comprehended my delight when I learned a new plant, and he didn't seem to mind if I wandered away from a group of chatty friends to gaze at birds and leaves. He got excited when I found berries hidden under a leaf that no one else could see. Nishiyama Sensei called me every time the season shifted—to show me what was happening in the woods—and he introduced me to other mountain meijin: Miyashita, Sakashita, and Shikijiya.

Miyashita-san is soft-spoken, obsessive, and contains volumes of encyclopedic knowledge. The cane he walks with doesn't keep him from going in the woods almost every day. He'll teach me dozens of plants rapid-fire and then quiz me on them playfully. I tell my friend Ai-chan that I wish my Japanese were better so I could understand more of what Miyashita and Nishiyama talk about. *No one can!* she answers. *They're maniacs!* What she means is, they speak in specialized language meaningful only to the deeply obsessed.

Nishiyama Sensei took me to meet another friend, Sakashita-san, at his wild wetland garden. Sakashita—wearing mud-splattered work clothes and a hat for shade—walked us around the pond and deciduous forest that he's populated with delicate wildflowers and rare mountain herbs from seeds he gathers all over Japan. People think he's strange for making a garden that looks like weeds, but he continues to grow his collection.

In the woods another day, they introduce me to Shikijiya-san, a diving instructor who has traveled the world with his scuba gear. He's a good cook and a dapper dresser (wearing leather loafers and polo shirts) when he's not bushwhacking deep into the mountains or scrambling along cliff sides.

My friend Mie Michiba, a retired lacquerware dealer, decided to host a wild plants lunch during Golden Week, the height of sansai season. She too is eager to learn from Nishiyama Sensei, so she suggested we ask him and the other mountain meijin to help us gather ingredients and then cook together in the garage she has converted into a semi-outdoor kitchen looking onto her flower garden.

Golden Week, at the end of April into the first week of May, is like Japanese spring break. It's called Golden Week because of the four national holidays it spans. Looking out at the light on new leaves and the flush of wildflowers, I think it could be named for the gleaming landscape.

Nishiyama Sensei tells me about going into the woods to collect zenmai, the fiddleheads of royal fern (*Osmunda japonica*), when he was in grade school. He sat by the river in awe of the five-petaled golden flowers of yamabuki bushes (*Kerria japonica*) blooming radiantly, and watched the sunlight dance on the water. That's when he knew he wanted to work with plants.

I must have been about the same age when I decided to make a dinner entirely from wild plants. I followed instructions from my parents' faded copy of *Stalking the Wild Asparagus* to dig up cattail roots, starchy rhizomes that I cooked like potatoes in soup made with canned chicken broth. I picked dandelion greens and chickweed for salad, and steeped tisane from the tiny purple deadnettle flowers in the lawn. I don't remember the meal so much as the harvesting—the excitement that there were useful and edible things all around me, if only I knew how to identify them.

That dinner felt like a beginning, a first try. Ever since, I've wanted to do it bigger and better (and without canned chicken broth, which even then seemed like cheating). I needed to know more plants and more ways to use them.

Instead, I moved to the city with my mother a few years later, when my parents divorced. I stopped playing in the woods and started going to punk shows. Still, in college, I picked the violets that grew between the bricks behind the faculty club and candied them in sparkling sugar. In Brooklyn, where I've lived almost a decade, I look longingly at lamb's-quarters growing in cracked sidewalks and mugwort filling empty lots; technically they're edible, but they are probably contaminated by industrial waste, exhaust fumes, dog piss, and residue from when Hurricane Sandy overflowed the Gowanus Canal Superfund site.

My father and his new wife live on the land where I grew up. There is a new house there. My mother's sprawling garden was taken over by weeds, then mowed down and replaced with pragmatic raised beds. I've forgotten the flowers' scientific names, but I remember the progression of colors and fragrances through the seasons—dark pink redbud, golden daffodil, pale pink peony, vermilion crocosmia, light purple aster. And which blossoms are edible—primrose, pansy, rose, nasturtium, calendula, borage. When I visit, I go out in the pasture and woods to find comfort. I search for ripe berries and pick the tart plums that have gone unnoticed or unappreciated.

ON A DRIZZLY late-April morning, three days before the wild plants lunch at Michiba's garage, we drove in a caravan up a mountain road from Mitani village (separated from Yamanaka by a tunnel) to collect ingredients. Shikijiya (the diving instructor) led the way with Sakashita (the gardener) in the passenger seat of his silver Jimny. Michiba followed in her clean white Prius, and I rode in the backseat with Akane-chan, a girlish twenty-four-year-old vintage fashion collector who'd brought an umbrella as rain gear (not exactly practical for hiking into the woods). Nishiyama Sensei drove behind us in his black Pajero Mini, taking up the rear to look out for everyone's safety. The plan was to collect enough wild food to feed a dozen people.

Mitani is Nishiyama's home village, and it's where wild herbs and vegetables are harvested every weekend and shipped to Narisawa, a whimsical modernist Michelin-starred restaurant in Tōkyō. Chef Narisawa chose to source his ingredients from Ishikawa because of its long history of hospitality and its rich biodiversity. This is where north and south, mountains and sea, meet: almost every wild edible that grows in Japan can be found here.

The mountains that day were a thousand colors of green, from the nearly white shimmer of new leaves to the deep blue green of sugi and Noto hiba cypress, all luminous under an overcast sky.

They stay that way—infinitely varied—only for a few days, and then the deciduous trees gradually darken into a more uniform green until the cold snap of autumn nights sets them alight in famously fiery hues.

We wound our way up the mountain in stops and starts, looking for tara-no-me, the leaf buds of prickly angelica trees (*Aralia elata*). But most of them had either been picked clean or the buds had grown too big for eating, guarding themselves with fierce little thorns that embed in your hands like splinters, even through gloves.

Shikijiya drove fast. He and Sakashita would spot something promising and stop suddenly, one of them leaping out of the car to inspect. Each time, we pulled in behind them to see what it might be. Nishiyama Sensei wandered the roadside, noticing smaller medicinal plants and wildflowers. He's always looking at the tiniest plants but seeing the whole ecosystem.

Sometimes, while Shikijiya showed us how to pick warabi (fiddleheads of *Pteridium aquilinum* var. *latiusculum*), or we watched as he cut a few buds from a lone angelica tree, Sakashita wandered off into the woods, returning with a bagful of edible buds and leaves or reappearing farther up the road. I wished I was allowed to do that too, but the mountain meijin worried I'd get hurt.

Below the trickle of a small waterfall, we scrambled to reach umbrella-like daimonjisō leaves (*Saxifraga fortunei*) clinging to the cliff, glistening with raindrops. Big frogs sang courtship songs from under the mud.

We drove farther up the mountain. Near the summit we crossed into Fukui prefecture and parked in a narrow pullout to pick koshiabura, the leaf buds of another tree in the Araliaceae family, *Chengiopanax sciadophylloides*.

I followed Sakashita into thick shrubs. He pulled down a speckled trunk—as thick around as my wrist and maybe twice my height—so I could reach the leaf buds at the top of its pliable branches. The buds snapped off easily: little clusters of tender green stems with pointy pale-green leaves not yet unfurled. The next one we found was harder to bend, and Sakashita threw his weight over the trunk, scaled it, and hung by his arms until his feet touched the ground and I could reach the end of the bowed tree to pick the tasty bits.

Soon, I could identify koshiabura too, and I scaled and bent the slender trunks. Hanging by my arms, toes reaching for the ground, I was tickled with joy. Once my feet were flat on the duff, I pulled down the top of the tree, hand over hand, picking the leaf buds. I left the smallest ones to open for the next forager (or for the tree itself) and avoided the big leaves that had passed the perfect point for tempura. Michiba and Akane followed cautiously into the brush, picking from the shrubs that Nishiyama Sensei and Shikijiya bent down for them. When we had enough, we kept picking, hooked on finding more and more.

We drove down in a U shape toward Yamanaka, collecting some tara-no-me on the way. We weren't far from joining the main road above the landmark Kayano cedar (the two-thousand-year-old enshrined tree at the south end of Yamanaka), but a cherry tree had fallen in our path. The three mountain meijin pulled saws from their bags and set to work. In minutes, our path was clear. As we descended, I recognized the road where Sakura sets her boar traps (with Sakura I'd always come from the town below, but today we came from the mountain above). We were not far from Moriguchi's wood-carving studio in Kazetani.

We brought bags and bags of leafy green things back to Michiba's garage to clean. Ai-chan joined us; she's an artist and a writer who grew up picking sansai with her grandmother. While she showed me how to rub the black fuzz off warabi fiddleheads with a cotton glove, she talked about how everyone used to eat sansai in the Jōmon period (about 14,000 B.C.E to 300 B.C.E.), before agriculture came to Japan. Even until recently, wild things were an important source of food. Most of Japan's land is unsuitable for large-scale cultivation. In the wake of World War II, hungry city dwellers went out to the country to forage for their survival.

We'd picked much more than we needed. I took a bag of koshiabura to my hunter friend Kawamoto and another to the sushi chef I like to chat with about local history at Saraku.

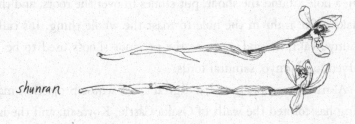

shunran

ON THE MORNING of our lunch party, my job was to go out early and pick edible wildflowers. I collected the lacy white heads of shaku (cow parsley, *Anthriscus sylvestris* subsp. *sylvestris*), dandelions, and bunches of violets. The meijin showed up with more leaves for tempura; frozen mushrooms they'd collected the previous fall; zenmai fiddleheads; and shunran (*Cymbidium goeringii* var. *goeringii*), a spring orchid with sweet-tasting pink stems in papery sheaths and pale purple sepals curling back from its mottled trumpet.

Michiba simmered fuki stalks in dashi seasoned heavily with soy sauce and mirin and folded them into vinegared rice. We scattered it with dark green watercress, purple-pink shunran heads, and the indigo, yellow, and white flowers I'd picked that morning.

Shikijiya, the scuba instructor, manned the tempura station, battering and frying the bitter green taste of spring: koshiabura and tara-no-me pinched from shrubs, round scalloped daimonjisō leaves plucked from a cliff, and frilly medicinal yomogi gathered by the roadside. They came out crisp and light, staining the serving platter but leaving no grease on the tongue.

Sakashita, the gardener, had brought bamboo shoots big as traffic cones, which he roasted in their scalelike prehistoric husks over charcoal. You harvest them by searching for the tiny tips that emerge from the ground and using a pickax to dig out the tender cone below and break it loose. Sakashita says that people used to dig a hole around the shoot, put stones in over the roots, and then make a fire right in the hole to roast the whole thing. It's called daimyō-yaki, he said, because the precious shoots used to be reserved for daimyō, samurai lords.

Akira Hasegawa arrived, a digital artist whose projection mapping has colored the walls of Ōsaka Castle, Kōyasan, and the hall hosting a Nobel Prize dinner. He brought aji (Japanese horse mackerel) he'd caught on his friend's fishing boat that morning, neatly sliced into sashimi, and a big bottle of Noguchi saké, one of the best in Ishikawa.

As it became abundantly clear that we had way too much food, phone calls were made and new guests showed up. Shōji Izukura, a soba chef and potter, arrived with wasabi greens pickled in creamy saké kasu, sweetened with mirin, and balanced with salt to counter the sinus-stinging bite of the stalks. Kuniharu Murai—

carpenter and part owner of a vegetarian café—arrived with an enormous bottle of another Ishikawa saké and told stories of catching river fish and chasing uribō (baby boars) as a boy.

How do you translate "satoyama"? Michiba's son, a medical student, asked me. It's something I've been thinking about, but in America we don't really have the concept: land is either wild or cultivated. Satoyama is village forest used lightly for food and industry, partly wild, but cared for and maintained. The word "stewardship" comes to mind, but satoyama isn't an activity, it's a kind of place. Satoyama is memorialized in folk songs and has recently become a buzzword for sustainable living—looking to (and perhaps romanticizing) the past to imagine a better future.

Nishiyama Sensei has been telling me about the pine trees on the coast. I helped him plant seedlings on the grassy hillside above Hashidate port, where there used to be a pine forest. That kind of coastal forest is critical for mitigating the impact of a tsunami or powerful typhoon. Until about fifty years ago, people went into the pines regularly to collect needles for kindling. Clearing the needles made the forest floor hospitable to pine seedlings and matsutake mushrooms. Growing together with the tree roots, the matsutake strengthened the pines' resistance to pests and parasites.

But hardly anyone was in the woods to notice when the trees started to die. They were busy modernizing their lives when a microscopic foreign parasite—the pine wood nematode—was introduced by imported lumber. The native pine sawyer beetle carries the parasite from tree to tree. The beetle gnaws at twigs, making an entry point for nematodes. Inside the tree, nematodes inhibit sap production, making a welcoming home for beetle larvae. Without matsutake growing nearby to fortify them, the defenseless pines are overwhelmed. The hunters at Katano Duck Pond mentioned it too; *there used to be more pine trees*.

Our glorious satoyama lunch went on until it was nearly dinnertime. *People in Tōkyō pay a fortune for food like this, but it's so much more delicious when you harvest and cook it yourself!* exclaimed Ai-chan, delighted for us and sad for those poor city people. For me, it was a dream fulfilled, to make such a marvelous meal from wild food. Still, I longed to go into the okuyama.

Toward the end of Golden Week, I went to visit Nimaida in Ōzuchi (the village where only he lives year-round and makes charcoal). Already the tender buds we'd picked for our sansai lunch were opening into broad foliage, their green stems hardening into twigs. But there were new things to harvest.

Nimaida and his brother had hiked into the okuyama before dawn, with the kinds of packs you'd take for multiday trekking, and come back with them full of zenmai. They were in the process of cleaning, boiling, and sun drying nests of the royal fern fronds, to sell to Tōkyō for an exorbitant price.

I asked if I could go with him next time. *It's too dangerous*, he said. *It's practically a cliff*. One guy rolled down the mountain last year, he said (but the guy did survive). *And there are bears*. Nimaida didn't want me to get hurt.

It was Shikijiya (the diving instructor) and Izukura (the soba chef) who finally took me into the okuyama. I had no idea where we were going or what to expect, only that we would pick udo (and I didn't know what udo was). We'd already been driving up-hill for miles when we pulled in to a small gravel lot.

They asked if I had water and a knife. Nobody had told me to bring anything, but I had both. I wore a pair of flexible hunter-green rubber boots (the preferred hiking footwear around Kaga) over my jeans and carried rubberized work gloves. The little bear bell attached to my backpack jingled as I followed them up a gravel path that reminded me of the logging roads in my hometown. They pointed to a verdant peak and said, *That's where we're going.* It took us fifteen or twenty minutes of ambling up the road to reach its base.

There was no trail, only a rocky streambed that cut through the low saplings. If the incline were any steeper, it would have been a cliff. Shikijiya led the way, and Izukura followed behind me, for safety. (I thought this was sweet, but I was certain if I were to slip and roll down the hill, I'd only take him with me.) I placed my feet carefully, testing each foothold before I put my weight on it. In the steepest spots Shikijiya pulled himself up by grasping the base of ferns and itadori (knotweed, *Fallopia japonica*). I held on to the plants too, but I'd only let them bear my weight as a last resort, I thought.

Sometimes, a rock loosened by our footsteps rolled down, tum-bling and tumbling until we couldn't hear it anymore. *It's not dan-gerous if you pay attention*, I told myself. But if you lost focus, a careless step could be deadly. *What made them think I could do this kind of thing?* I wondered. If I couldn't, I would have ruined their trip.

Shikijiya spotted the first few small udo and showed me how to dig the dirt away from the base of the stalk and cut the white tender part below the soil. At first, I identified the plants by checking off a list in my head: pointy seven-fingered leaves unfurling, spiny fuzz protecting the thick stem (there's a smooth-stemmed look-alike they called devil udo). But after a little while I scanned the landscape, and the recognition was instant, wordless. It was addictive.

We spread out in three directions—it was pointless to all scour the same area and easy to see each other over the low vegetation. I spotted a clump off to the left of the stream, and when I got there, I saw at least a dozen fat stalks to harvest. I sat on a ledge to dig away the soil and cut above the roots. From my perch, I could see a sweeping view of the valley far below, a cluster of tile roofs beyond a river, and that ever-present backdrop of dark triangular evergreens. The hill I sat on was spring green, and the sky was picture-perfect blue. I thought to myself, *This is one of the best days of my life.*

My backpack became heavy with udo. It changed my center of balance, and climbing was harder. As long as we were going up, I was fine, but I dreaded the descent. What if my fear of heights kicked in? I remember as a kid bouldering halfway up the big rock summit of Mount Si, then looking down and becoming paralyzed with fear (and humiliated that I was too scared to reach the top).

Izukura called from the summit, and Shikijiya and I climbed across to meet him. I was relieved to find a trail there. We paused to sip water and admire the view. We followed the path along the ridge but then made a wide U-turn and went down a different but equally steep hill. There was more udo, but I could fit only a few choice stalks in my full pack. I spotted the most plump and tender stalks I'd seen yet, across a dry, eroding streambed. I wanted them desperately, but I couldn't see a way to pick them while keeping my footing. *So this is how people die picking sansai*, I thought.

Moments later, Izukura slipped and rolled three times before a stand of saplings stopped his momentum. He stood up and brushed himself off. I followed Shikijiya, who paused occasionally to plot his course by the growth of strong itadori and saplings we could grip for support, like safety ropes.

We made it down to a river and scrambled along the boulders on its banks (I pulled two nice big wasabi roots along the way) until we reached the road we'd started on. Finally on steady ground, I realized every muscle in my body was tired. My knees trembled slightly as we ambled back to the car, stopping to dig up a rare tsuru-ninjin (*Codonopsis lanceolata*), a bellflower root resembling ginseng, and to admire plumes of white wildflowers growing between rocks.

Later that week, Michiba served the udo, like herbaceous asparagus, for guests from Tōkyō. She peeled the stems and soaked them in acidulated water, then sliced them thinly and plated them with hotaru-ika (firefly squid) and sweet vinegared miso. Meanwhile, Shikijiya battered and fried the tops.

I had fulfilled another dream, to go into the okuyama with mountain meijin. Later, I looked up the scientific name for udo (*Aralia cordata*) and was surprised to realize those asparagus-like shoots would grow into a plant I recognized from Pacific Northwest gardens: a lush shrub with green flower balls that look like a space-age 1950s textile. I learned that it was in the same family as the other trees I'd been eating, tara-no-me and koshiabura—and American sarsaparilla.

Sansai were becoming part of my regular pantry. I went again with Shikijiya to pick udo in a steep valley above Ōzuchi (that time, it was pouring rain), and my neighbor gave me her recipe for su-miso-ae, thin slices of raw udo marinated in sweetened vinegar with a little miso.

With Miyashita and Nishiyama Sensei, I collected salmon-pink azalea flowers that I macerated into drinking vinegar and sanshō pepper (actually a tiny citrus) that I dried for making chili oil.

On my own, I picked assortments of leaves for tempura and ohitashi—blanched greens with cold dashi and soy sauce—careful not to eat too much of any one thing (wild plants may be richer in nutrients but also haven't had the toxins bred out). As summer approached, the season for tender greens was winding down, but mulberries and wineberries promised to ripen soon, followed by mube and akebi fruits, tree nuts in fall, and finally, as winter approached, myriad mushrooms. Nishiyama Sensei teaches me new things every time the season changes.

I'm a long way still from being a mountain meijin, but I'm filling in my own mental map of the edible plants in Yamanaka. I know I can gather enough violets on the way to Kazetani to make deep purple syrup and sparkly candy, and that the easiest place to collect fuki is on my running route (I saw katakuri there too). I remember the cluster of tara-no-me up past Sakura's boar traps where I can pick buds for tempura. I can find tsuru-ninjin by the skunky smell of its leaves. And I came across a black walnut tree on the bike path, where I'll go to pick the unripe green nuts for liqueur.

THE LAST WEEKEND of May, I went with my two hunter friends, Kawamoto and Sakura, to help with the annual release of baby river trout called iwana. Dams have disrupted their natural spawning cycle. We'd let the baby iwana swim off, then spend the rest of the day catching mature fish and collecting sansai for a dinner prepared for us by a chef that night.

Early on a Sunday morning, big plastic bags of lively little fish were distributed to the two dozen men, plus me and Sakura. We split into small groups to go to different rivers and drove deep into the okuyama. On foot we passed a shrine gate at the mountain entrance, then veered immediately off trail, following the Dainichi River, making our way along its steep bank. The bags of baby fish sloshed in our backpacks. As underbrush whipped my face, I recognized kuromoji (*Lindera umbellata*); its fragrant twigs are used to make utensils for eating sweets.

We released our iwana babies into the river, then hiked upstream and started fishing. I had never fished in my life, and iwana are tricky. If they see your shadow, they'll hide, and once you've caught one, you have to move upstream to another spot. Kawamoto was a patient teacher, coaching me as I struggled to get the hang of fishing with a worm hooked to a telescoping pole. I seemed as if I'd never do it right—until I caught one, then another and another until I had five, including one of the biggest fish anyone caught that day.

Up high in the mountains, we came across udo and warabi. After a few hours of fishing, we ate our lunch sitting on huge slabs of rock below Nunoga Falls. I cooled my feet in the river while watching the water cascade down a cliff.

Rather than head back the way we came, we climbed up Mount Dainichi, Kaga's highest peak, only reaching an actual trail for the descent. On the ascent we traversed ravines more challenging than the hillsides where I'd picked udo with Shikijiya, and I was grateful it wasn't my first experience with that kind of climbing.

As we bushwhacked toward the summit, it was as if we climbed backward in time. There were koshiabura buds, still tender enough for tempura, and huge patches of katakuri flowers in full bloom, like early spring. But what was different now from a few months ago: I knew the plants with certainty. I felt at home.

Nandemo Tempura

TIME: *1 hour*
Makes about 50 pieces

Nandemo means "anything" or "whatever." Nine out of ten times, when I ask how to cook a wild vegetable, the answer is tempura. (The tenth time it's ohitashi: blanched and chilled in lightly seasoned dashi.) Tempura chefs make magic with flour, water, and egg—frying one piece of tempura at a time and serving it across the counter to be eaten immediately, while perfectly crisp.

For home cooks, it can be hard to get good results. In Japan, tempura mix (like pancake mix) is widely available and nearly foolproof. If you live near a Japanese grocery store, you could certainly go that route. Mie Michiba and Aiko Satō (Ai-chan), who both taught me a lot about sansai cooking, helped develop this recipe that nonprofessionals can execute successfully, with ingredients you can find anywhere. A lot of fuss is made about the best kind of oil for tempura, but more important than variety is freshness: open a new bottle just before cooking.

50 foraged leaf clusters, such as fuki-no-tō, koshiabura, tara-no-me, or yomogi; or vegetable pieces, such as 1 cm (½-inch) thick sweet potato slices, whole green beans, or mushrooms

50 grams (½ cup) cake flour, chilled

50 grams (⅓ cup) potato starch or cornstarch, chilled

1 can or small bottle seltzer, chilled and unopened

Cooking oil, such as canola/rapeseed, soybean, or rice bran

Toasted sesame oil (optional)

Flaky sea salt, for serving

Note: A skimmer (like a mesh ladle) is ideal for scooping loose bits of batter out of the oil, and long cooking chopsticks, called saibashi, are perfect for picking up hot tempura. Cheap ones from a dollar store or Chinese grocery are just fine.

1. Well ahead of when you start cooking, rinse the leaves or other vegetables, and dry them completely (spin in a salad spinner, or place in front of an electric fan). There should be no moisture on their surface. Keep them in the refrigerator until ready to fry.

2. Just before you heat the oil, mix together the flour and starch in a bowl or zip-top bag and place in the freezer. Place an unopened bottle or can of seltzer in the freezer. Chill a small mixing bowl in the freezer.

3. In a small aluminum or stainless steel pot, heat a few inches of cooking oil over medium high. For every cup of cooking oil, add about a teaspoon of sesame oil (if using) for flavor. The sweet spot for frying is 170°–180°C (330°–350°F), but you don't need a thermometer: you can use the batter to test (see step 5).

4. Take the chilled bowl out of the freezer. Make the batter in small batches as you go, using equal parts (by volume) flour mixture and seltzer. Combine about ¼ cup of each in a bowl. If it's too thick or too thin, add a little more flour or seltzer, but avoid overmixing. Mix it with chopsticks or a whisk just three or four times—seriously. The batter will be lumpy with pockets of flour. If you lift some batter with your finger or a spoon, it should drip into the bowl—not fall in clumps—but be slightly thicker than cream.

5. Drip a drop of batter into the hot oil. It should take 1 second to float to the top—it's not quite instant, there's the slightest pause before it quickly floats up. Dip a leaf cluster or vegetable piece in

the batter, let the excess drip off, and drop it into the oil. Cook for about 2 minutes, until it's crisp and barely blond; the sound of the oil bubbling will soften when it's ready. If the tempura is too brown, lower the temperature; if it's soft and oily, raise it.

6. Fry tempura a few pieces at a time so the oil temperature doesn't fluctuate too much. Set the cooked pieces on paper towels or a wire rack. Between each batch, scoop out the little bits of fried batter, called tenkasu, with a skimmer; save them to use as a crispy topping for udon noodles or salad.

7. Continue making batter in the same bowl (no need to wash) in small batches, as needed. Dredge heavier vegetables, such as sweet potato, in a little extra flour before dipping in the batter, and fry for about 3 minutes.

8. Serve tempura hot, with sea salt for sprinkling.

Cultivation

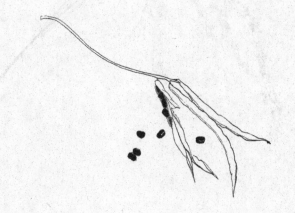

Thirteen

Eighty-eight Troubles

Tanbo is the Japanese word for rice paddy. Ishikawa prefecture is known for its terraced fields—stairs of tanbo climbing dark volcanic mountains or illuminated on bluffs above the sea. They shift from the brown of late winter soil, to the blue of water reflecting the May sky, to the green of summer as the rice grass fills out, to the gold of ripe grains in late August and September.

When samurai lords ruled Kaga, rice was currency, and they were rich because of their rice. The Kaga Domain was second in wealth only to the Tokugawa shogunate, the military government of Japan. Rice was the medium of tax payment and, since prehistoric times, an offering to the spirits.

In Japan, rice is the main dish of a meal—not the fish, or soup, or vegetables. Think of it this way: If you eat steak and potatoes, there might be more potatoes on your plate than steak, but the steak is the main event. If you're eating a Japanese meal, the rice is the important thing. It isn't the primary food people consume in terms of volume—it never was for all Japanese—but it is the most spiritually and socially significant. Noodles and bread, buckwheat and millet are part of the Japanese diet, but nearly every cereal besides rice is called zakkoku, a miscellaneous grain.

I remember an awkward dinner with my mother and my husband in Brooklyn. Hiroshi and I had lived together more than five years, but we were newly married. Our table was set with small bowls of rice. My mother still had a little in her bowl when she rested her chopsticks to talk. Hiroshi, who is often reserved and always kind to my parents, launched into a passioned speech about the importance of finishing every grain. *The rice farmer*, he'd been told throughout his childhood in Tōkyō, *goes through eighty-eight troubles to grow it*.

I could see that my mother felt humiliated. She takes care to be polite and culturally sensitive, but she didn't like being lectured to. But then, Hiroshi is the only person in his family to have left Tōkyō—much less Japan—so my parents (by sheer proximity) have more influence on our lives. He was asserting that this is *his* home. My loyalty was pulled in two directions, and I still squirm when I think about it.

In Yamanaka, I've often been asked, *If Japan is a rice culture, then what is America—a bread culture?* I don't know how to answer: the meals I grew up with had potatoes, or pasta, or rice, or bread to sop up sauce and fill our stomachs, but none of these starches had anything to do with my identity as far as I understood. I was always encouraged to join the "clean plate club," but the intensity of Japanese manners around rice feels stronger.

I know not to serve a rice bowl full—that's tacky—but to mound a little rice, never packed down, no more than two-thirds up the bowl. I know to place rice on the left side of a table setting. And I know, of course, to eat every last grain in front of me, even if I'm full. But I don't really know why it matters, other than to be polite. I thought if I could participate in growing it, maybe something would be revealed that no amount of reading—deeply researched books like *Rice as Self* and *Rice and Agricultural Policies in Japan*—had made clear.

IN THE VALLEYS, planting begins at the beginning of May during Golden Week—a long holiday when prodigal children return from the cities to help in the fields. I've watched farmers load trays of seedlings into planting machines that drive through the fields plugging clumps of rice grass into the mud at regular intervals in perfectly straight lines. Industrialization has cut out a few of the eighty-eight troubles that Japanese parents speak of—that left the backs of some farm women permanently hunched from leaning over to plant seedlings and pull weeds.

But in Yamanaka's Higashitani, the four small villages in its eastern mountains, it would be impractical or impossible to navigate a machine into the irregular-shaped terraced fields. In these villages a younger generation—who came of age aware of the damaging side effects of agricultural chemicals on people and ecosystems—is growing rice the old-fashioned way. Higashitani includes Aratani, Imadachi, Ōzuchi, and, farthest into the mountains, Suginomizu, where a man named Hayashi has given me a tiny tanbo to tend.

Up here it's not until mid-May that the nights are warm enough for our seedlings to thrive. In April, we're still preparing the field.

Hayashi picks me up in his kei truck. He's slim and tall, so his short-brimmed straw hat nearly brushes the ceiling. He leans forward as he drives up into the mountains, as if to get there faster. During the twenty-minute drive from town, the two cell phones he carries ring frequently. He's always counting off lists to himself or pointing at something that needs to get done.

Hayashi is a handyman, a boxing teacher, and an educator who runs a share house in Yamanaka for troubled young men and a free school for high school dropouts. One of his boxing students tells me that Hayashi is like a yakuza, a gangster—*not actually yakuza, but like yakuza*. He seems kind and friendly to me, so I asked another friend, what does that mean? *It means he's different; he follows his own path.*

No one lives in Suginomizu anymore, but there are two seasonal restaurants that draw sightseers on summer weekends. Hayashi has a house there, but the winters were too lonely for his daughter and wife, so they moved back to town. He uses the house—and its covered pavilion and work shed (where I butchered my first boar with Sakura)—for outdoor camps to help children experience nature. He's used the place for fasting and for yamabushi training, a spiritual practice of wilderness survival.

The field in Suginomizu is framed by sugi and keyaki trees, the native elms prized by woodturners. Hayashi shares it with the Shimoshita family, who have an eight-generation history in the village. Together, they revived the fallow land about twenty years ago. Hayashi's area consists of five tanbo: two big enough to grow all the rice his family eats in a year, and three smaller ones. I asked to help with his field work, but he wants me to have my own tanbo; that's the best way to learn. Not sure how much work I'm getting myself into, I choose the smallest one, a neat little rectangle (about the size of three queen beds).

We're going to grow Koshihikari, a relatively new strain of *japonica* developed not far from here in 1956 to be disease-resistant and well suited to cold climates. Its yield isn't as high as more recent cultivars, but it's the most popular rice in Japan because of its crisp, faintly sweet flavor and mochi-mochi texture—chewy but yielding, almost bouncy. Hayashi tried many varieties before finding that Koshihikari is best suited to this field. He tells me, *Nae-zukuri han shō*—growing seedlings is half the work.

THERE IS A Styrofoam cooler full of rice seeds floating in my bathtub. Hayashi will buy his seedlings from a farmer friend this year, but I want to learn how to grow them from seed, so I'm sprouting them with my friend Sakai, for his tanbo. Earlier in the day we put an egg in a bucket of salt water to test the water's density. When it had enough salt, the egg bobbed near the surface with an area the size of a ¥500 coin exposed above the water. We poured rice seeds into the bucket: the viable ones sank. We discarded the rotten, insect-eaten, and underdeveloped seeds that floated to the top. The good ones we rinsed off and packed into small Styrofoam coolers.

The warmth of the bath signals the seeds to germinate. In the morning, when I pick up a grain of rice, I can see a tiny sprout— not more than a millimeter—pushing out of the tip.

I meet Sakai and Sakura (the boar hunter) at Michiba's garage to fill seed trays. We scatter the seeds on BB-size pellets of soil and use a pheasant feather we found in the woods to spread the seeds out evenly. Then we cover them with more pelleted soil. Sakura soaks the full trays with a hose, the mist making rainbows in the sunlight.

I'm responsible for six trays, wrapped in garden cloth and stacked into two plastic bins. My job is to keep them at about 20 degrees Celsius (68 degrees Fahrenheit)—this isn't so hard, because I am at home writing most days, and below that is too cold for me too.

Every day, I rotate the stack, so one tray doesn't dry out more than another. Sakai tells me not to worry about the fluffy white mold that's growing on the soil, but I do. When the sprouts begin to make a second leaf, I line them up in front of the sliding glass doors to my balcony, to expose them to light. When a third leaf begins to grow, the seedlings are strong enough and the weather is warm enough to move them outside, to Sakai's tanbo.

Hayashi takes me to a hoop house in the plains northeast of Yamanaka to get seedlings for Suginomizu. We fill the bed of his little truck with trays of Koshihikari, soft and bright as Easter grass (the real thing, not the plastic stuff). In Suginomizu, we set the trays in the water to harden for a few weeks while we prepare the fields.

There are tadpoles and masses of frog eggs in the mud, and I carefully move them to the edges of the tanbo so they won't be disturbed. I scrape up the roots of weeds with a hoe, shake off the mud, and toss them onto the aze, the berms dividing flooded paddies. Uguisu sing *hō-ho-KE-kyo*. Wild wisteria blooms, entwined in the branches of the trees that are beginning to leaf.

THE NEXT TIME we come to the tanbo, Hayashi asks me if I can use a weed whacker to trim the grasses and wild herbs already growing tall on the aze. I say yes (I'm sure I can), but it's been a long time (this part is a lie; I have never used one). He gives me a quick demonstration, and off I go. I'm nervous at first—especially because I don't have eye protection—but then it's fun. Wild mint and mugwort perfume the air as I chop them short.

Hayashi says he doesn't mind the weeds; *they have their own reasons for growing*. But he'll keep them trimmed all summer to make nice scenery for the people passing by. It's a classic sight, like his parents' tanbo, where he learned to grow rice. But the way he works is informed by Yoshikazu Kawaguchi, a famous practitioner of natural farming whom Hayashi studied with. *Kawaguchi teaches you how to live rather than how to farm: We are made to live along with nature. We only assist; crops naturally grow on their own. Weeds and insects are not our enemy; everything exists for harmony.*

We follow the aqueduct up the road to where it meets the river. Hayashi turns a big orange crank to open a floodgate, letting more water flow down to the field. Since their advent, wet rice fields have been part of emergency infrastructure. They hold water that can keep crops and livestock alive in case of drought. During storms, they absorb overflow from rivers and ponds to avert flooding.

It's not that rice needs to grow in water; it's that it can—better than most of the weeds that compete with it. The farmer in the plains of Kaga who grows rice for Kayōtei has ducks in his tanbo. They eat aquatic plants and bugs, and their puddling makes the water cloudy, so weeds can't get enough sun to grow.

It takes a few days for the water to reach Hayashi's farthest tanbo. If some rice is in shallow water and some in deep, it won't mature at the same rate, so we grade the soil. My tanbo is built by Kawaguchi's method: there's a knee-deep moat around the edge, but the water is shallow in the middle, where the rice will grow.

With a hoe, we push the mud around until the water sits level across the surface. Each time I step, green and brown frogs leap into the deeper water. They sing to each other from their hiding places in the weeds.

The mud is heavy and the work is tiring, but when I finish my tanbo, I help with Hayashi's. He picks up a hawk's flight feather that has fallen in the field and gives it to me. I admire it, and then tuck it into my straw hat.

Another day we push the mud up onto the berms and press it flat with the back side of a hoe. This is called aze-nuri, berm painting. It's strenuous labor, but the smoothly painted aze are pleasing to look at. As it dries and hardens, the mud creates a barrier to keep the water in.

WHEN THE KEYAKI TREES unfurl their serrated lanceolate leaves, it's time to plant rice. It's a glorious late spring day—almost hot. The frog eggs have hatched into tadpoles, and some have already grown up. Girls run around catching the green-and-brown-striped tonosama frogs and red-bellied newts. A small boy clings to his parents. Hayashi's friends have come with their children to help. He's brought his whole family and some of the young men from the share house he runs. They are hikikomori, shut-ins, a growing affliction in Japan. It's a broad term that probably encompasses all kinds of struggles with mental health and emotional development.

He used to mentor "yankees" (the Japanese word for juvenile delinquents) who showed up at his boxing classes. But these days, he says, there aren't those kinds of troubled kids anymore. Society has changed and so has its problems. Now he supports young people who suffer from anxiety, depression, and lack of social skills and confidence. Hayashi says he's seen working in the rice fields cure them. He tells me, *It's important for people to connect and coexist not only with other human beings but with nature. The tanbo makes a bridge between nature and humans.*

We begin by marking where to put each plant. In Ōzuchi and Imadachi, they roll a long wooden scaffold (called a taue jōgi) across the tanbo to imprint a row of rectangles into the mud. Here in Suginomizu, we run strings from one end of the field to the other to define the rows, then plant the seedlings along the strings at twenty-centimeter intervals—about thumb tip to pinkie tip if you stretch your hand wide.

You grab a clump of seedlings and bend down to push two or three into the mud so the leaves stand up straight. The mud sucks at your boots as you try to lift your feet effortfully to plant the next one, and the next one, all the way to the end of the row. If you're not careful, the mud will pull your boots right off!

Grandma (Hayashi's mother-in-law) gets stuck and plays it up for laughs, reaching for the little boy and yelling, *Help me! Help me!* A few rows over, I work diligently to space the seedlings evenly, while the young men speed along hastily and unevenly. With each step forward in the mud to plant another seedling, Hayashi grunts, *Yoisho* (like an *umph* of self-encouragement). The little boy follows along, imitating, *Yoisho!*

When we take a break for sweets and tea, Grandma picks edible weeds from the aze and tells me how to cook them. Peel the fuki (butterbur) stems, snap them into short pieces, blanch and stir-fry them, and then season with a little soy sauce and sugar. The seri she recommends blanching and then tossing with ground sesame seeds, goma-ae. *This generation isn't interested in sansai*, she tells me. But I am, and I take home bags of fuki and seri to cook as she instructed.

I plant my tiny tanbo last, after lunch, pulling up weeds as I go. I take pleasure in making the rows neat and uniform. Later Hayashi will tell me, *Crops grow up in the same condition as your state of mind; if you cultivate crops with respect, they will grow properly.*

Hayashi and I spend a few more days planting under the hot sun, until my lower back aches and my hands are tanned. I see a big snake in the grass and hawks overhead. When we're done, we let a few more inches of water into the field. The color changes from brown to blue, reflecting the sky, with slender flags of green waving in the breeze.

RAINY SEASON COMES as it's time to start weeding the fields every few weeks. Moriao frog nests ornament the keyaki trees, like foamy spitballs the size of a grapefruit. I wear rain gear head to toe and a hat with a mesh screen to shield my face from biting flies and mosquitoes. Crouched in the tanbo, I pull up aquatic plants and strong grasses. The whole tanbo is green, and it's hard to distinguish rice from weeds, but the grid we planted on helps: I can work my way toward where I expect the rice to be and then carefully separate its bright green leaves from the other plants around it.

Each time, I weed a little of Hayashi's tanbo too; when I'm not there, he weeds mine. My friend Hiroko sometimes comes to help. She grew up in the countryside but has never cultivated rice. She wants to touch the soil and connect to her heritage.

After the rain, there are swallowtail butterflies. Grasshoppers as big as my index finger, called inago, leap between the grasses.

People used to pick them off by hand—so they wouldn't damage the rice—then simmer them in soy sauce and sugar to eat. Rice plants feed all kinds of bugs: leafhoppers and their nymphs that turn the stalks dry and yellow, stem borers, and small moths that eat holes in new leaves. But without pesticides, spiders and frogs also thrive in the tanbo, doing pest control for us.

Hayashi says, *If you have problems with insects, you might be giving too much fertilizer; you simply need to give less fertilizer.* The only fertilizer in our tanbo is the straw and hulls from last year's crop, and the minerals brought in by the mountain water. *To cure a disease, you have to take care of the cause of the sickness, not the sickness itself,* he says.

By late summer, the rice has grown into thick knee-high clumps. It flowers and goes to seed. The seeds grow plump, until they are so heavy they bow over. It's a shape I know from motifs carved and painted on lacquerware, dyed into fabric, and printed on packaging.

Wild boars test the fences around the tanbo, looking for weak spots. If they break through, they'll devour the rice, then wallow in the cool mud, crushing what remains. So far, the fence is holding, but I wonder if I'll get to eat the rice I've been working for since early spring.

THE GRAINS TURN GOLDEN; when the leaves turn golden too, it will be time to harvest. In Imadachi, Sakai shows a group of friends how to build a hasa, a rack for drying rice in the field. It has to be taken down each winter and built again each fall—otherwise it would be battered and broken by strong wind and heavy snow. We uncover a pile of chestnut-wood posts and thick bamboo poles.

Stakes mark the holes for the three vertical posts. We dig the holes deeper. In each, we plant a tall chestnut post. One person holds it vertical, while another tamps down the dirt and piles up big rocks for support.

We lash bamboo poles across the posts at shoulder height. Sakai teaches us a good knot for the heavy rope. We climb up a ladder onto the bamboo poles, one person at each of the three posts. We hoist up another set, secure them with rope, and then climb up onto those.

The view from up here is glorious: I look out at the terraced paddies climbing toward the forest and the blue sky. We lash the third and final horizontal pole into place and take pictures before we climb down.

In Suginomizu, birds have started nibbling the grains. Hayashi strings strips of silver Mylar ribbon all around to deter them. The keyaki leaves are kissed with bronze, and the days are cool enough to wear a jacket again. Red dragonflies hover over the rice.

The water needs to be drained from the field a few days before harvest. Too soon, and the weeds will grow back. Too late, and the mud will be viscid and hard to walk on.

The weather has turned warm and sticky again, the day we begin reaping. Closer to the water source—where my tanbo is—the bowed panicles have turned golden, but the leaves are still deep green. We begin with the most yellowed corner of Hayashi's ripest tanbo. In each place that we pushed two or three seedlings into the mud, there are now two dozen stalks; each stalk has fruited and ripened into over a hundred grains of rice. We grip each bunch of stalks and sever them with a sickle. Three young men make big piles, then grab handfuls of rice stalks and tie them together with pieces of rice straw saved from last year's harvest.

I follow the method an uncle in Imadachi taught me—he said this is the cool
way, because of its efficiency. As you cut
them, you place three handfuls on the
ground, crisscrossed. You tie the three
handfuls together in as few movements as
possible. You split the two outside legs
one direction and the middle leg the other
to hang them over the hasa, alternating
directions so the bundles interlock.

Near my tiny tanbo, I notice signs that
a boar has been rooting around. Hayashi
says he's patched the fence. His words are reassuring, but his face
looks concerned.

A few days later, the leaves of my rice are barely green gold, but
a typhoon is coming; it's best to cut the stalks before the heavy
rain pummels them into the mud. It's overcast but bright, and I'm
wearing my straw hat with the hawk's feather still tucked into it.
Doves eat gleanings in Hayashi's tanbo. The keyaki trees have
turned completely bronze.

Hayashi's mutts—Marvel, a Japanese hunting dog mix, and Lola,
a short-haired golden dog with a bum leg—sniff around at fresh
holes dug by boars. One must have gotten through the patched fence.

Hayashi helps me set up a small metal hasa. I cut handfuls
of rice and line them up on the ground, crisscrossing their stems,
practicing my efficiency as I tie each one. I like the scene of the
bundles all lined up on the aze.

I hoist five or six bundles onto each shoulder and carry them like
a real farmer. Marvel the hunting dog lolls under the hasa while I

fill it. My rice cascades down in uneven layers, reminding me of abstract designs on kimono silk. Within a day, the leaves will wilt. In a few weeks the grains will be dry enough to thresh.

The senior Shimoshita, who with his adult son works a tanbo in the same field, stops by to chat. *There's nothing better than rice dried in the sun*, he says. I tie a piece of the silver ribbon around the hasa to hold the bundles in place and scare away birds. I'm still worried about boars.

Dusk will fall by five, so we start gathering our tools and hanging the last bundles by half past four. Marvel runs off toward the woods, barking excitedly. We hear squealing. *He's got a boar*, says Hayashi. Lola, the golden dog with a bum leg, runs to help, and the squealing gets louder. I feel sorry for the boar, but glad for my rice.

The dogs flush a young boar into the field, and we go over to see. They have pinned it—it's not a baby but maybe a yearling— their same size. They tear at it for what feels like a very, very long time. I understand, in that moment, why farmers keep guns. I'd like to end that boar's suffering as quickly as possible.

We load up the truck, and the dogs trot over gleefully. Lola's yellow maw is stained with blood. They obediently hop into the bed of the pickup, and we drive away. On the way down toward town we see another boar—big as a black bear—run alongside the road and crash into the woods. The dogs bark madly.

WHILE THE RICE dries on the hasa, two or three typhoons pass. One is strong enough to knock down the bundles and tear off straws of rice, which Hayashi picks up and returns to the hasa. Every time the bundles are nearly dry enough to thresh, another typhoon soaks them, so they hang on the hasa for almost a month.

Finally, there's a sunny weekend. Hayashi picks me up in his wife's van, with Grandma and a gentle young man from the share house. We head up the narrow winding road into the mountain, past the Wagatani and Kutani dams, toward our rice fields. I gaze out the window.

A fox! It's red like one from a storybook, trotting along the side of the road. We pull over to look, and it stares back at us. Grandma rolls down the window and tosses a senbei (rice cracker) to the fox, who picks it up gingerly with its slender snout and crunches it. We watch for a while before continuing on our way to Suginomizu.

Hayashi has brought the rice to the covered pavilion at his old house, where we'll thresh, winnow, and mill it. The threshing machine is a spinning barrel barbed with triangles of heavy-gauge wire. As the barrel spins, the barbs catch the grains and knock them from the stalks. It's powered by a foot pedal and tented under a tarp to catch the flying grains. The grains rain down on another tarp spread over the ground.

The young man passes me one bundle at a time. I pump the foot pedal fast and hold the bundle firmly, touching down first the tip. The grains fly off, rattling against the tarp, and the stalks buzz against the barrel. I flip the bundle back and forth to get off every grain, working toward the base of the stalks. Before throwing the straw on a heap, I check it to make sure I didn't miss any rice.

Pumping the pedal makes your foot ache and tires your leg, so we take turns. An hour or so passes, until all the bundles from my tiny tanbo are stripped and separated into a pile of rice and a pile of straw.

We scoop up the rice, still covered in papery golden hulls, into a big plastic basin. I scramble around gathering stray grains. I worked hard for each and every one and can't stand to waste them.

We pick out and discard pieces of straw that have broken off along with the grains. Some of the grains are still connected to bits of stem, and we strip those by hand. Grandma has been sorting through Hayashi's rice all morning; the young man and I work on mine.

Next, we put the rice through a hand-cranked wooden winnowing machine. One person pours it through a funnel on top and pulls a tab to open the chute. The other cranks a wheel to generate wind. The wind blows dust, chaff, and tiny bits of straw out an exhaust vent. The good, heavy rice falls down one chute into a bucket, while the lighter (small and broken) pieces fall down a second chute.

It's raining lightly, and suddenly the sun comes through the rain, glittering off rice dust. *It's a fox wedding!* In Japanese folklore, sun during a rain shower means foxes (tricksters) are having a wedding.

A WEEK PASSES. The morning I hull my rice, dew glistens like a million Swarovski crystals on fluffy plumes of susuki grass and spiderwebs shivering between their stems. Steam rises through nearly horizontal beams of autumn sun. The sky is azure with a few still tufts of clouds.

Hayashi asks me if I want to mill my rice brown or white. I think for a moment before answering: brown. He says that's a good idea: the water is very clean (so we don't need to worry about contaminants like arsenic), and it's better not to waste the flavor by milling off the bran. His response surprises me, because most peo-

ple here eat white rice, but he says he used to follow genmai
saishoku—a vegan macrobiotic diet that emphasizes eating brown
rice and unpeeled vegetables.

Hayashi does mill most of his rice white, to please his family,
by putting it through a machine that polishes it into perfect pearls
by tumbling it like gemstones. He saves the bran, called nuka.
Grandma will use some for making pickles, nuka-zuke. It's used
for boiling with bamboo shoots to neutralize their tannic taste,
and as livestock feed and bait for boar traps.

In a rare concession to convenience, we use a machine with a
motor, but the mechanics are nearly the same as hulling manually.
The rice drops through a funnel and out of sight. Inside the metal
casing, the grains drop between two wheels that crush the hull; a
fan blows the hulls into an empty rice bag that we've tied to the
exhaust vent. The rice pours out a chute on the other side: smooth
grains of pale genmai (brown rice) some still faintly green. It feels
good to put my hands in the cool grains, running my fingers
through the product of my labor.

My rice fills a five-kilo sack—the kind made of paper with a tab
at the top for tying it closed, kind of like a coffee bag. For me
alone, that's almost half a year of rice; for my husband, it would
last a month. I press the air out of the brown paper sack and roll
down the top. I tie the tabs so they line up neatly with the top of
the bag. I pick up my newborn rice, and I cradle it in my arms—it
has the heft of a big baby.

HAYASHI SETS ASIDE a few armfuls of straw for tying next year's
bundles. I take some for making New Year's decorations, called

shimenawa, and twisting into twine that I'll use for hanging persimmons to dry. In old times, making things out of rice straw—ropes, baskets, sandals called waraji, and even raincoats—was winter work to do sitting around the hearth.

Hayashi shows me how to use a guillotine to cut the rest of the rice straw into short pieces to return to the field as mulch. Farmers who use fertilizer don't do that, but it's the old way—and the new natural farming way.

In the tanbo we sprinkle the rice hulls and scatter the cut straw—to nourish the soil and slow the growth of weeds. The frogs—whose eggs and tadpoles I saw in early spring while preparing for planting and who were still here only a week before—have gone into hibernation. The keyaki trees have dropped more than half their bronze leaves. I pick up one flecked with red and yellow and put it in my pocket. I look out at the deep blue sky, green-black sugi, and dusty yellow tanbo one last time. Until next year, our eighty-eight troubles are finished.

WITH MY RICE I eat umeboshi that I made from ume gleaned near Sakai's tanbo; I eat wild duck, cooked by Kazu the hunter-chef; I cook miso soup with the radish greens from my garden. For a meal shared with Moriguchi the wagatabon maker, Jessica the urushi apprentice, and Raku, a student from the wood-turning school, I make stew from mushrooms I foraged with Shikijiya, one of the mountain meijin, and venison from Sakura the hunter—all of it served with my rice.

If someone wasted a single grain, it would break my heart. This rice evokes uguisu singing as I labored to level the field with a hoe, wild wisteria blooming the day I painted the berms with mud, warm summer rain wetting my hair as I stooped to pull weeds, red dragonflies hovering above the rice while I cut down the stalks, and the picturesque scene of bundles drying on a hasa in the field. No wonder they say there are many spirits in each grain.

Usually, when I wash rice, I'm lazy. If a few grains escape down the drain, I don't care; it's not caviar! But when I wash the rice I grew, I make sure not one grain escapes. I take pleasure in swishing cold water through the bowl and feeling the grains between my fingers. I rinse and rinse until the water runs clear.

I bring my rice back to Brooklyn and cook it in a donabe that my friend from the Tōkyō suburbs made, an unglazed white clay pot, burned black on the bottom from years of use. I decide the water level by laying my hand on top of the grains. I listen for the steam to start hissing out the small hole in the lid. I turn the heat to the lowest low flame, barely a flicker, for twenty minutes—I can smell the rice cooking—starchy, musty, almost nutty—then fire it to high and hold my head low to listen for the last bit of moisture to rumble to a boil. I cut the heat, and walk away for five minutes before opening the lid to fluff my rice. The grains are toothsome and glossy, and a perfect crust has formed at the bottom. We scoop it into small lacquerware bowls.

Bad rice tastes like nothing. It's mushy, or it's hard. Good rice is almost bouncy, each grain firm yet yielding. It has a fragrance of rice and tastes so good you want to eat bowl after bowl. Hiroshi and I eat it together, savoring every last grain.

Ume Onigiri

TIME: *30 minutes*
Makes *6–8 onigiri*

There's no better way to eat good rice than a simple onigiri, rice gently packed into a ball or triangle shape. Fillings can be anything you like—tuna and mayonnaise, katsuobushi (bonito flakes) moistened with soy sauce, pickled vegetables—or nothing at all. You can wrap it in nori, or roll it in toasted sesame seeds, but when your rice is fresh and fragrant, you need nothing more than a little salt. I like mine with homemade umeboshi (page 228).

> 2 cups Japanese rice (short- or medium-grain "sushi" rice)
> 1 teaspoon kosher salt or flaky sea salt
> 6–8 umeboshi

1. In a mesh strainer set inside a bowl, rinse the rice in several changes of cold water, until it runs almost clear. Drain the rice, shaking off excess water.
2. Cook the rice in a rice cooker according to the manufacturer's instructions (and skip to step 5) or on the stovetop as follows. Place the drained rice in a small heavy-bottomed saucepan or donabe (clay pot). Add enough water so that if you rest your hand on top of the rice, the water covers your fingers, about 2 cups. If you measure the water this way, over time you will figure out the perfect amount based on your own hand and your preference for soft or hard rice. New-crop rice in the fall requires less water than the drier rice available year-round.

3. Cover the pot with a tight-fitting lid. Place it over high heat, and bring to a boil. When steam is spitting out the edges of the lid, reduce the heat to the lowest possible level, and set a timer for 18 minutes.

4. When the timer goes off, turn the heat to high for 60 seconds, or until you can hear the remaining water sizzle. Remove from the heat, without opening the lid. Let stand for 5 minutes; then remove the lid and fluff the rice.

5. Prepare a small bowl of cool salt water for wetting your hands— about ½ cup water and 1 teaspoon kosher salt or flaky sea salt—it should be at least as salty as the sea. Remove the pits from the umeboshi. Scoop some of the rice onto a plate, so it cools just enough to touch.

6. Wet your hands with the salt water. Place a mound of rice in your nondominant hand (about ¼ cup), and use your dominant hand to make a small indentation for the filling. Place the pitted umeboshi in the indentation. Cover it with a little more rice (about 2 tablespoons).

7. Gently pack the rice with your hands, not too tightly, but enough so that it holds its shape. To make a triangle, cup each hand into a right angle and alternately interlock your hands around the rice. A ball is easier: simply curve your hands around the rice and press gently, as if making a snowball, rotate, and repeat until the ball holds together.

8. Wrap each onigiri individually in foil or plastic wrap to pack in a lunch box. Or space them out on a plate (so they don't stick together), and cover the plate with plastic wrap. Keep at cool room temperature for up to a day (salt preserves the rice; refrigeration would harden it).

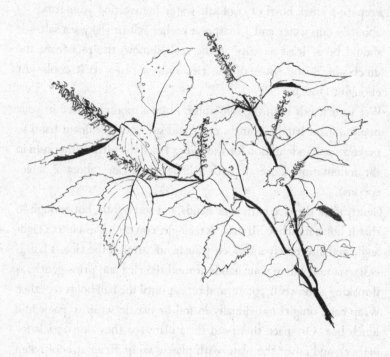

aka-jiso/red shiso

Fourteen

Totoro's Garden

Japan tells itself a story of exceptionalism and isolation, but its vegetables tell a different story. The beans I'm growing likely made their way from Africa to Asia about three thousand years ago. My sweet potatoes could be related to the ones Polynesians gathered from the American continent over a thousand years ago. Big white daikon radishes—which I eat pickled, boiled, grated, or dried—evolved from seeds brought along the Silk Road from the Mediterranean coast around the third century. Cucumbers, originally from the Himalayas, came to Japan via China in the sixth century but weren't widely cultivated until a millennium later. Purple-stem eggplant—one of Kaga's officially designated local vegetables—descends from seeds that arrived in Japan during the eighth century; their fruit was called Indian purple melon, denoting the plant's origin. Kabocha squash, ripening on vines that wind through the grass, appears to be named for Cambodia, where Portuguese sailors picked it up on the way to Japan in the sixteenth century. The hot peppers I'm growing to deter wild boars originated in the Americas and came with the Portuguese too (as did the idea of battering and frying vegetables: tempura). Tomatoes are here because of Dutch traders in the seventeenth century. Recently, exotic plants like basil and kale have taken root.

In suburbs and towns, vegetable gardens called hatake occupy spaces that would be paved over or planted with grass in America. It's not uncommon to see potatoes growing on a plot squeezed between an elementary school and a neighboring house, or onions on an awkward-shaped wedge at the edge of a rice paddy. Most are meant for sustenance, not sales. But even commercial enterprises are often cobbled together from several small plots. The mountainous geography of Honshu, Japan's main island, dictates patchwork agriculture. Only up north in Hokkaidō do farms near the size of those in Europe and America. In the 70-some percent of the country that is mountainous, you plant where you can.

The same summer I learned to grow rice, I made a hatake in a neglected field, beside a hundred-year-old farmhouse. The house, which has been empty for years, belongs to a friend of a friend who was more than happy to have me use the untended garden.

Miki-chan, my friend from tea lessons, calls it the Totoro House: it has a big weeping willow in front and fields and forest beyond. Even if the architecture is different, it has the feeling of the farmhouse full of magic in Miyazaki's animated film about two little girls moving to the country and befriending a big fluffy gray creature, named Totoro, in a hidden glen. When it rains, I half expect Totoro to come waddling out of the trees carrying a giant fuki leaf as an umbrella. Until I watched spring unfurl around my hatake,

I had seen such verdant clear colors only in Miyazaki's tenderly painted backgrounds.

Behind the house, I waded through a field where the weeds had grown taller than me to visit the two active hatake at the edge of the woods. One is neatly fenced and bordered by flowers, tended meticulously by an older woman. The other is haphazard, unevenly kept by a shy old man in a Yankees baseball cap named Ōshita (a distant relative of my tea-lesson friend Miki-chan and our tea sensei). He told me he was sick with cancer but that he ran away from the hospital. He'd planted a fig tree for his wife and was putting up poles for cucumber vines to climb. Looking out on the wild meadow, they told me this used to be tanbo, rice paddies, but everyone got too old and gave up.

I hoped the neighbors would become my teachers; at the very least, I needed to get along with them. I'd heard stories of young people moving to the countryside high on big dreams of a more natural life and then giving up because the community was so unwelcoming of outsiders. These young idealistic farmers, certain that organic is the best way, clash with an older generation who struggled for subsistence during food shortages and came to rely on industrial fertilizer and herbicides to make the work less strenuous. Vegetable plots are typically clustered together in one part of a village, so it's almost impossible to keep an organic garden uncontaminated by the pesticides and herbicides that most people use to keep their cabbages free from bugs and their walkways without weeds. I'm lucky, in that sense, that my hatake is buffered by vast untended fields. I can grow things the way I want to, without telling anyone else they're doing it wrong.

There's a shed next to my garden full of lumber and old tools. I found a hoe—rusted but better made than anything I could buy in a hardware store—that had been wired back together where its wooden handle was cracked. When I broke the earth with the mended hoe, I saw rich dark soil, alive with earthworms. This was the kind of garden I'd been reading about in *Farmers of Forty Centuries*, a book by the American soil scientist Franklin Hiram King.

In 1909, King traveled to Asia to learn about high-intensity organic farming. He wrote, "The United States as yet is a nation of but few people widely scattered over a broad virgin land with more than twenty acres to the support of every man, woman and child, while the people [of Asia] are toiling in fields tilled more than three thousand years and . . . have barely one acre per capita, more than one-half of which is uncultivable mountain land." King was impressed that in Japan inedible plant parts became mulch, ash became fertilizer, and all human and animal manure was fermented into compost—all the waste of daily life transformed into nutrients.

In contrast to the monocultures planted in America, he observed that "it is very common to see three crops growing upon the same field at one time, but in different stages of maturity" and that "even the narrow dividing ridges but a foot wide, which retain the water on the rice paddies, are bearing a heavy crop of soy beans." These beans not only yielded more food from limited land but enriched the soil with nitrogen.

King was concerned that the use of industrial fertilizers in America was not indefinitely sustainable: there was much we could learn from Asia about maintaining soil health. (I think we could learn from Indigenous Americans too.) Unfortunately, over the next century, the West had more influence on the agriculture of the East than the other way around.

My friend Sakai, an engineer-turned-organic-farmer, came by to look at my hatake. I showed him the healthy soil, and he got excited. We walked around the house and found clumps of alliums, with leaves like thick chives and each root like a single clove of garlic wrapped in papery purple skin. I brought some to the vegetable shop keeper next to my apartment to see if she knew what they were; we agreed they looked like rakkyō, Chinese wild onions, but she'd never seen them purple or tasted them so pungent. I pickled the bulbs in sweet vinegar to serve with Japanese curry.

We found udo and tara-no-me, wild Araliaceae bushes and shrubs that produce edible shoots in early spring. I wondered if someone had transplanted them so they could enjoy these treats without climbing a mountain. There was a yuzu shrub tangled with vines that belonged to a neighbor, and five or six tea bushes hidden in the tall grass. And there were lots of mulberry trees, so we guessed that the family who lived in the Totoro House had grown them as feed for silkworms and sold the raw thread to textile manufacturers in Fukui to be made into kimono.

I had just read Masanobu Fukuoka's manifesto on natural farming, *The One-Straw Revolution*, and was cultishly excited about low-intervention no-till cultivation. Writing in the 1970s, Fukuoka looks back even further than King: "A thousand years ago agriculture was practiced in Japan without plowing, and it was not until the Tokugawa Era 300–400 years ago that shallow cultivation was introduced." Fukuoka proves on his farm that he can get yields of grains as high as or higher than the modern farms around his—by following what he calls "do-nothing" agriculture. "The earth cultivates itself naturally by means of the penetration of plant roots and the activity of microorganisms, small animals, and earthworms," writes Fukuoka.

But it was nearly mid-May, and the grass had a head start. Part of the way that Fukuoka's method works is that you scatter the seeds for the plants you want—vegetables, grains, and helpful ground cover—before anything else can grow. The weeds in the hatake were up to my knees. I called my friend Shanti's mother, who ran an organic herb farm for twenty-five years (and gave me a job there when I was twelve). She has a tattered yellow copy of Fukuoka's manifesto from when it was first published in English in 1978, but she told me to go ahead and till. My mother—whose low-intervention farming I took for granted before I knew the word "organic"—said the same thing. If I wanted to harvest vegetables this season, turning over the soil would be the easiest way. And it would make the neighbors happy to see a tidy hatake.

Sakai agreed. If I wanted to plant in time for this year's summer season, I needed to clear the weeds and loosen the soil as quickly as possible. He told me I should make the rows in my hatake north to south, the same orientation as the house. Sakai said, *Let's call some friends and do it together!* He picked up his phone and began to recruit help.

I stood in the weeds, imagining the vegetables I would grow. It used to be that if you ate a carrot in Yamanaka, a carrot in Kyōto, a carrot in Tōkyō, a carrot in Fukuoka, each one would be different. People saved their own seeds, so the plants adapted over time to the environment and to local tastes. Now almost everyone buys their seeds from the national agricultural cooperative, so regional variation is disappearing. The local cooperative does carry Kaga Yasai, fifteen vegetables grown in this region since before 1945, some dating back to the Edo period. They're trademarked and heavily promoted by the Kanazawa City Agricultural Produce Branding Association and more representative of fancy Kanazawa city food than what was historically grown in Yamanaka. It's a streamlining of the variation that used to occur family to family, not just town to town, when people saved their own seeds.

Nishiyama Sensei (my wild plants teacher) gave me a list of the crops grown in the Yamanaka area a hundred years ago, around the time the Totoro House was built. He explained that long-term guests used to come to Yamanaka hoping the hot springs would cure what ailed them, and healthy food was part of their treatment. He wrote down the phone number of a seed shop in Nomi, about an hour's drive away.

I told my friend Ryo, who runs a small organic farm nearby, in Takigahara, about the shop and the traditional vegetables. For Ryo, it's more interesting to grow trendy kale and exotic things like Swiss chard, borage, and nasturtium—things I grew up with and have no need to plant in my Yamanaka garden. But Nishiyama's list contained vegetables Ryo had never heard of. Even common ones were listed under old-fashioned names or obscure varieties. Ryo's curiosity was piqued. I helped him work the fields in Takigahara for a morning under a beating sun so that he could take the afternoon off and drive me to the seed shop.

The owner of the seed shop said it was already late to plant some traditional crops, but he gave me seeds for leaf mustard that used to be sown in tanbo as green manure after rice was harvested; fuji-mame (hyacinth beans) that worked to put nitrogen back into depleted soil; and Kaga negi, fat green onions. He sold me seed-lings for small green-white melons, called nashi-uri, that he said dated back to the Meiji era. I bought the last three seedlings of Kaga tōgarashi, slender green and red chili peppers that would turn out more fragrant than mainstream varieties. (In Japanese cooking, chili peppers are rarely used for heat, but are added whole to pickling brines for their preservative qualities.)

I bought modern vegetables too: hybrid cucumbers that would grow long, thin-skinned, and nearly seedless; big fat pink toma-toes; and seeds for mixed greens that I could sow consecutively, for salad all summer. I even got a baby watermelon vine—something that would have rotted in the cool climate where I grew up.

When Ryo dropped me off at my hatake, he seemed dubious. Looking at the untilled weeds, he said, *That's going to be a lot of work*.

But the friends Sakai and I called came through. Sakura (the boar hunter) arrived on a warm evening with a brand-new weed whacker; the owner of the house had left one for me (and I'd learned to use one at my tanbo). We sweated through the last hours of sunlight. By dusk, we'd mowed down the weeds in the hatake and cleared a path all around the house. We moved some rocks to sit down on and have tea, and a baby snake slithered out from underneath. There were ticks attached to the poor little thing, and Sakura caught it and picked them off. *No wonder we are friends*, I thought.

Another evening, Nakajima (my woodturner friend) brought over his mother's cultivator machine—like a miniature version of the Gravely rototiller I remember my dad pushing across potato beds. Nakajima had sent me a how-to video that made it look easy, but when we tried to use the machine, it bit into the soil, then jumped ahead. We took turns tilling and laughing at each other, until I sort of had the hang of it.

The next morning, Sakai showed Sakura and me how to do it correctly. First, we used a small sickle to cut and remove the roots of weeds by hand. After that, the cultivator plowed through smoothly. He brought out a measuring tape and staked out the four corners of the hatake, then showed us a clever knot for running a string from pole to pole. Using the strings as a guide, we distributed the fluffy tilled earth, and hoed the soil into long mounds—*like kamaboko*, logs of fish cake, said Sakai. I was glad to be with people for whom a good time entailed working on a project together—even if it meant sweating through your clothes and getting dirt embedded so far under your fingernails it would stay for days.

The sun was high and the humidity thick, but after lunch we looked up companion plantings in books that Sakai brought. We followed their advice, tucking wild onions into the same hole as cucumber seedlings, and scattering basil and parsley seeds among the tomato plants. By evening—not a week after Ryo had looked dubiously at my field of weeds—I had a vegetable garden.

All the while, elderly neighbors came over to introduce themselves, and I was ready with a stash of gifts in the shed. I gave Mrs. Noguchi, who keeps a lovely flower garden, a small pretty package of cookies; she came back with a bouquet of lilacs. I also gave cookies to Mr. Yamane who was growing potatoes, cabbage, and onions west of the Totoro House; a few days later, he came over with a lacquered natsume that he'd made. He said it was not a fancy one, but it was nicer than any tea canister I had ever owned.

Ōshita, the hospital escapee, beamed when I gave him a bag of sweets; later, he lent me green netting to keep boars from trampling my beans.

One neighbor was a little gruff. It seemed he wanted to make it quite clear where the property line was. He accepted a box of cookies from me, but begrudgingly. Then, one morning, while I was tending my hatake, he and another man came over and started helping me. They pulled an old ladder out of the weeds and put it by the side of the house. They found some sturdy boards and replaced the rotten one bridging the irrigation ditch I had to cross to get to my garden. The whole time, they hardly spoke, but I understood that they were welcoming me. From then on, every time I passed the gruff man's house on the way to my hatake, he'd grin, wave, and say, *Hi, Hannah-chan!*

Without fail, the neighbors told me I would have trouble with boars. They warned me that crows would steal my tomatoes and melons, leaving behind a mess. I'd planted my Kaga sweet potatoes near the persimmon tree behind the house, hoping that the weeds would camouflage them (as I'd read about in *The One-Straw Revolution*). And I put hot peppers and a local green called kinjisō at the ends of the rows, because boars are said to despise them. I needed a good fence, but I wasn't sure I wanted to spend the money and effort to build one.

I STILL WANTED to plant more vegetables. I was looking for saved seeds from Yamanaka, but I could find only three kinds. Miyamana is a kind of mizuna grown only in the Sugatani neighborhood, where most of the woodturners live; the story goes that a bride brought the seeds with her from Fukui about fifty years ago. In Ōzuchi, Nimaida grows futo-kyūri, fat cucumbers, that have been passed down through his family for at least a century. Just on the other side of the mountain pass, in another of Yamanaka's eastern villages, Suginomizu, the Shimoshita family has grown egoma (perilla) for as long as anyone can recall. They tell me the seeds were an important source of omega-3s for mountain people, who couldn't easily get those nutrients from fish.

I couldn't get miyamana. Sugatani-machi is very protective of the crop, which could easily cross-pollinate with other brassicas.

Nimaida was also reluctant to give me futo-kyūri seeds. He told me he gave some to a friend in town once, but the cucumbers grew long instead of fat. They're so suited to the microclimate of Ōzuchi that even a few kilometers away they grew differently. But he finally gave me three seedlings. He instructed me to pinch off the top after every thirty centimeters of growth. Unlike modern cucumbers, he explained, the plant would grow one long vine with a single flower at the end if I didn't coax it to produce more fruit.

I got my egoma seedlings from the younger Shimoshita, whose nickname is Shimoshimo. He told me to bury each stalk up to the first set of leaves, mounding up the soil to support the plant and encourage a strong network of roots. He also told me about two seed stores nearby in Daishōji where I might find more local plants. I went looking for them, only to find that both had permanently closed.

By the time my seedlings were all planted, I'd been offered the fields in front of and behind the Totoro House—I could make a whole farm (if I had time)! My friends often came to help, and the neighbors were happy to see young people working the land. Their children left for modern conveniences in bigger towns, and you can't blame them. But it must be sad to watch fertile fields go to seed as your neighbors age and pass away.

LEAF MUSTARD WAS the first vegetable I harvested. My friend Michiba and I quick-pickled them, following a recipe in a book from a Kanazawa temple. We blanched them quickly, salted them, and sealed them in zip-top bags to keep in the gasses that make them spicy. They tasted green and peppery with a pleasant hint of bitterness.

A second crop of mustard was coming in, but little black cater-pillars and fat green ones (likely children of the neon-blue and lemon-yellow butterflies I'd thought were so pretty a few weeks earlier) ate them down to nothing but lace. Small orange beetles nibbled holes in the leaves of my cucumber seedlings, but they avoided the ones planted close to the wild onions.

I often saw a cute chartreuse tree frog hanging out on the cucumber trellis. I let the weeds on the side of the rows grow, hop-ing they would host spiders and more frogs who would eat the pesky beetles. But I trimmed these weeds and squared off the rows at the ends so it would look tidy. I didn't want to give the neighbors any-thing to object to, even if I did things a little differently.

There is a culvert, originating uphill next to a shrine, that di-verts water from a small river down along the road. When I need water for my plants, I slide a board into the culvert to direct some of the flow into the shallow ditch that runs toward my hatake and out into what used to be the tanbo.

For a few weeks, I filled a watering can in the culvert, to sprinkle on my tender seedlings. Then the first rainy season came. By the time it was over, the plants had strong deep roots that didn't need watering. The weather got hot and humid. My tomato plants thrived, growing taller by the day.

In Japanese you say that you are "making" vegetables. This construction strikes me as funny, because the plants are making the vegetables. The soil and rain and sun are feeding the plants. You simply set them up for success and coax them along with a little extra water or the support of a sturdy stake. The climate and soil around my hatake were so conducive to growth that I did hardly anything.

For three seasons—fall, winter, and spring—Yamanaka looks like the temperate almost–rainforest of the Pacific Northwest. But in summer—when the weeds grow thick as a jungle, with vines draping from trees that buzz with cicadas—it feels subtropical.

In June, I bought a single-speed peach mama-chari (the kind of shopping bike mamas ride) with a big basket. As I rode to my hatake in the evenings, I'd hear the whirring of wood-turning lathes coming from houses I passed. I filled my bike basket with ripe tomatoes, salad greens, chili peppers, and cucumbers. The hybrid cucumbers were so wildly productive that if I didn't make it to my hatake for a few days, they grew oversize and yellow. (I let one go, just for fun, and it grew as big as my arm, with a bend like an elbow.)

In the garden, I listened to insects and frogs. Of the four houses that border the field where my hatake is, three are empty. At first, I thought it was a radio playing opera that I heard carrying over the blue hydrangeas and tall susuki grass. Then, I realized, the man who lived in the one occupied house was singing enka, sentimental Japanese ballads.

Sakura had told me that the hunters had seen a black bear the other day, eating the rice bran bait in the boar trap by the river beyond this field. With that in mind, I left when dusk fell. By then, the lathes had stopped and the woodturners were at dinner.

I'd make my own dinner with vegetables from the garden. I ate sliced tomatoes on milk bread from the butcher shop, or cut them into wedges for hiyashi chūka, chilled Chinese noodles. Typically, this Japanese-Chinese summer noodle dish is piled with thin strips of omelet and deli ham, julienned cucumber, and wedges of tomato and dressed in a sweet and tangy shoyu dressing. I made it with whatever was ripe in my garden and left over in my fridge: radish sprouts and boiled eggs, golden mini tomatoes and pickled mustard greens, French radishes and young lettuce leaves.

I often got cooking advice from the ladies at the Sunday market in front of the onsen (which is more for the old folks to gather and drink coffee together than to buy and sell vegetables). One morning, a few of the ladies brought ippon-zuke, cucumber pickled whole overnight, that were mildly sweet and salty but still fresh tasting. I asked them for the recipe. *Salt the cucumber*, they said, miming a generous sprinkle, *and roll it*; they made a motion like shaping a log of Play-Doh. *Pickle it overnight in konbu-dashi with a little soy sauce and sugar*. It became my new favorite way to extend the shelf life of a cucumber for a few extra days, keeping its crunch and adding umami.

Nimaida's futo-kyūri did grow fat, as they were supposed to—a little rounder than a typical American supermarket cucumber, with skin striated lime green and pale yellow. Their flesh was firm and dense, with a faint lemony tartness. Nimaida taught me a quick and easy recipe his mother would make: *Peel the cucumber, halve it, and scoop out the seeds. Slice it thinly. Mix it with canned mackerel (no oil), soy sauce, and seasoned vinegar.* On summer days too hot to cook, I made this again and again and ate it with a bowl of rice or on the Scandinavian rye crackers I ordered online.

When the purple-stem eggplants, with their nearly black calyxes, ripened, the ladies at the Sunday market told me to peel the small eggplants, cut them into matchsticks, and sauté them in oil. When they're almost done, add a little sugar and miso to the pan. *That's how we do it around here.*

Red shiso sprouted here and there in my hatake and the field beyond, some of it from seeds I had scattered and some that had self-seeded from generations before. I salted handfuls of the leaves to color umeboshi I made in a tsubo (ceramic crock) borrowed from the Totoro House.

When their purple-green leaves grew back thicker, I made shiso juice following instructions from the proprietor of Eimi, the homey restaurant where I eat dinner when I want something healthy and comforting that I don't have to cook. Masumi Hayashibara (Eimi is a childhood nickname given by her baby sister) started the place at sixty-five, when she felt it was finally time to do whatever she wanted with her life. I watched her boil the shiso leaves one evening; the room perfumed with their fragrance. She gave me powdered citric acid to mix with the purple tisane, turning it bright pink.

One morning I noticed big pits in the field: boars had been

rooting around. I needed to protect my hatake. Online I found an article about high school kids who had figured out they could deter boars with hot chilis hung in cheap cotton gloves around a field. It worked even better if you flagged them with something blue—like plastic flowerpots left over from seedlings—because it's a color boars see clearly. So I devised a cute version: I tied the peppers in bundles of checkered blue cloth, and my friends helped string them from fence posts around my hatake. My elderly neighbors had never heard of such a thing and were as curious as I was to see if it would work.

I had imagined that these neighbors would mentor me, but they saw that I was doing fine and left me alone. Instead, I became a teacher to other young people. Sakai, who had helped me clear the field, introduced me to Chinatsu, a designer who had recently moved to Yamanaka so her husband, Yūma, could attend the wood-turning school. Chinatsu and Yūma wanted to grow vegetables too, and I wanted to expand my hatake for a new project—growing adzuki beans, one of the oldest crops in Japan.

I had a bag of seeds from Nishiyama Sensei, my mountain teacher. His idea was to create Kaga adzuki. His friend, a wagashi maker, could use them to make Japanese sweets. We began with organic beans from Noguchi seed company—a variety from the Noto Peninsula, in the same prefecture as Kaga. I was one of ten people growing them—each in our own way—and the idea was to see what kinds of conditions they thrived in. If we saved the seeds every year, within three generations the plants would adapt to this microclimate.

My garden neighbor Ōshita said we could use as much of the old rice paddy—stretching between my hatake and his—as we wanted to clear. Over the next week, Sakai, Sakura, Chinatsu and Yūma, and my friend Yōko (another artist in her thirties) helped till the soil and build rows.

When we were ready to plant, Yūma brought some of his classmates from the wood-turning school: eighteen-year-old Naoki and thirty-one-year-old Raku (whose name is written with the same character as "fun," "enjoy," "effortless"). Their parents' generation embraced convenience and modernity, but the young people who choose to be in Yamanaka are interested in understanding traditional culture and in making their own food. Surprisingly—because of my curiosity about Yamanaka and my own rural upbringing—I often know more than they do about plants and gardening.

We pressed the little red beans into the soil. The weeds we'd cut to make way for the hatake had been drying in the oppressive July sun, and we scattered them over the rows to keep the soil moist. Everyone was eager to help and to learn, and they promised to come back.

As the summer progressed, I saw my neighbors less. They worked their hatake early in the morning to avoid the worst heat, or not at all. I collected handfuls of chili peppers and dried them in the sun on wide flat baskets that I'd found in the shed and washed in the river. I mixed the sun-dried chilis with tingly-tasting wild sanshō—a tiny citrus, like Sichuan peppercorn, used as a spice in Japan since at least the Jōmon period—to make chili oil. In Japan, chili oil is a condiment for so-called Chinese food: ramen and gyōza. But I put it on everything: eggs, cucumber salad, plain bowls of rice.

The vigorous fuji-mame vines outgrew the trellis I'd built for them, until they looked like a brontosaurus-shaped topiary. They produced only a few handfuls of beans—the shape of snow peas with the texture and fuzz of old-fashioned green beans. I understood then why they'd fallen out of fashion as anything but a cover crop. I had eaten a few of the flowers raw, sweet and beany tasting, and some of the young leaves, boiled like mature spinach (they were fine, but nothing I'd crave). The beans, I read, could be toxic if overripe or undercooked, so I soaked them in cold water before boiling them well. They were tender and buttery, and I wished I had more.

By September, the egoma plants were at eye level, and the fujimame vines were reaching across and winding around their stalks. I picked the fragrant egoma leaves and followed Korean recipes for kimchi and soy-sauce pickling. No one could think of a Japanese use for the leaves, but they were so lush it seemed like a waste not to use them. By early October, they'd flowered, but I didn't know the best way or time to collect the seeds.

The senior Shimoshita said he'd learned from his grandmother to cut down the perilla on October 10, when the leaves begin to yellow. On the ninth, my plants were still green, but on the tenth they'd begun to yellow. Roughly following Shimoshita's instructions, I bundled the stalks and hung them across a laundry pole, with a sheet underneath to catch the seeds. As I worked I discovered the leaves were home to green spiders, green inchworms, and a giant green praying mantis—an entire green ecosystem.

The adzuki had lemon-yellow flowers that turned into slender pods like French green beans, bulging slightly with the ripening seeds inside. As the summer vegetables finished, making way for a fall planting, I checked the hatake around me to see what I should plant next. Wherever I looked, there were daikon and hakusai

(napa cabbage) seedlings coming up. Some people still had eggplant and okra. And they were putting in a fall crop of green onions.

My adzuki plants were laden with beans, but I noticed small
holes bored in some of the pods. When I opened one, there was a
small white worm wriggling inside. I told Nishiyama Sensei about
the problem, and he came to have a look.

I dreamed of making the Totoro House mine one day and nur-
turing a wild garden there with Sensei's advice. I was excited to
ask him which of the weeds were native and which were edible
besides the yomogi (mugwort) I already recognized. I wanted to
know which side of the house had the best conditions for each of
my favorite wildflowers that I planned to collect from the mountains.

He told me the little pink flowers blooming across the field
were called mizo-soba (*Persicaria thunbergii*). They look like buckwheat flowers (though they're not related) and grow where there's
lots of water. He knew before I told him that this was an old
tanbo. The tall stalks of yellow flowers towering over us were an
invasive goldenrod from America. He told me susuki grass, with
its fluffy plumes, was the only native plant strong enough to compete. To restore the native ecosystem, you could cut down the
goldenrod, or eat its shoots in early spring, and scatter susuki seeds
to replace it.

He took samples of the soil from the old tanbo where I was
growing the beans; beans like old rice fields he said. My soil is rich
in nitrogen, he explained, because it's near a steep mountain. De-
composing plant matter gets washed down from the slope. The
soil in the flatter areas of town is sandy and poor.

He watched closely and saw big black flies landing on the plants that dangled into the mud. Those might be the culprits: laying their eggs in the beans. They're attracted by the moisture and high nitrogen.

Don't worry about the bugs eating the beans, he said. If it was disease, the whole crop might be in danger, but if it's bugs, they'll only take part of it. *It's unlikely that they'll overpopulate, because if they do there will be nothing left for them to eat; these things naturally balance themselves out.* He'd said that before about the forest too: it can recover from anything—except herbicide.

The tea bushes in back were blooming; their white flowers made me understand they really are a kind of camellia. I cut some pretty branches for Nishiyama Sensei to take home, and he looked pleased. We searched for fruits on the sudachi tree and found them camouflaged under leaves exactly the same shade of green as the small perfumy citrus. I sent Sensei off with the last of the basil and waved until his car was out of sight. Then I returned to weed my hatake, thinking how nice it would be to have Nishiyama Sensei come back in every season. There's so much I want to learn from him it's almost endless.

My beans grew better than any others in the adzuki project. But it had nothing to do with me. I didn't add ash or compost to the soil, and I didn't water them once. They got all the moisture and nutrients they needed from the old rice paddy. When a typhoon knocked down the plants, I ran a few strings along each row to lift the stems out of the puddles; that's all.

Chinatsu, Yūma, Raku, Naoki, Sakai, Sakura, and Jessica (the maki-e apprentice) came to harvest the adzuki in late October, when the pods had dried papery beige and the little red beans had hardened inside. I spread the bean pods on baskets to dry.

The same day, we dug up the sweet potatoes I'd hidden among the weeds in the yard. The boars had come rooting around, but they hadn't found them all. The tubers were tiny—the soil was too heavy and damp for them to grow big—but they had the sweetest, most concentrated flavor of any sweet potato I've ever tasted.

As dusk approached, Raku and I climbed one of the shibu-gaki (astringent persimmon) trees that Ōshita told me no one uses anymore. We tossed the fruit down to Naoki, who collected them in a bucket.

Naoki had watched his grandmother make hoshi-gaki, dried persimmons, but he'd never done it himself. That evening we peeled them and hung them from rice straw rope (made with stalks from my tanbo) to dry on my balcony. The shibu-gaki sweeten as they shrivel in the cool autumn sun. In a few days they lose their astringency, and in a few weeks they are ready to eat.

A week later, the beans were dry enough to shell. Jessica and Raku came to my house in the evenings to help me peel open the papery pods. We ate the sweet, sticky hoshi-gaki while we worked, sitting on the kitchen floor.

We sorted the little red beans into three baskets: good, so-so, and no good. About half of the adzuki were tunneled through by worms. Still, the yield was generous, more than two kilos of good beans from the small handful of seeds we'd planted. Some of these I would return to Nishiyama Sensei for next year's seed stock. With the rest, I could do as I wished: simmer them with kabocha squash in dashi and soy sauce; steam them with new mochi rice to make sekihan, festive pink-tinted rice; or blanch and simmer them with sugar to make anko, adzuki jam for sweets.

I'd save the best ones—glossy and deep burgundy—for Nishiyama Sensei. He arranged for a meeting at the end of the growing season, for the ten of us who'd grown adzuki in different locations to gather and share what we'd learned. I thought I would make some adzuki sweets to bring and share with everyone.

A few days before the meeting, Nishiyama Sensei died suddenly of a brain hemorrhage. He was sixty-five.

I'd known him for only a year, but he had an enormous impact on my life. He reminded me who I am: a country girl, happiest in the woods or down in the weeds looking at flowers and insects, watching the seasons change day by day. I mourned the promise of decades more to learn from him and all the projects that he left unfinished. He was doing work, he had told me, *for the children's children—building society that coexists with nature so future generations can live happily.*

The adzuki project, at least, I could take forward. My beans had been the most successful, so it was my duty. It had seemed like a cliché: the Japanese master who will take his special knowledge to the grave as the world moves forward without him. But now it was real. It was my friend and teacher.

For weeks, every time I went outside, the trees and plants made me cry. I cried by the walnut trees on the bike path. I cried over the weeds in my hatake. I went to Nishiyama's friend Sakashita's wild plant garden and cried there too, thinking of the precious friendship between those two gentle men, always gazing down at the tiniest leaves. The other mountain meijin took me into the woods to pick natsuhaze berries (like a wild Japanese blueberry) and yellow shimokoshi mushrooms that emerged from the frost as fall turned to winter. It was their way of looking after me and managing their grief too. Standing among the trees, they told me, *Nishiyama is with us everywhere.*

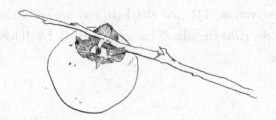

The last week in November, a few friends came to help prepare my hatake for winter. The sun glowed through thin cloud cover. The week before had been cold, with frost on the ground each morning. The bright red maples along the river had passed their peak. It felt like the onset of winter. But this day was warm enough to work without a jacket.

There was still some green: in the field, and in the fuzzy leaves of daikon and turnip in the hatake, and in the dark waxy foliage of the yuzu bush, still weighted with fragrant golden citrus. The persimmon trees had dropped their leaves, but bright orange fruits still hung like ornaments in the tops of the branches, out of reach. Deep pink winter camellias were starting to bloom.

I taught Jessica, Naoki, and Raku how to thin the daikon (later, I cooked the leaves for our dinner, with garlic from a neighbor's garden and yuzu from Ōshita's tree). We mulched the rows with the weeds we pulled. When we finished putting away all the tools, we scrambled up the river like kids, looking for sawa-gani, river crabs. We took off our shoes and waded in the icy water. I found red and orange berries that Nishiyama Sensei had taught me about and passed them out. They were sweet and tart and reminded me of the salmonberries I picked as a child.

In spring, I will plant the adzuki seeds I've saved. I trust the plants will tell me what they need. Through trial and error, and loving observation, I'll find the best way to grow them. And maybe by the time the adzuki have naturalized, I will have settled in here too.

Adzuki Jam and Butter Sandwich

TIME: *2 hours to make adzuki jam; 5 minutes to assemble sandwich*
Makes 4–6 sandwiches, plus extra adzuki jam

Whenever I see this treat in a Japanese bakery, I can't resist: a section of baguette spread with anko (adzuki jam) and fat slices of cold salted butter and sprinkled with kinako, nutty toasted soybean powder. When I grew my own adzuki beans, it was the first thing I made. I've adapted this recipe for anko from the Kurodas, at Sankaidō sweets shop; you can also use this homemade anko in the kuri yōkan on page 48.

FOR THE ADZUKI JAM
250 grams (1¼ cups) adzuki beans
110 grams (½ cup) brown zarame, demerara, or raw sugar
Pinch of salt

FOR THE SANDWICH
1 baguette (about 50 cm/20 inches)
1 stick (110 grams, or ½ cup) cold salted butter
About 1 cup adzuki jam
4 teaspoons kinako (optional)

TO MAKE THE ADZUKI JAM
1. In a small pot, cover the beans with a few inches of water. Bring to a boil over high heat. As soon as they boil, drain the beans, and discard the water. Return the beans to the pot with fresh water, and repeat.

2. For a third time, cover the beans with a few inches of water and bring to a boil, but this time continue to cook them. Reduce heat to keep the water at a simmer, stirring occasionally, until they are very soft, 30–50 minutes. (Add water, if necessary, to keep the beans covered.)

3. Drain the cooked beans, discard the water, and rinse. To make coarse tsubu-an, skip to step 5.

4. To make smooth koshi-an, place a mesh strainer over a large glass bowl. Mash the beans through the strainer to remove the skins. To help get the bean pulp through, periodically pour cool water through the strainer as you mash, 1 or 2 cups at a time (about 8 cups total). When all the pulp has been washed through, discard the skins. Let the bean pulp settle to the bottom of the bowl, about 10 minutes. The water will still be cloudy, but you'll see two distinct layers. Pour off as much water as you can without losing the settled pulp.

5. Return the pulp (for koshi-an) or whole beans (for tsubu-an) to the pan. If you're using whole beans, add enough water to cover; if you're using pulp, there's already enough water. Add the sugar and salt, and bring to a simmer over medium heat. Lower the heat until the mixture bubbles a little but doesn't splatter or scorch. Cook, stirring frequently with a silicone spatula, for about 30 minutes. If using whole beans, smash them slightly as you stir.

6. It's done when the mixture thickens to a loose, jammy consistency and your spatula leaves a slight trail. It will thicken more as it cools. If you're uncertain whether it's cooked enough, put a little on a dish and keep in the freezer for a few minutes; it won't gel like fruit jam, but it should thicken to a spreadable consistency.

7. Transfer to a container—you should have about 660 grams (2½ cups). Keep in the refrigerator for up to a week or in the freezer for a few months.

TO MAKE THE SANDWICH

1. Slice the baguette open lengthwise, so it hinges like a hot dog bun, and cut it into 4–6 pieces.
2. Cut the butter into slices about 5 mm (¼-inch) thick. Line one side of each baguette piece with butter slices. Smear the other side with adzuki jam. (The sandwiches can be wrapped and stored at cool room temperature for a few hours.)
3. Sprinkle with kinako (if using) just before serving.

jika-tabi

Fifteen

Koi Koi Matsuri

E very year on the third weekend in September, the town of
Yamanaka transforms into a two-day party called Koi Koi
Matsuri, which translates roughly to "Come on! Come on! Festival." Strings of red lanterns sway above the streets. Vendors called
yatai pop up selling deep golden fried chicken; okonomiyaki glistening with salty-sweet sauce and sunny-side-up eggs; chocolate-
dipped bananas with rainbow sprinkles; cream-filled crepes in
pink paper cones; and sweet-smelling baby castella cakes, like
balls of pancake with a dark crust. Late into the night teenagers
dance around a tall circular stage to a Eurobeat version of Yamanaka's festival song, shouting, *Koi! Koi!* Come! Come!

In pop-up tents, garages, and empty storefronts open to the
street, people gather in honjin, a military term for headquarters.
Each neighborhood has a honjin, and then there are honjin for
business groups, alumni groups, professional organizations, and
yokinkō (like informal credit unions). Inside, people sit on plastic

tatami mats or at folding tables cluttered with plates of colorful kaki-no-ha-zushi (persimmon-leaf sushi) and skewers of yakitori. They call in their friends from the street and pour them beer, saké, and highballs.

The first time I attended the festival, I had no idea what these party tents were, but it looked like a lot of fun that I wasn't in on. Now—after years of visiting Yamanaka on and off and more than a year of living here—I have my own role to play. I'll wear a yukata in my neighborhood colors to dance in the plaza, and I'll help carry a mikoshi with a rowdy group of two dozen craftsmen.

A mikoshi is an elaborately adorned palanquin—like a carriage with no wheels—supported by four long poles that at least two dozen men lift onto their shoulders. But it's not for transporting royalty or a wealthy bride; a mikoshi is for parading a spirit through a festival.

We call them *o*-mikoshi (the *o* is honorific) out of respect. But the one I'll join is an *owan*-mikoshi, shaped like an owan (a miso soup bowl). Three years ago, my woodturner friend Nakajima made me an honorary member. Last year, he took me to the hardware store to buy my own pair of jika-tabi, split-toed black canvas shoes, for my costume.

This festival is a tangle of Shintō, Buddhist, and secular meanings, but with all the partying it's easy to overlook its spiritual agrarian roots. It's held during higan, the autumnal equinox—a time for Buddhists to commune with ancestors who have crossed to the other side. But its form comes from the Shintō Aki Matsuri, Autumn Festival, an occasion to thank the spirits for a successful harvest.

Aki Matsuri—part ceremony, part celebration—is the most important occasion for Shintō shrines. In the past—when food came not just from a supermarket but from land you tended yourself or saw your neighbors cultivate—everyone gathered to express gratitude for the rice and vegetables that would sustain them until the next growing season. People offered some of this bounty to the spirits and then ate it with them. There was a spring festival too, but the autumn one was bigger—a collective sigh of relief that there would be food for another winter.

Each year, there are fewer people working the land. Like towns all over Japan, Yamanaka is losing young people to the cities. The old people who remain become physically unable to tend their fields. (Each time I chat with Yamane, an old man with a hatake near mine, he tells me he'll probably be dead soon.) Tanbo and hatake are abandoned faster than people like my friends Hayashi and Sakai can revive them.

When the outer villages were incorporated into central Yamanaka in 1961, the town created a new festival—Koi Koi Matsuri. Each village had its own small Aki Matsuri, but the town hoped to attract more people with a bigger, centralized one that combined the Shintō tradition with Yamanaka's Commerce and Industry Festival.

At first, Koi Koi was held in front of Hakusan Shrine, up three long flights of steep stone stairs from the onsen, next to the temple, Iōji, on the mountainside overlooking the tile roofs of the town. Shrines belong to Shintō, and temples to Buddhism. But this shrine used to be inside Iōji. That was common until the Meiji era, when Japan unified into a centrally governed country and opened its borders to international trade. The government made Shintō the state religion—to help define Japan's identity against Christian nations— and a few sects became more like churches. After World War II, the Allied occupation required all shrines to register as religious organizations, reinforcing the idea that Shintō is a religion.

Shintō has no holy books, only nature, Yamanaka's shrine keeper tells me. Yūji Yamashita is a fourteenth-generation kannushi. He doesn't like "Shintō priest" as a translation of "kannushi." Shintō is not a church, he says, it's a path. You don't look up to learn: you look down at the earth as you walk. His job is not to instruct but to mediate between people and the spirits that inhabit all things. When a Buddhist monk leads a ceremony, he faces the altar. A pastor faces his parishioners. A kannushi orients himself sideways— one eye to the shrine and one to the people.

This site is a branch of the main Hakusan Shrine, named for the 300,000-year-old volcano. Before there was a Hakusan shrine, the mountain itself was considered a holy place, and people were forbidden to enter. There are three thousand Hakusan shrines—seven of them in Yamanaka. Yamashita explains that most are connected to Mount Hakusan by sight lines or rivers. *Water is important; it's related to tanbo*, Yamashita tells me. He takes care of Yamanaka's seven Hakusan shrines, plus other shrines that were constructed during the Meiji-era shrine-building boom that accompanied the declaration of Shintō as the state religion.

Over the years, Koi Koi Matsuri shifted away from the shrine. First the yatai selling snacks and toys moved down around the onsen, then the dancing, and eventually the mikoshi too. People got too lazy to hike up the hill, says Yamashita. Now the festival's significance is more social than spiritual.

IN THE DAYS leading up to Koi Koi Matsuri, the town buzzes with preparations. Matsuura delivers beer taps and two thousand large bottles of saké—that I helped fill and cap—to various honjin. And men in pale green work wear start building the precariously tall octagonal stage, called a yagura, at the center of the plaza between the men's and the women's bathhouses, dressing it in festive red and white banners. The yagura stage will have two levels with railings running all the way around, high above the heads of the crowds that will gather, and a roof sheltering the top tier.

The night before the festival, I go over to Youko-san's house. She owns the vegetable shop a few doors down from my apartment, where I shop almost every day (and ask her how to cook this or that, like slimy yellow nameko mushrooms or enormous quince fruits). Together we make about two hundred kaki-no-ha-zushi.

On each waxy dark green persimmon leaf, she places a hand-formed disk of seasoned sushi rice. On top of the rice, I arrange a piece of vinegar-pickled salt-cured salmon or mackerel, a wafer-thin triangle of lemon, some tiny pink dried shrimp or red pickled ginger, and a pinch of blue seaweed threads. We layer the sushi in a wooden box with a heavy lid, where they press overnight. All over Yamanaka, women are doing the same thing. They'll distribute kaki-no-ha-zushi and other festive foods (like sekihan, sticky rice tinted pink with adzuki beans) to important friends and customers and send them to their sons' and husbands' honjin.

THIS YEAR, there were rumors that the festival would be canceled because of an incoming typhoon. But typhoons aren't unusual in the late summer and early fall, and their path is never certain. I met my friend from tea lessons Miki-chan in the early afternoon. She was dressed up in a shirt with a bow, and I wore red lipstick. In spite of light rain the yatai sizzled with pork fat and chicken grease. Excited children were playing games—trying to knock boxes of candy off a shelf with cork guns or scoop up goldfish with paper—and carrying plastic swords flashing with colored lights, and cups of rainbow cotton candy. Miki and I wandered from honjin to honjin, chatting with friends and acquaintances.

Yūichi Kano, the son-in-law of Iōji's head monk, beckoned us into one of the tents. He served me a highball and Miki-chan a juice and urged us to eat from a tray of fried panko-breaded fish and vegetables. He told us that once a typhoon did hit during the festival. A carpenter friend helped him add a flap to the front of his honjin, and he and his friends stayed inside drinking while the rain pelted the tent so hard they could hear nothing else. When Kano peeked outside to see what was going on, it was strangely quiet and everyone was gone. He called a friend and found out there had been a mudslide. The hillside beyond Iōji had poured into the town, trapping a few people in their cars, and everyone had gone to dig them out. (Thanks to cell phones, Kano tells me, the people were found quickly and survived.)

Kano said that this year the rental company wanted to take back the tents early, before the typhoon made landfall, but Yamanaka people had negotiated to keep them. It appeared that the worst of the storm would veer out to sea tonight, toward Korea, so the second day could go off without a hitch.

At another honjin, we were welcomed in by people we didn't even know. Someone poured us Moët & Chandon in plastic cups. My hunter friend Kawamoto came over from a tent across the way to serve us sashimi from fish he'd caught that morning, with real, freshly grated wasabi.

Around five I went to Youko's house, where I'd made kakai-no-ha-zushi the night before. It had become our routine over the past few years to have dinner together on the first night of the festival. She brought out squid fished by her son, roast pork, and salad made with peaches from her shop and basil from my garden.

When we heard the flute and drums of lion dancers, we abandoned our meal to run to the window. From the third-floor balcony we watched the lion's cloth body undulate and its wooden jaws snap menacingly at the tamer twirling a tasseled baton. When the music slowed, the beast knelt in the doorway of the shop across the street—waiting for money to pacify him. We returned to pouring each other saké and passing around kaki-no-ha-zushi.

After dinner I hurried to meet Mika, the paper artist, at my neighborhood honjin. We were each handed a black and yellow yukata and an obi checkered in gold, black, and silver. Two older ladies rushed to dress us so we could join the dancing that had already started. While they tied the bow on Mika's obi, I belted my yukata into place. Only a year earlier, I'd have had no idea how, but after taking Culture Class from the strict senior geigi, Botan Sensei, I had lots of practice.

We slipped our feet into yellow and black geta and trotted toward the rhythmic shamisen and percussion of "Koi Koi Ondo," the festival song. Two concentric circles of dancers moved in opposite directions around the plaza, grouped by costume—happi jackets or yukata in blue, white, silver, or magenta, each color signifying belonging to a club or neighborhood.

We slipped into line with the other people dressed in blocks of yellow and black. I'd forgotten the dance since last year but copied the slow simple arm movements of the woman in front of me. I tried to look cute by keeping my fingers closed and toes pointed inward as Botan Sensei had taught me.

As we progressed around the towering yagura stage in trance-like choreography, I passed faces I recognized from Culture Class and from the sushi counter at Saraku. Friends broke step to wave at me. As the hour wore on, my arms grew tired and my feet ached, but I didn't want the spell of the dance to be broken.

Suddenly the music changed to pop rock with a driving techno beat; teenagers rushed into the middle of the plaza and started to bounce around the stage to "Shin Koi Koi" (New Koi Koi). Most of the adults fell away, but my landlady, Yoshiko, and her club of women business managers climbed up to the first level of the circular stage. Dressed in magenta happi, they led the dance: a blend of traditional movements and the kind of coordinated routine you see in J-pop videos. Above them, on the top level, a rock band wailed on electric guitar and belted out the song.

The women business managers' club commissioned the choreography about fifteen years ago, to draw more young people (who thought the traditional dance was boring) and keep them out of trouble. Remarkably, it worked! Teenagers flock to participate in something dreamed up by their moms and grandmas.

I nudged Mika to join—*let's just try*—and quickly we were swept up into the manic energy and unself-conscious silliness of it all. We spun past Nimaida, who'd come down from Ōzuchi to watch. Hariya, an accomplished artisan who would help carry the owan-mikoshi, swooped into the crowd and danced over to say hello. There is a saying in Japan: *We're fools whether we dance or not, so we may as well dance.*

When the music stopped, we joined more friends at the biggest honjin, an enclosed tent with cubbies for shoes, at least half a dozen low tables on top of tatami mats, and a menu of draft beer, highballs, and juice. It's run by the town's forty-year-old men: forty is said to be an unlucky year, so they must appease the spirits by being generous—so they can have small bad luck instead of big bad luck. I went home before midnight to get a good sleep: I was excited about the owan-mikoshi in the morning.

Strong wind and heavy rain woke me in the night. The forecast for the second day of the festival worried me, but Nakajima had said that the only time the owan-mikoshi had been canceled was the year of the mudslide. And they still did it the next day.

I wanted to carry the mikoshi for a third time, with men who were now my friends. The first time I was so shy! I timidly followed Nakajima and barely spoke to anyone. The second year I was more at ease. This year, I was sure, would be the best yet.

Nakajima had even invited two veteran mikoshi men from Tōkyō's famous Sanja Matsuri. Sanja is a rowdy spring festival that attracts about two million attendees, to watch a hundred mikoshi, carried by men in short shorts or loincloths—often yakuza, Japanese mafia—crash into one another in sport. Koi Koi, with its seven amateur mikoshi and only twenty-five thousand attendees, is quaint in comparison. But it's fun, because extra hands are always welcome, and the old prohibition against co-ed mikoshi has been discarded.

When I got the owan-mikoshi schedule in the mail a week before Koi Koi Matsuri, I recognized the blue envelope. I already knew the plan. We'd meet in the morning to assemble the mikoshi. Yamashita, the kannushi, would come—wearing wide turquoise pants, a sheer peach outer robe, and a sparkling black fez-like hat—to start the ceremony. As we squinted into the late-morning sun, he would shake the paper tassels of his ōnusa and call a spirit into the enormous red bowl atop the owan-mikoshi (later, someone would make the joke that it was a miso soup spirit). We'd toast with cups of saké and receive protective talismans to wear around our necks. Nakajima would tell me to tie the string short so it looks *kakkoii*, cool.

Inside we'd change into split-toed black jika-tabi shoes, slim black pants, white shirts, and crimson happi jackets. We'd belt our happi, slip it off our shoulders, fold it down, and tie the sleeves around our waists—like a backward apron—so the white bowl insignia was centered on our behinds.

After lunch—at tables littered with pink paper bentō boxes, half-size cans of beer, ashtrays, and green tea—we'd roll out. We'd line up along the four lacquered poles that support the owan by height, tallest in front. Leaders with whistles around their necks like PE teachers would direct traffic, and a few wood-turning students would follow with uchiwa (paddle-shaped fans) so big they took two people to carry.

Our first stop would be Matsuura's saké shop. Nakajima would clap together hyōshigi, rhythm sticks, *ka ka ka!* We'd hoist the owan-mikoshi onto our shoulders and march toward the shop in lockstep, chanting—*orya, saa*—in call-and-response (the words have as much meaning as "hey-ho"). Then, on Nakajima's cue, we'd lift it above our heads, practically tossing it into the air, its purple tassels swinging wildly. Matsuura and his mother would pass out cups of the new autumn saké.

We'd gather in the plaza with the other mikoshi. The rowdiest would be the one for twenty-five-year-old men, and the ōshishi (giant beast) carried by teenagers with their hair sprayed neon colors. The senior Kano, head monk of Iōji, would read a prayer from the high stage; then he and other town leaders would bless the mikoshi with onsen water, splashing it by the bucketful on the crowd, to cheers and squeals.

We'd depart in procession, geigi leading the way, playing shamisen, and singing from the bed of a truck decorated in red and white banners. Behind us ryokan girls—with fancy hairdos, short shorts, white tabi shoes, and polka-dot tenugui twisted into hachi-maki and tied around their heads—carried another mikoshi. Nakajima might give me the honor for a while of the front position, called the hana-bō, usually reserved for whoever has high status and good looks. We'd relish the play on words—in Japanese "Hannah" becomes "Hana," meaning flower—Hana on the hana-bō.

At each hotel or honjin where we performed, we'd be rewarded with refreshments. Kobayashi, the eighty-something neighbor from my first trip to Yamanaka, would wave from the assisted living place where she'd moved. Ishikura, the boss of the morning market, whose son was part of the team, would run out from her house when she heard us coming. My landlady, Yoshiko, and Youko the veggie lady would be waiting for us on the main street, yelling my name and clapping (to my embarrassment and delight) as we passed. It would be mid-afternoon by the time we finally looped back to the Lacquerware Hall, shoulders and feet aching.

But none of that happened this year.

Fearing dangerously high winds and heavy rain, the organizers decided to cancel most of the festival events. We still gathered at 10:00 A.M., but only to pick up the pink bentō boxes that had been prepared for us, which we would take home and eat alone. They were packed into plastic bags with bottles of green tea and small cans of beer. I saw my friend Raku, a first-year wood-turning student, but he was too disappointed to talk. By 11:00 A.M., as I passed from one end of town to the other on the way home, all of the honjin tents had been dismantled, and the yatai had folded down their awnings; some of them were already packing their portable kitchens onto trucks to head home or on to the next festival in another town.

I put the two mini-cans of beer in my refrigerator, opened the bentō, and nearly cried. I had set aside the day to play, and I didn't want to work. So many times I'd felt excluded and lonely because I didn't understand or I didn't belong, but then I'd come to accept that fitting in is not my thing—anywhere in the world—so I may as well be an outsider in a place I love. I'm comfortable with solitude. But today, I didn't want to be alone; I wanted to be part of something. I went outside to see what I could find.

The diminished festival felt sad. The tents were gone, but where honjin had been set up in open garages and empty storefronts, people still gathered. Botan Sensei passed me in a big black car and rolled down the window to say hello; she was in full makeup and a wig cap, on her way to perform somewhere. One brave vendor kept his yatai open, selling paper bags of warm baby castella.

As the day wore on and the typhoon never landed, others lifted their awnings and started cooking. In the space that used to be a bookstore, a lively group of uncles and aunties called me over and insisted on feeding me yakitori. *Come in! Sit down! Do you want beer or a highball?* Someone served us slices of chilled nashi, crisp Japanese pear. One man told me he was a carpenter helping to restore the old houses in Ōzuchi—he knew all about Nimaida's charcoal kiln. Another had heard about me working at the saké brewery and was curious what it was like (most people will never see inside a sakagura). The next couple they pulled in were Kawamoto and his wife, who always says hi to me at the onsen and tells me her husband loves me like a daughter.

It was starting to feel like a party.

I followed the Kawamotos to another honjin, gathering up Miki-chan and her friend along the way. This honjin was a garage in my neighborhood, with folding chairs and tables cluttered with plastic cups, potato chips, and all kinds of bottles. I was excited to recognize Hibino and his wife, who had taught me about Yamanaka folk music over the many evenings I spent in their sushi shop. It was my first time to see them without a counter between us.

There was no soda water for making a highball, so someone poured me a whisky on the rocks. When I asked what was in another bottle—shōchu—they poured me some of that too. As I slowly sipped my two cups, everyone talked over each other. Hibino asked Miki-chan her name and got excited when he realized he knew her parents well. Miki-chan's friend was the daughter of the couple who owns the drugstore, and he knew them too. He was so flabbergasted you would have thought it was a remarkable and rare coincidence, not the kind of thing that happens every day in a small town.

Mochi throwing in front of the onsen hadn't been canceled. The forty-year-old men would stand on top of the yagura stage and toss plastic-wrapped disks of pink and white mochi into the large crowd that gathered. (Asami, who makes Japanese sweets at Sankaidō, told me that they and three other shops worked for days to make all the mochi.)

We spilled out of the honjin toward the onsen to join the crowd. Hibino and another guy raced ahead on bicycles, laughing like boys. Kawamoto put a fatherly hand on my shoulder and hustled me into a good spot. He waved his arms and yelled gleefully, catching mochi in midair. The grandma in front of me let go of her walker and crawled on the ground to gather the pieces that fell. Adults became kids, and the kids had their own fenced-off area so they wouldn't get trampled.

The forty-year-olds hollered and grinned from high above us as they flung mochi. One piece hit me in the head, and I understood why Miki-chan had slipped away to watch from the sidelines.

It was fun trying to get as much mochi as I could, but I didn't need it. I gave some to the grandma who'd abandoned her walker, and some to grandchildren of Hashizume-san, a restaurant owner who had rented a room to me a few years ago on one of my shorter visits to Yamanaka. I lost Kawamoto in the crowd, and it was getting chilly, so I went home to get a jacket. Hashizume's daughter knocked on my door. She was holding a shiny double-decker bentō of food for me—more kaki-no-ha-zushi, and long-simmered pieces of fish swaddled in soft kelp. She thanked me sincerely for the mochi. This seemed absurdly kind to me, and I nearly cried for (at least) the second time that day.

I ended this year's matsuri at my neighborhood honjin. Everyone had received a ticket to enter into a drawing by 8:00 P.M. We placed the tickets in a red box, and someone drew them out, one by one. The prizes—enough for everyone—were contributed by local businesses. I was hoping for a big box of fruit or a bottle of saké, but my name was drawn for a purple lacquered basket, lined in cloth to use as a purse. It would look perfect with a yukata and geta, but I don't like purple, so I discreetly gave it to the lady next to me, who in turn insisted on giving me the coffee cup she'd won.

The cup was thin, with scalloped edges, a narrow blue line on the inside rim, and a graceful handle, like a teacup. It looked as though it belonged in a classic kissaten, the sort of Japanese diner where I like to read a book over a leisurely breakfast. On the front it was printed with bright flowers, and it said, *Ii hana mitsuketa, Yamanaka Onsen*. It means "I found a good flower"—something special and beautiful—in Yamanaka.

THE DAY AFTER Koi Koi Matsuri all of Yamanaka is hungover. The town is even quieter than usual. By the time I emerge to get a coffee at the convenience store and sit in the plaza soaking up the autumn sun, the yatai and tents are entirely gone, and the stage is being disassembled. I feel full of friendship and festivities, satiated and tired.

I was disappointed that the festival was cut short, but I also think gaudy revelry had lost some of its luster for me. The Yamanaka I love most is going into the woods with mountain masters and hunters, cooking with grandmas, and tending fields with my friends.

Yamashita, Yamanaka's shrine keeper, thinks the typhoon was an opportunity to reconsider what the festival has become. *It's funny, but not funny*, he says. Now the party has taken over. He misses when all the mikoshi used to depart from his shrine. *The celebration is important*, he says, *but so is the ceremony*.

I can't imagine the festival will go back to how it was. People's lives are hurtling further and further away from agriculture and forestry.

But I think of Nimaida keeping his village alive with the help of young volunteers who come from around the world. I think of Hayashi, Shimoshita, and Sakai bringing fallow tanbo back to life with natural farming. Mika harvesting forgotten ganpi shrubs to make paper for her photographs. Nakajima pushing the boundaries of what can be expressed through functional woodenware. Moriguchi reviving a forgotten craft.

Not all traditions are worth keeping. But for the ones that are, it's possible to maintain their integrity while letting go of the parts that are oppressive or irrelevant. Matsuura broke with fourteen generations of precedent to let me work in his sakagura. Sakura ignored the people who said hunting wasn't for her. And I suspect that in the future, faced with dwindling membership, the duck hunters at Kamoike will open their ranks to women. It takes progressive thinking to keep old ways relevant. And as Nakajima says, tradition is something we are always creating.

Yamashita tells me, *The Japanese spirit developed with nature, feeling the seasons, and accepting changes*. He says we can invite new things and still keep the essence of that spirit.

Persimmon-Leaf Sushi

TIME: *1 hour, plus 6 hours marinating,*
and overnight pressing
Makes 20 pieces

K aki-no-ha-zushi, persimmon-leaf sushi, is Yamanaka's festival food. Pickled fish and a confetti of toppings are pressed into seasoned rice on top of a wide leathery leaf. The leaf is a wrapper, a plate, and a mild preservative; you don't eat it, but it does add fragrance. This is mountain sushi: prepared from salted fish, and laced through with vinegar and sugar so it doesn't spoil easily. I learned the recipe from Youko Nakano.

They make a kind of persimmon-leaf sushi in Nara too, but it's rectangular and completely wrapped. In Ishikawa, the rice is formed into a round disk, and the leaves are left open. These can be made with salmon, but I prefer the more traditional mackerel version. Some cooks use tiny pink dried shrimp instead of red pickled ginger.

If you don't have access to a persimmon tree to collect leaves from, you can use bamboo leaves (cut in half), available online and at some Asian markets.

The process of making kaki-no-ha-zushi begins at least 24 hours in advance of serving. In the morning, you'll pickle the fish. In the evening, you'll assemble the sushi. Then press it overnight, and serve it the next day.

> *Note:* Shio-saba is available in Japanese markets. To make it from scratch, rinse mackerel fillets in a little saké, pat dry, and sprinkle generously with salt (3–5 percent of the fish's weight). Wrap in paper towels or a clean dishcloth, place in a nonreactive container, and refrigerate for 12–24 hours. Salting and pickling fish reduces but does not eliminate the risk

of parasites; fish previously frozen below −20° Celsius (−4° Fahrenheit) for at least 24 hours is the safest to eat uncooked.

FOR THE FISH

120 mL (½ cup) rice vinegar

6 tablespoons granulated sugar

140 grams (5 ounces) shio-saba (salted mackerel; see note)

FOR THE RICE

2 cups Japanese rice (short- or medium-grain "sushi" rice)

120 mL (½ cup) rice vinegar

3 tablespoons granulated sugar

2 teaspoons fine sea salt

FOR THE SUSHI

20 persimmon leaves (or 10 bamboo leaves, cut in half), plus more for covering the sushi

1 tablespoon beni-shōga (julienned red pickled ginger), cut into 1 cm (½-inch) lengths

1 lemon, cut into very thin triangles

1. Begin at least 6 hours (and up to 24 hours) before assembling the sushi by pickling the fish. In a small saucepan, combine the rice vinegar and sugar. Bring to a boil, and stir until the sugar dissolves, making a brine. Cool completely before using. Place the fish in a tight-fitting nonreactive container. Pour the cooled brine over the fish, and refrigerate for 6–24 hours (it will get firmer the longer it pickles).

2. When the fish has pickled, it becomes firm and opaque. Place the fish on a cutting board and discard the brine. Carefully peel away the tough translucent skin and discard it, leaving the silvery part on the fish. Use tweezers to remove large bones from the middle of the fillet.

3. Cut 5 mm (¼-inch) slices from the fish, crosswise, keeping your knife at a 45-degree angle to the fillet. At this point, the fish can be refrigerated until you are ready to use it.

4. In a mesh strainer set inside a bowl, rinse the rice in several changes of cold water, until it runs almost clear. Drain the rice, shaking off excess water.

5. Cook the rice in a rice cooker according to the manufacturer's instructions or on the stovetop as follows. Place the drained rice in a small heavy-bottomed saucepan or donabe (clay pot). Add enough water so that if you rest your hand on top of the rice, the water covers your fingers, about 2 cups. Cover the pot with a tight-fitting lid. Place it over high heat, and bring to a boil. When steam is spitting out the edges of the lid, reduce the heat to the lowest possible level, and set a timer for 18 minutes. When the timer goes off, turn the heat to high for 60 seconds, or until you can hear the remaining water sizzle. Remove from heat, without opening the lid. Let stand for 5 minutes.

6. Meanwhile, in a small saucepan, combine the rice vinegar, sugar, and salt. Bring to a simmer, and stir until the sugar and salt dissolve; remove from the heat. This is your rice seasoning.

7. You will need to set up an electric fan or get another person to fan the rice with a paper fan or piece of cardboard while you cut in the seasoning. Transfer the cooked rice to a shallow wooden tub called a sushi-oke, a sheet pan, or a large cutting board. With the fan blowing, pour the seasoning over the rice, and cut it in with a shamoji (rice paddle) or silicone spatula. The idea is to quickly incorporate the seasoning and dry it, without crushing the rice. Use a vertical cutting motion, or fold the rice over onto itself, until the seasoning dries and the rice becomes glossy and sticky.

8. Now you're ready to make sushi. Get your *mise en place* set: persimmon leaves, beni-shōga, and lemon triangles. Pick up about 40 grams (¼ cup) of rice, and flatten it into a small disk to fit on top

of a leaf. Place the rice on a leaf. Arrange a piece of fish, a pinch of beni-shōga, and a triangle of lemon on the rice. Repeat until you have used all the rice.

9. Assuming you don't have a large wooden sushi press, you'll need to jury-rig something. I use half-sheet pans (rimmed baking sheets): fill one pan with sushi, cover the sushi with extra leaves or baking parchment, then stack another half sheet on top. Weight it with one or two more pans or a couple of books: the idea is to press the toppings into the sushi, but not to crush it.

10. Wrap this whole thing in plastic wrap, or drape it with a dish towel, and let it press overnight in a cool room (do not refrigerate; the rice will get hard). In the morning, take the sushi out of the press, and arrange it on platters or in bentō containers. Serve at room temperature (leftovers can be refrigerated for a day or two, but the texture will not be as good).

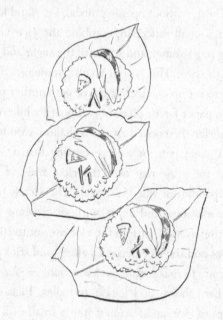

Author's Note

When the research for this book was done, I had to go back to New York—at least for a while. Before I did, Kawamoto took me out in his fishing skiff from Shioya, a port that used to bring merchant seamen to Yamanaka. He navigated the little boat fifteen minutes out to sea, until the mountains became small. From the water, he pointed to Dainichi, the tallest peak in Kaga, which we'd climbed together when we released trout in the river. Then he pointed to the back of Mizunashi Mountain: Iōji and Hakusan Shrine were on its other side, the water for Shishi no sato saké underneath. In the narrow valley beyond was Yamanaka. I thought of lyrics from the town's folk song:

> The Yamanaka bushi I learned last night,
> A parting song it's become this morning.
>
> Into the tall mountains I cannot see.
> Missing Yamanaka, so hating the mountains.

I was seeing from the same perspective as the merchant seamen who sang those words. This was the port from which they'd head back out to sea. When I boarded a flight a few weeks later, I didn't know that the coronavirus pandemic would make it almost a year before I could return.

As of December 2020, no one in Yamanaka has fallen ill from COVID-19, but the loss of foreign tourism has altered their lives. In anticipation of the 2020 Olympics, Fumiaki Matsuura filled lots of extralarge bottles of saké for restaurants and parties. But instead of an increase in sales, he faced a dramatic drop when people stopped going out to restaurants and hosting parties. Takehito Nakajima does not sell his work to tourists anyway, but business has slowed because of the economic recession; he's using the time to reorganize his workshop so he'll be able produce table- and teaware more efficiently when people start buying fancy things again.

Mika canceled her overseas travel to exhibitions this year, but after a few months of quiet art making she's begun to welcome occasional visitors from Tōkyō and Kansai for papermaking workshops beside the brook outside her studio. Yamanaka's ryokan and hotels were struggling with staffing and profitability even before the pandemic; so far, all have reopened as Japan cautiously encourages domestic tourism, but for some there are painfully few guests.

For a little while, the public onsen was closed—not because of the pandemic, but because the boiler broke down. I hear that for many Yamanaka people this was a bigger disruption—and topic of conversation—than the national state of emergency that forced restaurants and bars to limit business from April through May.

While Kenichi Hibino's sushi shop was closed during the national state of emergency, he enjoyed having more time for amateur astronomy. Yūsuke Shimoki reconfigured his bar with screen doors for ventilation and expanded outdoor seating. My landlady, Yoshiko Tsuji, reduced the hours of her saké and gift shop over the summer, but by October the autumn leaves and the famous Ishikawa snow crab drew enough domestic tourists to keep her staff busy six days a week. In public, at least, Yamanaka people face the pandemic and the recession with stoicism.

Noboru Nimaida tells me that while the town is struggling, things are the same in Ōzuchi: the vegetables and rice are growing as usual. But he missed the volunteers that would usually help with spring planting. My friends took over my tiny tanbo, and by the time I got back to Yamanaka they were threshing their first harvest.

The adzuki seeds I'd saved, for continuing Nishiyama Sensei's project, were crawling with bugs and covered in mold; I discarded them ruefully. But in my neglected hatake, among the shoulder-high weeds, I found five adzuki plants that had grown on their own from last year's fallen beans—enough to save seeds for the future.

In its thirteen-hundred-year history, Yamanaka has survived wars, fires, typhoons, and mudslides. The town will adapt and endure this hardship, but not without losses. I miss the warm meals at Eimi: Masumi Hayashibara permanently closed her teishoku restaurant. It breaks my heart to think of other businesses that may not make it through the winter. But, remarkably, three new cafés opened this year.

There are places like Yamanaka—with their own special crafts and culture—all over Japan and all over the world. I hope I've made you fall in love with Yamanaka, but also that you will think about the unique and interesting culture wherever you are.

THE NARRATIVE OF this book emerged from my own experiences but was enriched by interviews and research conducted with the help of native speakers and information from books and experts. I relied on Yū Mizukami, Hiroko Kimura-Myōkam, Natsuko Higa, and Takuya Kodama to translate interviews—to make sure my observations were accurate, and to ask the things I didn't know how to in my limited Japanese. Mika Horie, Jessica Ho, Hiroshi Kumagai, and Raku Terai helped with informal interviews and fact checking.

Yū Mizukami—who previously did his own ethnographic study in Yamanaka of the relationship of artisans to society—assisted me with research in Japanese. While I was immersed in brewing saké or carving wagatabon, he was answering my questions by traveling to libraries, calling government offices, and reading stacks of books I mailed to him. We gathered information and inspiration from the following sources, as well as countless news articles, blog posts, pamphlets, and casual conversations with Yamanaka people.

WATER

James C. Baxter, *The Meiji Unification Through the Lens of Ishikawa Prefecture*; Rebecca Corbett, *Cultivating Femininity: Women and Tea Culture in Edo and Meiji Japan*; Fushin'an Foundation Library, *Japanese Tea Culture, the Omotesenké Tradition*, www.omotesenke.jp; 加藤恵津子『<お茶>はなぜ女のものになったか: 茶道から見る戦後の家族』(Etsuko Katō, *The Tea Ceremony and Women's Empowerment in Modern Japan: Bodies Re-presenting the Past*); 西島明正 編『山中町史 完結編』(Myōshō Nishijima, *Yamanaka Town History: Complete Edition*); Sadako Ohki with Takeshi Watanabe, *Tea Culture of Japan* (exhibition catalogue); Kakuzo Okakura, *The Book of Tea*; A. L. Sadler, *Cha-No-Yu: The Japanese Tea Ceremony*; SSI International, *Master of Sake: The Textbook for Kikisake-shi*;『総務省 統計局『平成28年社会生活基本調査』(Statistics Bureau of Japan, *2016 Survey on Time Use and Leisure Activities*); 淡交社編集局 編『茶席で話す英会話』(Tankosha, *Tea Room Conversation in English*); 山中温泉ゆけむり倶楽部・山中節覚え書編集部会『山中節覚え書』(Yamanaka Onsen Yukemuri Club, *Yamanaka Bushi Memorandum*); 米岡威『特集 土木遺産(5)日本の国づくりの心 美に隠された先端技術<兼六園>』『Civil Engineering Consultant』, vol. 234、建設コンサルタンツ協会 (Takeshi Yoneoka, "Hidden High Technology Behind Beauty (Kenroku-en)," Engineering's Heritage 5: The Spirit of Building Japan, *Civil Engineering Consultant*, vol. 234).

WOOD

Kim Brandt, *Kingdom of Beauty: Mingei and the Politics of Folk Art in Imperial Japan*; 樋口清之『ものと人間の文化史 71：木炭』(Kiyoyuki Higuchi, *Wood Charcoal, The Cultural History of Things and Humans*, vol. 71); 石川

県農村文化協会　編『石川県農村文化関係史料第5集：石川のむらとくらし』 (Ishikawa Rural Culture Association, *Life and Village in Ishikawa Prefecture: Rural Culture-Related Historical Materials*, vol. 5); 岸本定吉『木炭の博物誌』(Sadakichi Kishimoto, *Natural History of Charcoal*); 農林水産省林野庁『平成28年度 森林・林業白書』(Ministry of Agriculture, Forestry, and Fisheries, Forestry Agency, *Annual Report on Forest and Forestry in Japan, Fiscal Year 2016*); 本谷文雄「我谷盆について」『石川県立歴史博物館紀要17』石川県立歴史博物館 (Fumio Motoya, "About Wagatabon," *Bulletin of the Ishikawa-ken History Museum*, vol. 17); Barbra Teri Okada, *Symbol and Substance in Japanese Lacquerware: Lacquer Boxes from the Collection of Elaine Ehrenkranz* (exhibition catalogue); 瀬良陽介『盆百選』 (Yōsuke Sera, *100 Selected Trays*); Junichirō Tanizaki, *In Praise of Shadows*; Conrad Totman, *The Green Archipelago: Forestry in Pre-industrial Japan*; Conrad Totman, *The Lumber Industry in Early Modern Japan*; Sōetsu Yanagi, *The Beauty of Everyday Things*.

WILD THINGS

Karl F. Friday, "Bushidō or Bull? A Medieval Historian's Perspective on the Imperial Army and the Japanese Warrior Tradition," *The History Teacher*, vol. 27, no. 3; Sukey Hughes, *Washi: The World of Japanese Paper*; G. Cameron Hurst III, "Death, Honor, and Loyalty: The Bushidō Ideal," *Philosophy East and West*, vol. 40, no. 4, *Understanding Japanese Values*; Yoshiko Iida, *Learning About the Satoyama and Satoumi of the Hokuriku Region Through Maps*; 公益財団法人日本食肉消費総合センター『日本人と食肉』(The Japan Meat Information Service Center, *Japanese and Meat*); 加賀市片野鴨池坂網猟保存会編『片野鴨池と村田安太郎』 (Kaga City Katano Kamoike Saka-ami Hunting Preservation Society, *Katano Kamoike and Murata Yasutarō*); 加賀市片野鴨池坂網猟保存会 編『片野鴨池と坂網猟』(Kaga City Katano Kamoike Saka-ami Hunting Preservation Society, *Katano Kamoike and Saka-ami Hunting*); 加賀市片野鴨池坂網猟保存会編『坂網猟Q&A続け名人の技！』 (Kaga City Katano Kamoike Saka-ami Hunting Preservation Society, *Saka-ami Hunting Q&A; Long Live Masters' Skills!*); 加賀市片野鴨池坂網猟保存会編『坂網猟：人と自然

の付き合い方を考える』(Kaga City Katano Kamoike Saka-ami Hunting Preservation Society, *Saka-ami Hunting: Thinking About How People Interact with Nature*); 金子浩昌『日本史のなかの動物事典』(Hiromasa Kaneko, *Encyclopedia of Animals in Japanese History*); John Knight, *Waiting for Wolves in Japan*; Mario Melletti and Erik Meijaard, eds., *Ecology, Conservation and Management of Wild Pigs and Peccaries*; 守田良子 監修『おばあちゃんの味ごよみ：加賀・能登』(Ryokō Morita, *Grandma's Taste: Kaga/Noto*); 守田良子と「日本の食生活全集石川」編集委員会『日本の食生活全集 17：聞き書 石川の食事』(Ryōko Morita and the Complete Collection of Japanese Foodways Ishikawa Editors' Association, *Writing Down What We Hear: Ishikawa's Meals,* Complete Collection of Japanese Foodways, vol. 17); 中井将善『たのしい山菜とりと料理』(Masayoshi Nakai, *Fun Picking and Cooking Wild Vegetables*); Inazō Nitobe, *Bushidō: The Soul of Japan*; Annalena Stüwe, "Jibie: Reinventing Hunting in 21st Century Japan"; 高橋春成編『イノシシと人間：共に生きる』(Shunjō Takahashi, *Inoshishi and Humans: Living Together*); Brett L. Walker, *The Lost Wolves of Japan*; Wild Bird Society of Japan, *A Field Guide to the Birds of Japan.*

CULTIVATION

Nicole L. Freiner, *Rice and Agricultural Policies in Japan: The Loss of a Traditional Lifestyle*; Masanobu Fukuoka, *The One-Straw Revolution*; 井上雪『加賀の田舎料理』(Yuki Inoue, *Countryside Cuisine of Kaga*); 加賀市文化財総合活用事業実行委員会『加賀市歴史文化学習帳』(Kaga City Cultural Heritage Comprehensive Utilization Executive Committee, *A Study Book for Learning History and Culture in Kaga City*); F. H. King, *Farmers of Forty Centuries*; 北川賢佑「11.我谷ダムの影響」『金沢大学文化人類学研究室調査実習報告書第23集』(Kensuke Kitagawa, "Influence of Wagatani Dam," Field Work Reports of Kanazawa University Cultural Anthropology Laboratory, vol. 2); Kokugakuin University, *The Online Encyclopedia of Shintō*, http://k-amc.kokugakuin.ac.jp; 丸果石川中央青果『野菜の知識』(Maruka-ishikawa-chuō-seika, *Knowledge of Vegetables*, http://www.maruka-ishikawa.co.jp/vegetables/vegetables.htm); 中島一

三 編『杉水の歴史』(Kazumi Nakashima, *History of Suginomizu*); Emiko Ohnuki-Tierny, *Rice as Self: Japanese Identities Through Time.*

IN ADDITION, I learned directly from experts and scholars who graciously shared their knowledge: writer and forager Winifred Bird, librarian and tea scholar Rebecca Corbett, woodworker Jarrod Dahl, saké educator Jamie Graves, ethnomusicologist David Hughes, woodworking professor Masashi Kutsuwa, tea seller Zach Mangan, and Shintō expert Mirato Takada. Takeshi Watanabe, who teaches Japanese food history (among other things) at Wesleyan University, was particularly generous, advising me on historical accuracy and linguistic precision.

The meijin and shokunin I've written about spend a lifetime honing their knowledge and craft; I've only scratched the surface of Yamanaka's deep culture.

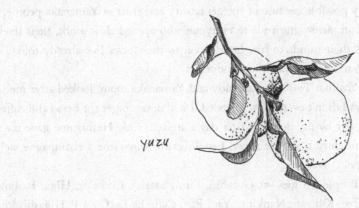

yuzu

Acknowledgments

In the solitary final months of drafting this manuscript, a pigeon named Hato-chan kept me company. I found her, lost and out of place on a Yamanaka sidewalk, too exhausted to fly. When I took her in, my mother and husband both thought she must be a writing spirit who arrived to help me finish my first book.

It's true that a book is not made by its author alone. This one was only possible because of the generosity and trust of Yamanaka people. I feel immense gratitude to everyone who opened their work, their lives, and their minds to me. In addition to the stories I've already told, I'd like to honor some other kindnesses.

Yoshiko Tsuji, my landlady and Yamanaka mom, looked after me in ways I didn't even know I needed. I will never forget the bread and coffee she left by my door the first day I arrived. Chie Hashizume gave me a home during shorter stays. Jirō Takeuchi threw me a champagne welcome.

People fed me—at Gyoshin, Eimi, Saraku, Chōraku, Higa, Bashow Coffee, Kūnyan, Nanking, Yagi Pan, Caffé La-La, Coya-P, Higashiyama Bonheur, and the Tsurutarō Kataoka museum café—and took the time to chat with me even though my Japanese was poor. Others helped me at the supermarket or post office. Each week I looked forward to seeing folks at the Sunday morning market, especially my dear Mie Kobayashi, and the boss lady, Yoshie Ishikura—maybe someday you'll let me pay for my coffee!

Takuya Kodama made trouble, told tall tales, and is probably my fairy godfather. Noriko Matsuura gave me free soft serve and always had my back. Gumpu and Kimiko Nakamura smoothed the way for conversations with saka-ami hunters and the chef at Bantei, Kiyotaka Mizuguchi, who was generous with his knowledge. Yoshiki Mishima introduced me to Yoshiharu Nishiyama Sensei, who became one of the most important teachers in my life. Emiko Mizukami and the women who pick sansai for Narisawa taught me about wild edibles too. Kayo Takeuchi, I hope you make all your dreams come true (especially the sheep).

Takehito Nakajima, Sadao Tsuchiya, Sam Sifton, Yūichi Kano, and Masanori Kamiguchi wrote letters in support of my artist visa; I can die happy knowing they all said nice things about me. Elizabeth Andoh shared advice and encouragement. Ann Hood: I think I still owe you a final project from that independent study; will you accept this book?

While I revised in Brooklyn, Susie Plaisted, Mesha Hamilton, and Devra Ferst made sure I ate well. There are times when every writer needs a "wife" to take care of them, or better yet a cavalry of supportive friends. If it weren't for them, I might have eaten an awful lot of instant noodles.

Susie also read early versions of some chapters; so did Shelley Sather, Rosie Schaap, Michele Paladino, and Robin Calderon. My brother Owen Kirshner and sister-in-law Erin Pham did too, and they tested recipes, along with Chuck Kuan, Nancy Matsumoto, Saori Kurioka, Caroline Lange, Michael Harlan Turkell, Katherine Sacks, Devra Ferst, Emilie Hsu, and Jean Lee and Dylan Davis. David Paul Eck, L. Nichols, Bob Hazelbrook, Bob Jackson, and Nora Chase helped with details about woodworking, hunting, geology, and papermaking.

Brendan Francis Newnam, Jason Schwartz, and Gina Rae LaCerva reminded me to celebrate my successes; so did Ralph Rodriguez. Isaac Gertman, Alicia Cheng, Sohui Kim, Shannon Mustipher, Sydne Gooden, and Sarah Kirshner provided perspective when I needed it. Rebecca Kirshner showed me, by example, how to claim space for my work. Rosie

Jablonsky, Shanti Giese, and Lynn Yarne are a constellation of inspiration.

My agent, Lori Galvin, believed in my vison; my editor, Allison Lorentzen, guided me through its execution, and her assistant, Camille LeBlanc, helped shepherd my manuscript through many stages. Publisher Brian Tart, associate publisher Kate Stark, and editor in chief Andrea Schulz all did behind-the-scenes magic. Production editor Bruce Giffords and copy editor Ingrid Sterner saved me from embarrassing mistakes. Designer Meighan Cavanaugh took my binders full of pen-and-ink drawings and made them part of the book you're holding. Burcu Avsar and Zach DeSart photographed the jacket, and Brianna Harden designed it. Lindsay Prevette, Mary Stone, Kristina Fazzalaro, and Nora Alice Demick made sure people would know this book exists.

It's possible I never would have become a writer if it weren't for the bravery of my parents, Robin Pringle and Bill Kirshner: they didn't listen to the first-grade teachers who said I would never learn to read.

To the publications where I got to work on early iterations of some chapters: *Mata yoroshiku onegaishimasu!* A version of "A Saké Evangelist" appeared in *Roads & Kingdoms* as "The Saké Ambassador"; a karaage recipe similar to Midnight Fried Chicken lives on the *New York Times Cooking* website; and I wrote a little about Nimaida's work in Ōzuchi for *Gastro Obscura*, and about Mika Horie's artwork for *Saveur* with photos by Max Falkowitz.

About my pigeon: Hato-chan regained her strength after a few months of sharing my apartment. I took her to live with some other pigeons, cared for by a Pakistani-Emirati man outside Tōkyō who told me he likes to talk to birds because they are close to the spirits. In her new aviary, Hato-chan adopted two orphaned chicks, found a mate, and hatched chicks of her own. This family of birds flies together over the rice fields and junkyard where they reside.

With all my heart, I thank Hiroshi Kumagai, for always letting me go, and giving me a place to fly home to.